Rethinking Humanitarian Intervention

Alex J. Bellamy
Stephen McLoughlin

First published 2018 by
PALGRAVE

Palgrave in the UK is an imprint of Macmillan Publishers Limited,
registered in England, company number 785998, of 4 Crinan Street,
London, N1 9XW.

Palgrave® and Macmillan® are registered trademarks in the United States,
the United Kingdom, Europe and other countries.

ISBN 978–1–137–48809–1 hardback
ISBN 978–1–137–48808–4 paperback

This book is printed on paper suitable for recycling and made from fully
managed and sustained forest sources. Logging, pulping and manufacturing
processes are expected to conform to the environmental regulations of the
country of origin.

A catalogue record for this book is available from the British Library.

A catalog record for this book is available from the Library of Congress.

Dedicated to

William Cooper (1860–1941)
elder of the Yorta Yorta people.

Contents

List of Illustrative Material

Tables

Figure

Acknowledgements

It has been a huge pleasure working on this book together, which is the culmination of a decade of shared thought, discussion, and research. There are numerous people whose support, advice, and guidance have been crucial along the way.

First, we owe a debt of gratitude to our publisher. This book sprang out of conversations with Palgrave's indefatigable Steven Kennedy, and it was his energy and enthusiasm for the project that drove it forward. When Steven retired, Lloyd Langman and Tuur Driesser helped drive the project forward and showed remarkable forbearance when things were delayed. Many thanks.

Stephen would also like to thank former and current colleagues – both at Griffith University and Liverpool Hope University, the two institutions that have housed him during this project. Over the last few years his own learning curve as an academic and researcher has been steep, and he is grateful for the mentorship, friendship, and collaboration of many. In particular, he would like to thank Jason Sharman, Lee Morgenbesser, and Shannon Brincat at Griffith, as well as Michael Holmes, Catalina Montoya Londono, and Yazid Said at Liverpool Hope. Likewise, many thanks to the Griffith Asia Institute, and Liverpool Hope's Department of History and Politics, for the collegial and institutional support, without which writing this would not have been possible.

Alex is grateful for the ongoing support received from the University of Queensland and colleagues there, especially Roland Bleiker, Tim Dunne, Phil Orchard, and Richard Devetak. He is also deeply grateful to his colleagues in the Asia Pacific Centre for the Responsibility to Protect, especially the Centre's utterly indispensable manager, Arna Chancellor.

We both owe debts of gratitude to some of our fellow travellers over the years. We would like to thank Jess Gifkins, friend, former doctoral student, and colleague, whose feedback and friendship have been much valued. Thanks also to Luke Glanville, Charles Hunt, and Sarah Teitt for their friendship, and for working through these issues with us over the years. Sara Davies, too, has been a significant help to us both over the years.

Cumulatively, this book represents nearly two decades of research and thinking on humanitarian intervention. While all the text has been written afresh for this book, inevitably, some of the arguments and pieces of evidence presented here draw upon our earlier work. These include: Alex J. Bellamy, 'The Humanization of Security? Towards an International Human Protection Regime?', *European Journal of International Security*, vol. 1, no. 1 (2016); Alex J. Bellamy, 'The Changing Face of Humanitarian Intervention', *St. Anthony's International Review*, vol. 11, no. 1 (2015), pp. 15–43; Alex J. Bellamy, 'The Responsibility to Protect Turns Ten', *Ethics and International Affairs*, vol. 29, no. 2 (2015), pp. 161–185; Alex J. Bellamy, 'When States Go Bad: The Termination of State Based Mass Killing', *Journal of Peace Research*, vol. 52, no. 5 (2015), pp. 565–76; Alex J. Bellamy and Paul D. Williams, 'Libya' in David Malone et al. (eds), *The UN Security Council in the Twenty-First Century* (Boulder, CO: Lynne Rienner, 2015); Alex J. Bellamy, 'The UN Security Council and the Problem of Mass Atrocities: Towards a Grand Bargain?', in Anthony Burke and Rita Parker (eds), *Global Insecurity* (London: Palgrave, 2017); Alex J. Bellamy, 'Protecting Responsibly: The UN Security Council and the Use of Force for Human Protection Purposes', in Hilary Charlesworth and Jeremy Farrell (eds), *Strengthening the Rule of Law through the UN Security Council* (London: Routledge, 2015); Alex J. Bellamy, 'The Responsibility to Protect and Regime Change', in Don Scheid (ed.), *Armed Humanitarian Intervention: Ideas and Reconsiderations* (Cambridge: Cambridge University Press, 2014).

Finally, our greatest debt of thanks goes to our families. We would like to thank them for their continued love and support.

AJB & SM
Brisbane, August 2017

Introduction

This book is about a minor revolution in humanitarian affairs: the transformation of ad hoc humanitarian intervention into an international regime for human protection.

'Never Again', the world proclaimed after the Holocaust. More than 6 million Jews lay dead, victims of the Nazis' campaign of mass extermination. Around the world, ten times that number died as a result of Nazi, fascist, and Japanese attempts to violently reorder the world – attempts that from the very outset were always doomed to fail because of the sheer numbers aligned against them.[1] This book is about the challenge of making 'Never Again' a lived reality in those most difficult of cases when governments and armed groups begin killing, raping, torturing, and displacing civilians on a massive scale – that is, when foreign armed intervention may be the only way to protect populations from their tormenters.

The use of military force to 'save strangers' from atrocities in other countries is not new.[2] During the nineteenth century, for example, European powers intervened repeatedly in the Balkans and the Middle East to protect Christian populations from abuse by the Ottoman Empire.[3] Nor is the idea that we have a duty to save our fellow humans from tyranny, irrespective of national boundaries, an invention of our modern – more cosmopolitan – era. As Luke Glanville points out, as early as the eighteenth century, the great jurist Emmerich de Vattel wrote that states had 'duties to contribute to the perfection of those beyond their borders insofar as they can without doing an "essential injury" to themselves'.[4]

Yet although the practice of humanitarian intervention is not new, it has undergone a minor revolution since the end of the Cold War. For most of its history, humanitarian intervention has been a rare, ad hoc activity undertaken by individual states or groups of states motivated by a mixture of compassion for the victims of atrocities and self-interest. Since the 1990s, however, it has evolved into one of the instruments employed collectively by the society of states as a whole to prevent atrocity crimes and protect vulnerable populations. Where it was once a largely unilateral affair, humanitarian intervention has become a more collective endeavour; and one that is regulated, more often than not, by international institutions. And where it was once an entirely ad hoc response to atrocities in faraway places, humanitarian intervention has become but one – rarely used – component of an international regime focused on the protection of populations from atrocities. So, while populations in peril today are no more likely to experience armed intervention on their behalf than they were during the Cold War, or in the nineteenth century for that matter, they are much more likely to experience other forms of collective international action in their name. Although far from perfect, the norms and practices this minor revolution instantiated have helped reduce both the incidence and the lethality of atrocity crimes by increasing the costs to the perpetrators, diminishing their chances of success, and improving the protection afforded to the vulnerable.[5] In the pages that follow, we explain how humanitarian intervention is changing and examine some of the practical, political, and moral questions that it continues to pose.

Rights beyond states

The Statute of the Nuremberg Tribunal, created in the autumn of 1945 to hold senior Nazis accountable for their crimes, established new categories of crimes committed against individuals (crimes against humanity) and groups (genocide). 'The individual must transcend the state', Britain's chief prosecutor Sir Hartley Shawcross told the tribunal in his opening submission.[6] In 1947, the newly established United Nations (UN) General Assembly passed the Genocide Convention, which prohibited the crime of genocide, established a legal duty to prevent it, and demanded that states prosecute alleged perpetrators – as the wartime allies had done through the Nuremberg and Tokyo trials.[7] Genocide refers to one subset of what we now typically refer to as 'atrocity crimes' – those committed with the intent to destroy a whole group. In 2007, the International Court of Justice (ICJ) judged that, because of the Genocide Convention, all states have a legal responsibility to do what they reasonably can, within existing law, to prevent genocide.[8] Specifically, the Court found that

states had a legal responsibility to take positive steps to prevent genocide when they have prior knowledge about its likely commission
and the capacity to influence the would-be perpetrators.

Two years after the passage of the Genocide Convention, the four
Geneva Conventions (1949) codified the laws of war. Among other
things, they prohibited intentional and indiscriminate attacks on
civilians and prisoners during international wars. These earned the
label 'war crimes' – the second cluster of crimes collectively labelled
as 'atrocity crimes'. The subsequent Protocols (1977) to the Geneva
Convention established the immunity of all non-combatants, whether
in international or non-international armed conflicts, from the intentional use of armed force against them and required that parties
cooperate with one another to prevent violations of the law. When
committed in non-international armed conflicts these could be considered 'crimes against humanity'.[9] A little more than two decades later,
in 1998, international society established the International Criminal
Court (ICC) by adopting the Rome Statute. The Statute insisted that
'crimes against humanity' were international crimes irrespective of
whether they were committed in situations of armed conflict. Around
the same time, the International Criminal Tribunal for Yugoslavia
(ICTY) confirmed that the practice of 'ethnic cleansing' – the use
of violence and other means to forcibly displace a population from
its home – constituted one such crime against humanity. This is the
fourth crime commonly labelled an 'atrocity crime'. Not specifically prohibited by international treaty, international law recognizes
that those who practice ethnic cleansing must, by necessity, commit
either genocide, war crimes, or crimes against humanity. Thus, since
Nuremberg, international society has recognized and prohibited four
sets of atrocity crimes – genocide, war crimes, crimes against humanity, and ethnic cleansing.[10]

Gradually, these normative developments reshaped our expectations about the state's relationship with its own population and
about how the world ought to respond to atrocity crimes. They
helped establish the point in positive international law that states
are not entitled to treat their populations however they see fit; that
sovereignty entails responsibilities for protection as much as rights
to autonomy and independence.[11] It established the once revolutionary idea that individuals and groups had legal rights that, to
echo Sir Hartley Shawcross, transcended the state, the satisfaction
and denial of which individual leaders could be held accountable

for. So well ingrained are these ideas in contemporary international society that we forget just how recent – and revolutionary – they were. It bears remembering that immediately after the Nuremberg judgments, Raphael Lemkin – the jurist whose determined campaigning resulted in the Genocide Convention – lamented that Nazis were not prosecuted for crimes against Jews committed prior to the outbreak of war; it was only the fact of Germany's war of aggression that made the Nazis' abuse of Germany's Jews an international crime. Had there been no invasion of Poland, France, and the rest, Lemkin recognized, there would in all likelihood have been no prosecution of Nazis even had they killed every last German Jew.[12] Today, however, atrocity crimes – genocide, war crimes, ethnic cleansing, and crimes against humanity – are recognized as international crimes. Of these, only war crimes are limited to situations of armed conflict. International lawyers describe these laws as *jus cogens*, meaning that they have universal jurisdiction (they apply even to non-signatory states) and that no derogation is possible from them.

The corpus of international law is not limited to simply prohibiting atrocity crimes, however. States also have duties to prevent these crimes, protect their victims, and promote compliance with the law. All states have an extraterritorial obligation to take all reasonable measures to prevent genocide. They have an additional responsibility to raise the alarm when genocide is committed or thought to be imminent by bringing the matter to international attention.[13] In relation to war crimes, Common Article 1 of the 1949 Geneva Conventions points to an obligation not just to abide by the law but to 'ensure respect' for the Conventions around the world. Additional Protocol I (1977) to the 1949 Geneva Conventions established a duty for state parties to cooperate by acting, individually or jointly, to address serious violations committed in the context of an international armed conflict in cooperation with the UN (Article 89). The Convention relating to the Status of Refugees and the 1967 Protocol thereto required that states provide asylum and ensure *non-refoulement* for people fleeing persecution because of their membership of a particular race, religion, nationality, or social group or because of their political opinions. The more recent Arms Trade Treaty, which came into force on Christmas Eve 2014, prohibits the sale of arms in situations where a state party recognizes that that 'the arms or items would be used in the commission of genocide, crimes against humanity, grave breaches of the Geneva Conventions of 1949, attacks directed against civilian objects or civilians protected as such, or other war crimes'.[14]

As we observed earlier, this basic idea – that states have positive duties towards outsiders – is hardly new. What is new, and unique to contemporary international society, however, is the idea that the duty to uphold the most fundamental rights of individuals and groups in other countries is itself a *legal* obligation; and one invested not only in the natural law but also in positive international law.

Yet it is one thing to create legal duties and obligations in international society and quite another to ensure compliance with them. States, as Hedley Bull – one of the progenitors of the 'English School' approach to world politics – understood, inhabit an 'anarchical society', one constituted and regulated by law but lacking a supreme authority capable of enforcing compliance with it.[15] And while it is certainly true that most states abide by most rules, most of the time, when it comes to the prohibition of atrocity crimes, international practice after the Holocaust seldom fully satisfied the demands of international law.

With concern for human dignity trumped by the global struggle for geopolitical supremacy during the Cold War years that followed Nuremberg, atrocity crimes remained a common feature of world politics. What is more, despite the aforementioned advances in international law, perpetrators of these crimes enjoyed impunity more often than not.[16] Communist regimes, for example, employed atrocity crimes against civilian populations to eradicate 'bad elements', forcibly transform societies, and suppress dissent. Stalin, Mao, and Pol Pot, communist leaders in the Soviet Union, China, and Cambodia, respectively, used atrocity crimes on a massive scale to achieve their goals, resulting in the premature deaths of tens of millions of people. Historians nowadays argue about whether Stalin killed more people than Hitler. Whichever of them was the bloodiest, it was a relatively close-run thing – the Nazis probably killed 11 million to 12 million people, while Stalin's communists killed up to 9 million.[17] Both may have been outdone by Mao. New research on the scale of mass killing in Maoist China might prompt us to the conclusion that no people have been killed in so large a number by their own government than the Chinese. One study suggests that as many as 45 million Chinese were worked, starved, or beaten to death during the four years of the Great Leap Forward (1958–62), only one of the massive bouts of violence unleashed by China's communists.[18] While smaller in absolute numbers, the lunacy of Khmer Rouge rule in Cambodia led to the death of more than a quarter of that country's population in just three and a half years.[19] Ironically, when Vietnam invaded and put an end to the slaughter in Cambodia, it was condemned by states other than those in the Soviet bloc for violating Cambodia's sovereignty.[20] Vietnam was also subjected to economic sanctions by the West – a clear signal of how unimportant the principles set out at Nuremberg had become in the face of Cold War rivalries. Some other communist regimes, including that in North Korea were equally brutal.[21]

But it was not only communist regimes that used extreme violence against civilian populations to prosecute their own political agendas. On the eve of the Korean War, South Korea's military regime rounded up and executed suspected communists and their families. Precisely how many were killed will never be known, but estimates suggest that, at the very least, some 100,000 people perished.[22] These massacres were barely reported at the time. A decade later, nationalist extremists in Indonesia and their allies massacred approximately 600,000 suspected and actual communists during a six-month purge in 1965–6.[23] These atrocities raised barely a ripple of international press coverage, let alone condemnation. Similar stories could be told of right-wing regimes in Argentina, Chile, El Salvador, and Guatemala, though the sheer scale of killing was significantly smaller, and by the 1980s these governments started to come under intense pressure to mend their ways. Nationalism and bloody self-interest, too, were a cause of mass killing – as with Pakistan's bloody suppression of East Pakistan (Bangladesh) and Idi Amin's reign of terror in Uganda.[24]

Despite the advance of international laws prohibiting atrocity crimes and establishing positive duties to prevent them, in the years that followed Nuremberg international society failed to establish institutions or to legitimate practices designed to enforce the law. Where intervention against atrocities occurred at all – as with India's 1971 intervention into East Pakistan, Vietnam's 1978 intervention into Cambodia, and Tanzania's intervention in Uganda the following year – it was ad hoc, unilateral, and motivated by a combination of humanitarian concern and self-interest.[25] And it was condemned by international society as a breach of state sovereignty. The service Vietnam performed for humanity by defeating the murderous Khmer Rouge was rewarded by the imposition of economic sanctions that retarded its economic development by decades.

This was all primarily because the Cold War politics that followed Nuremberg, and the global ideological struggle it engendered, tended to trump concern for human rights. Sometimes, as in the cases of Indonesia and North Korea, the perpetrators of atrocities were protected from opprobrium and punishment by superpower allies. Other times, states with the capacity to step in and end atrocities preferred not to expend their resources this way, holding them back for use when the national interest dictated. Sometimes, and despite the legacy of Nuremberg and the laws it bequeathed, states and scholars argued that the sovereign right to non-interference was more important than the protection of the most fundamental human rights.[26] Yet it remains true that otherwise willing states have never refrained from protecting the rights of others *because* of the sovereignty of others.[27] There were always other reasons for inaction. Nonetheless, intervention to save strangers from atrocity crimes remained ad hoc and controversial.

With the end of the Cold War, some of these political constraints were lifted and new opportunities for collective action emerged. Yet, initially, the gap between international legal responsibilities and actual lived experience became, if anything, more obvious than it was before. Genocide in Rwanda and Srebrenica; mass killing and ethnic cleansing in Angola, Bosnia, Burundi, Croatia, East Timor, Kosovo, Liberia, Sierra Leone, and Zaire/Congo; state repression in northern and southern Iraq; and acute state fragility and civil war leading to mass human suffering in Somalia exposed the hollowness of legal niceties in the face of governments and armed groups willing and able to generate and use mass civilian suffering for their own ends. International society was initially ill-prepared to respond: UN peacekeepers recoiled in the face of the *genocidaires* in Rwanda, where 800,000 people were massacred in one hundred days; they stood aside as UN 'safe areas' collapsed in Bosnia – the worst coming in Srebrenica in 1995, when more than 8,000 men and boys from the safe area there were massacred by Bosnian Serb forces; US forces were hounded out of Mogadishu in Somalia taking with them the UN peacekeepers and any hope of delivering humanitarian aid to civilians; political and diplomatic efforts were insufficient to stop Angola's slide back into war or the widely predicted mass violence that greeted East Timor's vote for independence.[28] These, and other, crises also created a global crisis of internal displacement, as millions of people were forced from their homes.

Why were governments so reluctant to act to fulfil their pledge of 'Never Again'? As an ad hoc and mainly unilateral endeavour, in which the intervening states bore all the costs of blood and treasure, humanitarian intervention was a risky and expensive undertaking. Consequently, it was rare. Thus, while it certainly had the potential to save lives, armed intervention for humanitarian purposes would always be an incomplete and inadequate response to the problem of atrocity crimes. A politics of protection in which armed intervention played a primary or exclusive role would never be able to comprehensively protect the rights of individuals and groups to live lives free of atrocities. It would always lack the coverage, consistency, and sustainability needed.

'Never Again' all over again: reluctant state actors

A tension runs right through the politics of humanitarian intervention: between the widely held aspiration of 'Never Again' and the practical realities – and costs – associated with achieving that goal through the ad hoc use of military force by self-selected states and groups of states. Only if the prevention of atrocities and protection of populations were given a surer institutional and normative footing in international society would practice become sufficiently consistent and comprehensive to close this gap between normative aspiration and daily lived reality. Indeed, there are at least three reasons for thinking that the pledge of 'Never Again' could not be satisfied without a move away from the traditional politics of ad hoc military intervention.

The first was the lingering power of state sovereignty. Or, more accurately, the lingering view that sovereignty, on the one hand, shielded the perpetrators of atrocity crimes from accountability (territorial sovereignty) and, on the other, precluded collective action against them by allowing each state to make up its own mind about whether and how to respond to atrocity crimes in other states (decision-making sovereignty).[29] International society is comprised of sovereign states that pursue their own interests (however defined), privilege domestic over foreign concerns, and generally cherish their legal right to determine their own affairs. Any account of contemporary world politics has to take this reality as a starting point. Sovereignty, which in many parts of the world was hard-won from colonial powers, is not likely to be given away easily. Most states do not self-identify as 'cosmopolitan' and are bound to place their own interests – and those of their populations – above those of outsiders.

This has several implications. States – especially, but not only, those experiencing genocide and mass atrocities – are protective of their own sovereignty and can impose limitations on international action through the conferring and denial of consent. Since 1945, the UN Charter has bestowed upon the Security Council the authority to override these limits and enforce its decisions but it has seldom chosen to do so for a range of practical, political, and principled reasons. It is worth observing that when the Council has extended its authority to its farthest reach by establishing transitional governments under its own authority it has always done so with the express consent – indeed at the invitation of – the relevant parties. Transitional administrations in Eastern Slavonia, Bosnia, Kosovo, and East Timor were all established with the consent of the parties involved. Indeed, not until Libya in 2011 did the Security Council see fit to authorize the use of force to protect a population from atrocities without the government's consent. Sometimes the absence of consent has blocked collective action, with disastrous consequences. During the 2011 NATO-led intervention in Libya, for example, the UN began planning for a post-conflict reconstruction mission led by Ian Martin. The plans were leaked and Libya's new government declared that it would not accept an international peacekeeping mission.[30] While it might certainly have suited some Western governments eager to avoid long-term entanglements in Libya, the formal initial blockage to an international mission came from the Libyan authorities and not international society.

The underlying problem here is that states jealously guard their decision-making sovereignty: their right to decide for themselves, on an entirely ad hoc and case-by-case basis, how to respond to atrocity crimes. It is common to read that failures of protection are failures of political will, but they stem, in fact, from decision-making sovereignty.[31] Traditionally, this worked in at least two ways to inhibit collective action to protect people from atrocity crimes and promote ad hoc responses. The first, and least discussed, is not about 'failure' at all. It is to do with the *presence* of countervailing interests. In other words, states fail to protect civilians not just because those with the capacity to do so are sometimes reluctant to incur the costs involved, but also because they sometimes prefer to support or shield the perpetrators, as doing so serves their interests better. For example, the link between China's interest in Sudanese oil and arms sales and its obstinate refusal to impose sanctions or other measures on that country's government despite its clear responsibility for crimes against humanity and possibly even genocide in Darfur is well known.[32] More recently, Russia's decisions to repeatedly block UN action on Syria were prompted by its interest in preventing the spread of radical Islamism to its southern Caucasus region and protecting a friendly regime.[33] The West has also put its own interests ahead of the protection of vulnerable populations from time to time. During the Cold War, it supplied arms to the Indonesian government just as that government slaughtered communists and brutally suppressed East Timor. In the early 1980s, the USA supported, funded, and armed the genocidal regime in Guatemala and prevented international efforts from ending the conflict there as well as in El Salvador.[34] Motivated mainly by its interest in preserving Francophone influence in Africa, France funded and armed the Hutu government in Rwanda and supplied a substantial proportion of the machetes used for genocide. At the very least, France's position muddied the international political waters when it came to responding to the Rwandan genocide in 1994.[35] Sometimes, therefore, states simply choose to protect or assist the perpetrators of atrocity crimes because it suits them to do so. When those states are permanent veto-wielding members of the UN Security Council, the interests of one can make it impossible for all the others to marshal effective responses to atrocity crimes.

The second, and more commonly discussed, aspect of decision-making sovereignty (or 'political will') relates to the fact that each state is primarily responsible for the well-being of its own citizens. As a result, they prefer to direct their resources to the achievement of domestic goals rather than to the saving of foreigners in faraway places. The costs of humanitarian intervention are rarely low – a problem made only more acute by our age of austerity. The NATO-led intervention in Libya, for example, cost British taxpayers between £300 million and £400 million – the equivalent of servicing nearly 3,000 hospital beds for a year. During that campaign, both France and Britain came close to exhausting their stockpiles of expensive precision-guided munitions. Moreover, the cost of replacing those munitions placed a heavy burden on already stretched defence budgets. And while public opinion in democratic countries might tolerate the deployment of military forces to protect people in other counties from grave inhumanity, it generally does not look kindly on more than very modest casualties in these operations because they are seen as wars of choice and not necessity. Moreover, while sometimes prepared to support the expenditure of relatively small amounts of money for saving strangers, most publics baulk at the prospect of sacrificing public spending at home to support intervention abroad. Charity really does begin at home.

However understandable it may be from the perspective of domestic politics, this reluctance to commit resources to the protection of foreigners from mass atrocities can have devastating effects. Some were detailed by the Report of the Independent Inquiry into the UN's failure to prevent or halt the Rwandan genocide in 1994. The Inquiry found that this abject failure was caused by 'the lack of resources and political commitment devoted to developments in Rwanda ... There was a persistent lack of political will by Member States to act, or to act with enough assertiveness.' The absence of will affected the UN's own response and 'was also evident in the recurrent difficulties to get the necessary troops' for the UN's peacekeeping mission in Rwanda.[36] This 'overriding failure' of will in Rwanda resulted in the deployment of international forces on the ground that lacked the resources they needed to protect people from genocide. The UN's mission there was smaller than had been recommended, slow to deploy owing to the reluctance of states to contribute effective troops, and debilitated by administrative difficulties. When troops did arrive, many were inadequately trained and equipped. That it saved any lives at all was due entirely to the heroism of individuals – and none more so than Force Commander General Roméo Dallaire.[37] Both the UN and RAND found that a properly mandated, configured, and robustly equipped additional numbering around 2,500 could have been sufficient to stop the genocide in its tracks. But the world could not muster these additional resources for the UN Assistance Mission for Rwanda (UNAMIR) when it mattered most.

The UN's failure to prevent or respond effectively to the genocide in Rwanda was a failure caused by decision-making sovereignty. UNAMIR was conceived as a small, cheap, and consent-dependent operation despite the misgivings of those who thought that this would prove sorely inadequate. It was a tragic coincidence of history that the UN's mandate for Rwanda was decided upon just one week after the killing of American peacekeepers in Somalia in the now famous

'Black Hawk down' incident. At that time, the USA was in no mood to support or pay for the dispatch of more peacekeepers to Africa.[38]

There is much debate about the capacity of public opinion to influence governments towards greater activism in response to mass atrocities. The crisis in Darfur, for example, gave cause for the emergence of a major global campaign (the 'Save Darfur Coalition') which tried to persuade Western governments, and the USA especially, to take action. The campaign succeeded in putting and keeping the issue on the international agenda for longer than it otherwise would have been. Although slow, hesitant, and inadequate, international society did eventually muster the will to deploy peacekeepers, refer the matter to the ICC, sponsor a series of major peace initiatives, and organize one of the largest-ever humanitarian operations. These efforts, the latter especially, undoubtedly saved lives and might not have happened without determined public agitation in the West.[39]

But the capacity of public opinion to influence foreign policy and generate the impulse to act where none already exists in government is limited. The so-called 'CNN effect' has never pushed a democratic government to do something it did not want to do. The simple and brutal reason for this is that very few, if any, voters change the way they vote over a government's record of responding or not responding to foreign atrocities. That is because atrocities in foreign places do not rank highly on any national list of political priorities. As a result, governments – especially democratic ones – are risk-averse and unlikely to be moved by transient public opinion. In most cases, as in Kosovo in 1998–9, governments themselves lead public opinion on foreign affairs.[40] In others, such as Darfur, public pressure might push governments to take diplomatic or other forms of action that do not incur significant costs. Generally speaking, international activism is more likely where the political, financial, and material costs associated with the desired policy are low. As expected costs increase, so the capacity of activists to persuade governments to shoulder them diminishes.[41]

Prudence is, of course, an additional inhibitor of humanitarian intervention. Even when states have genuine moral concerns about atrocity crimes in distant lands, prudential considerations may counsel against expensive and risky measures such as armed information. Sometimes, leaders may judge that a proposed policy could do more harm than good, for instance by provoking a wider conflict, jeopardizing the support of groups thought necessary for the delivery of vital humanitarian assistance, or by creating false hopes of a military victory that could encourage parties to avoid good faith negotiations. Other times, states might simply prioritize other humanitarian concerns. Alternatively, they might lack the capacity to intervene effectively. These considerations are evident in most debates about how best to respond to atrocity crimes.

For instance, when the UN Security Council debated what to do about Kosovo in 1999, prudential considerations were at least as important as principled ones. A few days after NATO began its bombing campaign over Yugoslavia, Russia introduced a draft resolution to the Security Council condemning the intervention. Russia's criticisms centred on two points: the legal point that NATO did not have the authority to use force without authorization from the Security Council, and the prudential point that the intervention was likely to do more harm than good.[42]

In relation to Darfur, where some 100,000 civilians were killed between 2003 and 2005, primarily by 'Janjaweed' militia aligned with the government of Sudan, those who preferred a cautious international approach argued that trying to coerce the Sudanese government would do more harm than good by provoking a wider crisis. It would also, they thought, jeopardize the pursuit of other goals such as a negotiated peace agreement to end the decades-long civil war between the government and the Sudanese People's Liberation Army in the south, a war which had claimed more than 2 million lives. Moreover, with ongoing commitments in Iraq, Afghanistan, and the Balkans, the West lacked the military capacity to intervene effectively and there were few who thought that Western intervention in another Arab-led country seemed like a good idea.[43]

More recently, prudential arguments came to the fore against proposed intervention in Syria to prevent Bashar al-Assad's regime there from continuing its indiscriminate campaign against civilians. Here, there were concerns that outside force would be met with counter-intervention by Russia, Iran, and Hezbollah; that it would escalate the overall level of violence; that it would weaken key neighbours such as Lebanon, Turkey, and Iraq; and that it could precipitate the regime's collapse and the rise of an Islamist extremist government there.[44]

For these, and other, reasons, humanitarian intervention has always been a poor and unreliable substitute for a more systematic approach to preventing and responding to atrocity crimes. Yet despite these limitations, there has been a steady decrease in the frequency and severity of episodes of atrocities over the past few decades and a con-comitant increase in international engagement to limit and halt them. Multiple datasets measuring interrelated phenomena such as govern-ment-sponsored mass killings, one-sided violence, and mass atrocities all point to the same trend – that of declining levels of violence, in terms of both episodes and casualty numbers.[45] R. J. Rummel's mul-tiple surveys of 'democide' – the mass killing of people by their own government – in the twentieth century show a clear pattern of decline from a peak around the time of the Second World War.[46] This general trend was also found by the Political Instability Task Force, which focuses on the incidence of government-sponsored mass killings and shows a sustained decline since 1993.[47] A similar picture was painted by the Uppsala Conflict Data Program and the 2013 Human Security Report, which showed a steady decline in the number of cases from a peak in 2001 and a decline in the number of violent deaths globally.[48] There were especially marked declines in the Americas, Central and South Asia, East Asia and Oceania, Europe, and sub-Saharan Africa.[49] Smaller datasets pointed in the same direction, towards a decline in both the overall frequency and the lethality of mass vio-lence against civilians.[50] Although the trajectory of decline reversed between 2011 and 2015 (followed by slight reductions of violence in 2016–17), as civil wars and atrocities increased, the average inci-dence remained lower than it had been in the 1990s and significantly lower than during the Cold War.

In this context, debates came to focus more on the *causes* of decline than on the *fact* of decline.[51] On the one hand, structural forces such as state consolidation, economic growth, and trade, as well as factors that Azar Gat conjoins under the rubric of 'modernization', put downwards pressure on violence and pushed societies towards greater peacefulness.[52] On the other, these structural forces were aug-mented by a minor revolution in international responses to atrocities – a transition from ad hoc humanitarian intervention towards more institutionalized human protection.

From humanitarian intervention to human protection

The downwards trends in the incidence and lethality of atrocity crimes coincided with a minor revolution in international prac-tice with respect to such violence. Since the end of the 1990s, the

Security Council has become much more active in responding to atrocity crimes than it ever was prior to this time. International society is more likely to respond to atrocities than it was once, and when it does, responses are more comprehensive and much more likely to foreground protection than in the past. Nowadays, it is common to see international actors utilize a bewildering array of strategies and measures in response to atrocities: peacekeeping, diplomacy, mediation, investigations, sanctions, embargoes, judicial actions, humanitarian relief, and informational operations, to name but a few.

Among these measures, armed humanitarian intervention is the most intrusive and controversial approach to halting atrocities. It is also among the least likely forms of response – something that has grown more salient as the scope of potential action has increased. In this book, we define humanitarian intervention as the use of force by international actors without the host state's consent and undertaken for the purposes of protecting populations from atrocity crimes committed by either state or non-state armed groups.[53] Because of its military dimension, it is not uncommon to see humanitarian intervention described as the most effective weapon in international society's arsenal. High-profile cases such as Rwanda and Kosovo hold a promise for international action – that if the requisite political will can be found, the use of force can be effective against mass killings. Yet reality is not so straightforward. In some situations, military intervention can make matters worse or may be simply incapable of creating the protection sought.

How then, should humanitarian intervention be understood? Too often, intervention for humanitarian purposes is studied in isolation of the broader configurations of laws, morals, institutions, and practices designed to give meaning to 'Never Again'. The purpose of this book is to resituate intervention as one of the many measures that can be used to prevent atrocity crimes and protect populations from them. This is a growing repertoire of mainly non-violent measures, most of which are wielded under the rubric of international institutions such as the UN, the ICC, and regional arrangements. Understood in this way, the issues surrounding humanitarian intervention become less of a binary dilemma (do we send in the Marines to save strangers?) and more of a question of what combination of actions are the most appropriate for preventing or halting atrocities in any given situation. Indeed, this approach encapsulates how the thinking and practice of humanitarian intervention have changed since the late

1990s. Before, during the Cold War and immediately afterwards, international society's response to atrocity crimes was framed by humanitarian intervention: an ad hoc, unilateral, uncertain, military, and selective way of responding to the problem of atrocities. Owing to the limits described above, humanitarian intervention was never likely to represent a compelling response to the problem of atrocity crimes – an answer to the call of 'Never Again'. These old ways of thought and practice have been gradually supplanted by new, more comprehensive, ways that focus on the prevention of atrocity crimes, the utilization of a far wider range of measures and tools, and the engagement of a much broader spectrum of actors. In place of the ad hoc, is an emerging international regime that takes the focus away from questions of intervention and places it squarely on the protection needs of vulnerable groups and individuals.

In this book, we argue that humanitarian intervention needs to be placed within the context of changing international responses to atrocity crimes. We argue that emerging norms and practices of human protection, which have their roots in the development of International Humanitarian Law (IHL) after the Holocaust, gradually coalesced into an international human protection regime that has changed how states and international organizations think about, and practice, responses to atrocity crimes. This, in turn, has changed the place of humanitarian intervention in international society: responses to the problem have become more comprehensive and have come to involve more actors.

Since the 1990s, international society has utilized a growing range of measures to protect populations from atrocity crimes. These include diplomacy and mediation, information gathering, embargoes and sanctions, judicial measures, humanitarian protection for refugees and displaced persons, and post-conflict peacebuilding. With this has come a new focus on the *prevention* of these crimes – a topic that received little, if any, consideration prior to 2005 but which is today a burgeoning field of thought and practice.[54] What is more, the field's expansion has brought new actors to the fore – not just states and international organizations, but also regional and sub-regional organizations, judicial institutions, civil society actors, the private sector, and individuals have all become invested – to a greater or lesser extent – in human protection.[55] Even in extreme cases where atrocities are either imminent or unfolding, non-violent measures by non-traditional actors can prove effective. In Kenya, in early 2008, when post-election violence escalated into inter-ethnic violence that led to the killing of over 1,000 people and the displacement of 500,000, it was mediation efforts by a joint UN–African Union team that helped end the violence.[56] Five years later, private sector and civil society groups in Kenya worked together in a highly effective campaign to prevent a repeat of the electoral violence.

All this has contributed to increased global activism in relation to the prevention of atrocity crimes and protection of vulnerable populations. One measure of this increase can be seen in the greater willingness of the UN Security Council to authorize responses to such violence. As we point out in Chapter 2, the Security Council has become more consistent in the adoption of measures to support human protection, particularly since the mid-2000s. While such responses are not always effective in halting atrocities or protecting populations – as Syria tragically illustrates – they are indicative of international society's increasing activism.

Overview

We begin where few accounts of humanitarian intervention start – with the causes of atrocity crimes themselves. We ask why atrocities occur, and how they end. The key to developing strategies that prevent atrocities or protect vulnerable populations lies in a thorough understanding of why atrocities happen and why they unfold in the ways that they do. Yet simply posing these questions pushes our analysis beyond humanitarian intervention, since the causes of atrocity and the long-term refashioning of sustainable peace afterwards are often not conducive to external intervention. This is borne out of the fact that humanitarian interventions have historically played a minor role in ending atrocities, which raises questions about precisely what combinations of measures are most likely – and suitable – for responding to these crimes. This involves a shift in emphasis, from the rights (and wrongs) of armed intervention and towards the broader sets of engagements, strategies, and measures that may be needed to protect populations from atrocities. It is this fundamental shift in thinking that, we argue, underscored a minor revolution in humanitarian affairs: the shift from ad hoc humanitarian intervention towards the International Human Protection Regime (IHPR).

In the second chapter, we identify two interrelated trends that have unfolded, particularly since the end of the 1990s. The first – confirmed by multiple datasets – is the steady decline in the frequency and severity of cases of mass violence described earlier. We argue that this decline was – at least in part – the product of increasing global activism to both prevent and halt such episodes, reflected in the growing commitment of the UN Security Council to authorize action for the purposes of human protection, the engagement of a wider number of actors in atrocity prevention, and the adoption of more comprehensive approaches. These innovations pointed towards the emergence of an international human protection regime comprising rules, norms, institutions, and practices that have together supported the decline of atrocity crimes.

Precisely what these different measures are, and how well they are utilized, is the subject of Chapter 3, which focuses on the development of non-violent responses to atrocity crimes. In order to better understand humanitarian intervention, it is necessary to situate it at one end of a broader spectrum of measures. Chapter 3 charts strategies and actors involved in these non-violent approaches to human protection, demonstrating that the use of force for the purposes of human protection can be best understood as only one among many options, and one of the more rarely deployed.

It is within this broader context of the human protection regime that the 2011 NATO-led intervention in Libya is analysed in Chapter 4. The UN Security Council's decision to authorize the use of force in this case was significant because it was the first time that the UN Security Council had authorized the use of force for human protection purposes without the consent of the state involved. Security Council Resolution 1973, which sanctioned the use of all necessary means to protect unarmed civilians in Libya, was not issued in isolation. Indeed, the Council's Resolution 1970, issued three weeks earlier, authorized a range of non-violent measures to halt the state-led violence that was rapidly escalating. It was only after all these measures were exhausted that the use of force was considered, and only then after strong appeals by regional organizations such as the League of Arab States (LAS), the Gulf Cooperation Council (GCC) and the Organisation of Islamic Conference (OIC). While the circumstances that facilitated the passing of the resolution were unique, and although NATO members and their partners have been criticized for not investing in rebuilding, this intervention marked a turning point in international society's response to mass atrocities, particularly in terms of the Security Council's increased willingness to mandate action for the purposes of human protection.

At the same time, the NATO-led intervention provoked much controversy, not least in relation to regime change, with a number of member states accusing the coalition of conflating the protection of civilians with regime change. Yet how should the international community respond in cases where the perpetrators of atrocities are states themselves? Chapter 5 takes up the issue of regime change more directly, arguing that although activities designed to protect populations should not be used for regime change, sometimes regime change is necessary in order to protect populations who are being targeted by their own government, albeit in highly exceptional cases.

Chapter 6 explores two apparently divergent trends that have emerged since implementing Resolution 1973 in Libya. The first is the growing international commitment and consensus on the 'Responsibility to Protect' (R2P) and protecting civilians affected by violent conflict, which has prompted greater expectations on the Security Council. The second trend concerns the increased demand for accountability in the wake of this growing commitment, particularly when resolutions mandate the use of force for protection purposes, as it did in Libya. This chapter examines the evolution of these two trends, particularly in relation to the ongoing crisis in Syria, and emerging discussions around the Brazilian proposal of 'responsibility while protecting'.

Chapter 7 then takes up the issue of consistency. It argues that the use of force is always going to be inconsistent, contingent as it is on context, political will, and capacity. That is why the transition towards a more institutionalized international human protection regime is a significant – and positive – development. Even when the use of force is authorized, there are always consequences, many of which may not be anticipated. To compensate for these problems, it is important to emphasize and invigorate aspects of the human protection regime that can mitigate the adverse effects of intervention, including a greater emphasis on preventive action which promises to reduce the number of situations that escalate into atrocities.

The measure of effectiveness of humanitarian intervention is based not on how frequent and robust such responses to mass atrocities become, but in terms of its position as a rare option within a broader repertoire of responses to such violence. In every case, the ideal is to prevent atrocities from starting, and to use non-violent means to bring about their cessation when they are committed. The decision to commit atrocities is never the first option of bellicose actors – more often than not, it is the last resort when other options have failed, as Benjamin Valentino has pointed out.[57] Given this, there are always opportunities for prevention prior to utilizing 'final solutions'. Indeed, as I. William Zartman has argued, it is rare for opportunities for prevention not to exist, even in the most extreme of cases.[58] Thus, as Catherine Lu argues, a more accountable world is not one in which progress is measured by more legitimate humanitarian interventions, but one where there is continued development of a robust human protection regime that helps to diminish risk through non-violent strategies, thus decreasing the need for international society to consider the use of force in the first place.[59] Yet in the most dire and desperate of situations, unilateral force may still be the only means by which protection from atrocity crimes can be afforded.

In the final chapter, Chapter 8, we cast our gaze to the present and future. Here, we argue that human protection today confronts a series of challenges which, if left unaddressed, threaten to wind back the decades of progress charted in the first parts of the book. We examine the nature of the challenges and their causes, and identify a series of steps that could be taken to address them and reinvigorate human protection. Ultimately, though, much depends on the choices made by political leaders, their followers, civil society groups, members of the security forces, religious leaders, analysts, journalists, and ordinary individuals. That is why we have dedicated this book to William Cooper, a man who by his thoughts and actions has inspired a new generation to continue to work against atrocity crimes and discrimination. His is a legacy that has influenced us both, profoundly.

William Cooper was a Yorta Yorta Aboriginal Elder and tireless campaigner for indigenous rights in Australia. On 6 December 1938, some weeks after Kristallnacht in Germany, Cooper led a march of petitioners to the German Consulate in Melbourne to present a petition protesting 'the cruel persecution of the Jewish people by the Nazi people in Germany'. The consulate kept its door closed and refused to accept the petition. Yet William Cooper's action still stands today as the *only* formal protest to Kristallnacht presented to the Nazi government. Especially given the context of the destruction of the Indigenous community in Australia, this was an immensely powerful story of how one group of people – itself subjected to violence, dispossession, and institutionalized discrimination – took a stand to speak out on behalf of another. The bonds established between the Yorta Yorta people and Australia's Jewish community are bonds that remain strong to this day.

We found this story, and witnessing first-hand the bonds of solidarity that it forged, was both deeply moving and deeply disturbing. It was deeply moving because it shows the depth of our common humanity and its capacity to reach across great geographical, historical, and cultural distance in opposition to cruel persecution. It is upon these bonds of common humanity – whether created or discovered – that the whole theory and practice of human protection rests. But we also found it deeply disturbing because it served a painful reminder that those who were much more empowered than William Cooper did far too little to stand up to the Nazis in the 1930s. This remains the challenge of our time: to translate the fundamental principles spoken of at Nuremberg into a daily lived reality for the world's vulnerable peoples. That, we believe, is the goal of the international human protection regime, an endeavour that – however imperfect and incomplete – marks a steep change from the old politics of humanitarian intervention.

Notes

1. Cathal J. Nolan, *The Allure of Battle: A History of How Wars Have Been Won and Lost* (Oxford: Oxford University Press, 2017), pp. 364–440.
2. The phrase 'save strangers' is coined from Nicholas J. Wheeler's landmark book on the subject of humanitarian intervention, *Saving Strangers: Humanitarian Intervention in International Society* (Oxford: Oxford University Press, 2000).
3. The two best books on humanitarian intervention's history are Fabian Klose (ed.), *The Emergence of Humanitarian Intervention: Ideas and Practice from the Nineteenth Century to the Present* (Oxford: Oxford University Press, 2015); and Brendan Simms (ed.), *Humanitarian Intervention: A History* (Oxford: Oxford University Press, 2013).
4. Luke HYPERLINK "https://researchers.anu.edu.au/publications/ 84040" Glanville, 'Responsibility to Perfect: Vattel's Conception of Duties beyond Borders', *International Studies Quarterly*, 61, no. 2 (2017), pp. 385–95.

5. These are claims we return to in Chapter 2. See, among others, Joshua S. Goldstein, *Winning the War on War: The Decline of Armed Conflict Worldwide* (New York: Penguin, 2011); and Gary Goertz, Paul F. Diehl, and Alexandru Balas, *The Puzzle of Peace: The Evolution of Peace in the International System* (Oxford: Oxford University Press, 2016).

6. As cited in Philippe Sands, *East West Street: On the Origins of Genocide and Crimes Against Humanity* (London: Weidenfeld and Nicolson, 2016), p. 349.

7. The story behind the Genocide Convention is conveyed by Samantha Power, *A Problem from Hell: America and the Age of Genocide* (New York: Basic Books, 2002), pp. 17–47.

8. *Application of the Convention on the Prevention and Punishment of the Crime of Genocide (Bosnia and Herzegovina v. Serbia and Montenegro), Judgment*, 26 February 2007, paras. 428–438.

9. The best accounts of the evolution of these legal rules are Geoffrey Best, *War and Law Since 1945* (Oxford: Clarendon Press, 1997); and William Schabas, *Unimaginable Atrocities: Justice, Politics and Rights at War Crimes Tribunals* (Oxford: Oxford University Press, 2012).

10. We share Payam Akhaven's view that these four crimes ought to be regarded on an even footing, and we label them collectively as 'atrocity crimes'. See Payam Akhaven, *Reducing Genocide to Law: Definition, Meaning, and the Ultimate Crime* (Cambridge: Cambridge University Press, 2015).

11. A point long recognized by theorists of sovereignty, if not by positive international law. See Luke Glanville, *Sovereignty and Responsibility to Protect: A New History* (Chicago, IL: Chicago University Press, 2014).

12. See John Q. Barrett, 'Raphael Lemkin and "Genocide" and Nuremberg, 1945–1946', in Christoph Safferling and Eckart Conze (eds), *The Genocide Convention Seventy Years After its Adoption* (The Hague: TMC Asser Press, 2010), p. 52.

13. William Schabas, *Genocide in International Law: The Crime of Crimes* (Cambridge: Cambridge University Press, 2009).

14. United Nations, *The Arms Trade Treaty* (2013), para 6.

15. Hedley Bull, *The Anarchical Society: A Study of Order in World Politics* (London: Macmillan, 1977).

16. Recounted in Alex J. Bellamy, *Massacres and Morality: Mass Killing in an Age of Civilian Immunity* (Oxford: Oxford University Press, 2012). East Asia accounted for much of the bloodletting, see Alex J. Bellamy, *East Asia's Other Miracle: Explaining the Decline of Mass Atrocities* (Oxford: Oxford University Press, 2017).

17. Timothy Snyder, 'Hitler vs. Stalin: Who Killed More?', *New York Review of Books,* 10 March 2011. For a more detailed explanation see his *Bloodlands: Europe Between Hitler and Stalin* (New York: Basic Books, 2010).

18. Frank Dikötter, *Mao's Great Famine: The History of China's Most Devastating Famine, 1958–1962* (London: Bloomsbury, 2010); Frank Dikötter, *The Tragedy of Liberation: A History of the Chinese Revolution 1945–1957* (London: Bloomsbury, 2013); and Frank Dikötter, *The Cultural Revolution: A People's History, 1962–1976* (London: Bloomsbury, 2016).
19. Ben Kiernan, *The Pol Pot Regime: Race, Power, and Genocide in Cambodia under the Khmer Rouge, 1975–79* (New Haven, CT: Yale University Press, 1996).
20. See Wheeler, *Saving Strangers*, pp. 78–110.
21. Andrei Lankov, *The Real North Korea: Life and Politics in the Failed Stalinist Utopia* (Oxford: Oxford University Press, 2013).
22. Hun Joon Kim, *The Massacres at Mt. Halla: Sixty Years of Truth Seeking in South Korea* (Ithaca, NY: Cornell University Press, 2014).
23. Robert Cribb (ed.), *The Indonesian Killings 1965–1966: Studies from Java and Bali* (Melbourne: Centre of Southeast Asian Studies, Monash University, 1995).
24. On the former see A. Dirk Moses, 'The United Nations, Humanitarianism and Human Rights: War Crimes/Genocide Trials for Pakistani Soldiers in Bangladesh', in Stefan-Ludwig Hoffman (ed.), *Human Rights in the Twentieth Century* (Cambridge: Cambridge University Press, 2011) 1971–1974', pp. 258–279. On the latter see Kurt Mills, *International Responses to Mass Atrocities in Africa: Responsibility to Protect, Punish and Palliate* (Philadelphia, PA: University of Pennsylvania, 2015), pp. 132 ff.
25. See Wheeler, *Saving Strangers.*
26. For the best account see Wheeler, *Saving Strangers.*
27. The core argument of Simon Chesterman, *Just and Unjust Interventions: Humanitarian Intervention in International Law* (Oxford: Oxford University Press, 2001).
28. Respectively, Linda Melvern, *A People Betrayed: The Role of the West in Rwanda's Genocide* (London: Zed Books, 2000); David Rohde, *Endgame: The Betrayal and Fall of Srebrenica, Europe's Worst Massacre since World War II* (New York: Penguin, 2012); Walter S. Clarke and Jeffrey Herbst (eds.), *Learning from Somalia: Lessons of Armed Humanitarian Intervention* (Boulder, CO: Westview, 1997); and Lise Marje Howard, *UN Peacekeeping in Civil Wars* (Cambridge: Cambridge University Press, 2007).
29. These are terms developed from Stephen Krasner's typology. They form a central part of the argument of Alex J. Bellamy and Edward C. Luck (eds), *The Responsibility to Protect: Promise to Practice* (Cambridge: Polity, 2018).

30. Emily O'Brien with Richard Gowan, *The International Role in Libya's Transition: August 2011–March 2012*, report of the Centre on International Cooperation, New York University, July 2012.

31. For example, quintessentially, James Gow, *Triumph of the Lack of Will: International Diplomacy and the Lack of Will* (London: C. Hurst and Co., 1997).

32. Nicola P. Contessi, 'Multilateralism, Intervention and Norm Contestation: China's Stance on Darfur in the UN Security Council', *Security Dialogue*, 41, no. 3 (2010), pp. 323–343.

33. Detailed in Christopher Phillips, *The Battle for Syria: International Rivalry in the New Middle East* (New Haven, CT: Yale University Press, 2016), pp. 28–30.

34. All these cases documented in Bellamy, *Massacres and Morality*, ch. 5.

35. Daniela Kroslak, *The Role of France in the Rwandan Genocide* (London: C. Hurst and Co., 2008).

36. Independent Commission, *Report of the Independent Inquiry into the Actions of the United Nations During the 1994 Genocide in Rwanda*, 12 December 1999, p. 1.

37. For his account see Roméo Dallaire, *Shake Hands with the Devil: The Failure of Humanity in Rwanda* (New York: Cornerstone, 2011).

38. Recounted in Melvern, *A People Betrayed*. Also Gerard Prunier, *The Rwanda Crisis: History of a Genocide* (London: C. Hurst and Co., 1998).

39. Rebecca Hamilton, *Fighting for Darfur: Public Action and the Struggle to Stop Genocide* (London: Palgrave Macmillan, 2011).

40. Tony Blair's role was especially instructive. See Alex J. Bellamy, *Kosovo and International Society* (London: Palgrave, 2001).

41. A point recognized by Robert A. Pape, 'When Duty Calls: A Pragmatic Standard of Humanitarian Intervention', *International Security*, 37, no. 1 (2012), pp. 41–80.

42. UN Security Council minutes, S/PV.3989, 26 March 1999.

43. Detailed in Julie Flint and Alex de Waal, *Darfur: A New History of a Long War* (London: Zed, 2008).

44. All canvassed in Phillips, *Battle for Syria.*

45. See, for example, Benjamin A. Valentino, 'Why We Kill: The Political Science of Political Violence against Civilians', *Annual Review of Political Science,* 17, 2014, p. 100; and Human Security Report, *Human Security Report 2013: The Decline in Global Violence: Evidence, Explanation and Contestation*, (Burnaby: Simon Frazer University, 2013), p. 107. For more on this trend, see Chapter 2 in this book.

46. R. J. Rummel, *Death by Government* (Piscataway, NJ: Transaction, Piscataway, 1994); and R. J. Rummel, *Statistics of Democide* (Piscataway, NJ: Transaction, 1997).

47. Valentino, 'Why We Kill', p. 100.
48. Human Security Report, *Human Security*, p. 107.
49. Human Security Report, *Human Security*, pp. 107–113.
50. Alex J. Bellamy, *Mass Atrocities and Armed Conflict: Links, Distinctions and Implications for the Responsibility to Protect.* Policy Analysis Brief for the Stanley Foundation, February 2011; Bellamy, *Massacres and Morality*; Benjamin A. Valentino and Paul Huth, 'Mass Killing of Civilians in Time of War', in J. Joseph Hewitt, Jonathan Wilkenfield, and Ted Robert Gurr (eds), *Peace and Conflict 2008* (Boulder, CO: Paradigm 2008), pp. 79–92; and Scott Straus, *Making and Unmaking Nations: War, Leadership and Genocide in Modern Africa* (Ithaca, NY: Cornell University Press, 2015), pp. 96–97.
51. For example, Bradley Thayer, 'Humans, Not Angels: Reasons to Doubt the Decline of War Thesis', *International Studies Review*, 15, no. 3 (2013), pp. 411–416; and Jack Levy and William R. Thompson, 'The Decline of War? Multiple Trajectories and Diverging Trends', *International Studies Review*, 15, no. 3 (2013), pp. 405–411.
52. Azar Gat, *The Causes of War and the Spread of Peace: But Will War Rebound?* (Oxford: Oxford University Press, 2017).
53. See, for example, the International Commission on Intervention and State Sovereignty, *The Responsibility to Protect* (Ottawa: International Development Research Centre, 2001), p. 8. Other sources which have defined humanitarian intervention along these lines include J. L. Holzgrefe, 'The Humanitarian Intervention Debate', in J. L. Holzgrefe and R. Keohane (eds), *Humanitarian Intervention: Ethical, Legal and Political Dilemmas* (Cambridge: Cambridge University Press, 2005), p. 18; Jennifer Welsh, *Humanitarian Intervention and International Relations* (Oxford: Oxford University Press, 2006), p. 3.
54. See, for example, Serena Sharma and Jennifer Welsh (eds), *The Responsibility to Prevent: Overcoming the Challenges of Atrocity Prevention* (Oxford: Oxford University Press, 2015); and Sheri Rosenberg, Tiberiu Galis, and Alex Zucker (eds), *Reconstructing Atrocity Prevention* (Cambridge: Cambridge University Press, 2015).
55. See Edward C. Luck and Dana Luck, 'The Individual Responsibility to Protect', in Sheri P. Rosenberg, Tibi Galis and Alex Zucker (eds), *Reconstructing Atrocity Prevention* (Cambridge: Cambridge University Press, 2015). Also John Forrer and Conor Seyle (eds), *The Role of Business in the Responsibility to Protect* (Cambridge: Cambridge University Press, 2016).

56. Serena K. Sharma, *The Responsibility to Protect and the International Criminal Court: Protection and Prosecution in Kenya* (London: Routledge, 2015).

57. See Benjamin A. Valentino, *Final Solutions: Mass Killing and Genocide in the Twentieth Century* (Ithaca, NY and London: Cornell University Press, 2004), pp. 3–4.

58. I. William Zartman (2005), *Cowardly Lions: Missed Opportunities to Prevent Deadly Conflict and State Collapse* (Boulder, CO: Lynne Rienner), p. 2.

59. Catherine Lu, *Just and Unjust Interventions in World Politics: Public and Private* (New York: Palgrave, 2006), p. 10.

1
Atrocities and Responses

Atrocity crimes are extreme forms of identity-based conflict in which one group deliberately targets another. As such, they are often the culmination of processes that have deep roots within states and societies. There are significant limits to what outsiders can do to prevent them and protect vulnerable peoples from atrocity crimes. What is more, a mode of response prefaced on the use of military force once atrocities occur is likely to provide imperfect protection at best – protection limited to those situations where humanitarian concern, national interest, and prudence converge within those states capable of intervening. Many of the internal conflicts that give rise to atrocity are complex and deep-rooted, not readily susceptible to outside mediation whether because one or more of the parties have embarked implacably on a course of action leading to atrocities – as in the case of Rwanda or Iraq (Islamic State) – or – as in the case of Syria and South Sudan – because a situation is so complex and fraught with danger as to defy easy resolution. It is not for the want of trying that international society's record of supporting transitions from war to peace is so mixed.[1] The endeavour itself is difficult and fraught with obstacles, its success often determined not by the interveners but by the local actors themselves.

Any account of humanitarian intervention needs to confront this reality head-on – yet few ever do, preferring instead to focus on the rights, responsibilities, and strategies of external actors while overlooking the internal dynamics that give rise to atrocities and – more often than not – terminate them too. International efforts can support protection where there is local will and capacity, and the levels and types of resilience can differ in various parts of a country, producing different patterns of violence,[2] but the so-called 'structural'

1

or 'root' causes of genocide and mass atrocities are often not easily influenced by external actors. While outsiders can play important enabling and facilitative roles, foreign assistance cannot by itself achieve structural change except through massive intervention followed up by equally massive and sustained commitments to peacebuilding and statebuilding. And even when states are prepared to take these great risks and make immense investments in the welfare of other peoples, there remain inherent limits to what can be achieved by outsiders.[3] As Scott Straus observed, when it comes to protecting populations from mass atrocities, '[i]n the long-run ... domestic actors are likely to be more effective than international ones'.[4] Well-targeted interventions or other forms of engagement can, however, support local sources of resilience to genocide and mass atrocities and change the cost–benefit calculations of would-be perpetrators. But although concerted international action can sometimes halt mass atrocities (e.g. as in Côte d'Ivoire, Kenya, Libya), in the long-term the avoidance of these crimes depends on what happens within the countries themselves – and this is typically driven by local actors, not international ones.[5]

This problem is compounded by the fact that intervention or other forms of large-scale engagement tend to be reserved for the most difficult and severe of cases.[6] As a rule of thumb, where conflicts have an easy remedy or are modest in their scale, solutions tend to be found without the need for debate about intervention. In such circumstances, a modest success rate might partly reflect the sheer difficulty of the cases presented.

To understand the dilemmas that atrocity crimes present for international society, it makes sense to start with the problem itself. This chapter attempts to do that by looking first at the causes of atrocity crimes and pathways of escalation and then at the issue of how these crimes are most commonly brought to an end. Our central arguments here are that atrocities tend to arise out of conflicts and deep-seated patterns of discrimination within and between societies that are often not readily amenable to external military intervention and that, historically, humanitarian intervention has tended to play only a marginal role in the termination of atrocities. As such, it is important to understand practices of humanitarian intervention as part of a broader set of questions about how the world ought to prevent as well as respond to atrocity crimes.[7]

Why atrocities happen

Because mass atrocities are products of their historical, political, and social context, analytical models can never perfectly identify their general causes or predict their coming.[8] However, as former UN Secretary-General Ban Ki-moon argued repeatedly during his tenure, atrocities are processes and not singular events.[9] As such, though each case is different in crucial respects, we can identify some of the main contributory factors that are often at play in pushing states and societies towards atrocities.

Atrocities are not new phenomena. Although every case needs to be viewed within its proper historical context, evidence of what we now recognize as genocidal killing reaches back into antiquity with the destruction of Melos in the Peloponnesian War and the Roman annihilation of Carthage standing out as only two notorious cases that are still studied today.[10] Indeed, countries that have recent histories of atrocities are at much greater risk of succumbing again than those that have not.[11] A recent violent past creates cultures of suffering and resentment that breed and validate future violence.[12]

Most of the major episodes of genocide or mass atrocity since the start of the twentieth century can be thought of as falling into one of five broad types:

- *State repression*: the use of genocide and mass atrocities to maintain state power, usually in the context of relatively weak states.
- *Counter-insurgency*: the use of genocide and mass atrocities to defeat an insurgent organization by denying it access to a civilian population.
- *Radical social transformation*: the use of genocide and mass atrocities to impose radical social transformation on a society, usually by eliminating a particular ethnic, religious, political, or socio-economic group.
- *Rebellion*: the use of genocide and mass atrocities as a strategy of rebellion against the state, sometimes through terrorism.
- *Major war*: the use of genocide and mass atrocities as a strategy for winning a major war at the lowest cost.

Although not synonymous with war, because genocide and mass atrocities can occur in the absence of armed conflict, and – contra Martin Shaw[13] – because armed conflict does not lead inextricably to atrocities, most modern atrocities are perpetrated in times of war.[14] Indeed, around two-thirds of the atrocities committed since 1945 occurred during wartime, a figure rising to more than three-quarters in the post-Cold War era.[15]

Genocide, the use of mass violence and other means to destroy an ethnic, national, racial, or religious group, is almost exclusively a crime of governments or other political elites. It is not spontaneous, but is premeditated and planned.[16] Practices of genocide and mass killing are rooted in the world historical contexts they inhabit.[17] The same usually applies to other forms of mass atrocity though there are some relatively rare instances where these crimes are genuinely spontaneous, occurring without elite-level planning and orchestration (such as the mass communal violence that accompanied the partition of India in 1948, or the anti-Chinese violence in Indonesia in 1998). But this is the exception rather than the rule. The main instigators of genocide and mass atrocities can usually be found in a society's political elite.[18] The goal of genocidal violence (and, often, other forms of mass atrocity) is to eliminate or suppress a group, either to prevail in an armed conflict, to protect putative interests of 'progress', or because the victim groups are perceived as hostile to the political goals of the state or a particular elite. Typically, in these circumstances genocide and mass atrocities are used to fulfil one of three goals, whether on behalf of a state or non-state entity: (1) *regime consolidation* – establishing a new or emerging regime's control within its domain; (2) *regime expansion* – expanding the domain of control to encompass more peoples, territory or resources; and (3) *regime maintenance* – regimes that consolidate their power initially through genocide and mass atrocities typically continue to conduct massacres when challenged.[19]

With this in mind, it is important to understand the motives of the decision-makers themselves, as the dynamics of collective violence alone do not explain why some states and armed groups revert to genocide and other atrocities. Almost always, atrocities are planned and purposeful; they are not committed in a social and historical vacuum.[20] There are a number of conditions that allow conflicts to escalate into genocide and mass atrocities and permit actors to believe that committing these terrible crimes is a rational response to their circumstances and a legitimate means of advancing their interests and those of their group. These conditions, which are not themselves necessarily the result of particular government or elite policies (though they might be), create the structural foundations for genocide and mass atrocities. Although the existence of these conditions does not always presage atrocities (in fact they generally do not), in the twentieth century and beyond, these crimes have rarely occurred in their absence.[21]

What, then, are the main factors that sow the underlying seeds of genocide and mass atrocities? A prerequisite, of course, is established divisions between different groups, be they of an ethnic, political, socio-economic, or religious nature.[22] According to Barbara Harff, one of the pioneers of risk assessment for atrocities, ethnic conflict has preceded nearly two-thirds of the genocides and 'politicides' of the last century, and various forms of discrimination against a minority group are a serious cause for concern. This also applies in circumstances where the minority group holds political power. Indeed, where a political elite is represented entirely by one minority group, the risk is two and a half times greater than in other circumstances.[23] The principal problem here, of course, is that most countries have some degree of entrenched ethnic, socio-economic, political, or religious division. For this reason, it is not simply the existence of division that constitutes a problem but the *politicization* of at least one identity group and the entrenching of practices of discrimination.[24] In these situations, ordinary political battles over the allocation of resources become entrenched conflicts *between groups* – setting out parameters for future conflict.

The politicization of identity groups is deeply connected to practices of discrimination. Discrimination takes many forms, but most notably there is political discrimination (denial of equal voting rights or under-representation in public institutions, the military, etc.), social discrimination (denial of education, etc.), economic discrimination (unequal employment opportunities, differentiation in wages according to identity groups, as well as variations in access to the means of production, denial of basic goods such as food, shelter medicine), and gender discrimination. These practices of discrimination are, of course, associated with deeply ingrained, often widespread and systematic, violations of human rights.

Often related to aspects of discrimination, economic factors can play a role in shaping the risk of civil war in general, as well as genocide and mass atrocities. Although overall levels of wealth (measured in terms of GDP per capita) matter in terms of overall risk, the relative economic position of groups within a country is especially important. These are *horizontal* inequalities (across groups) rather than the more commonly measured *vertical* inequalities (referring to relative wealth of rich and poor measured by Gini coefficients).[25] Sometimes, conflict erupts as an outcome of competition between groups for scarce resources. The role that the increasing scarcity of water and grazing land, both necessary for survival in Darfur, played in sharpening the conflict there is a case in point.[26]

These underlying identity, historical, and economic issues can be either mitigated or exacerbated by the nature of a political regime. What the UN Secretary-General called 'inhibitors' to atrocity crimes can, in their absence, also serve as 'accelerators' towards atrocities. Perhaps the most fundamental of these is the rule of law. Political stability, human rights, and economic prosperity are premised on the rule of law. When the rule of law breaks down, civilian populations become subject to the arbitrary exercise of power in which the absence, for example, of an impartial judiciary allows for impunity in acts of discrimination and violence against vulnerable groups, by an arbitrary power. Adherence to the rule of law provides accountability even in the face of discriminatory policies from governments, ensuring a safety net for minority groups.

More generally speaking, democratic and accountable regimes are more likely to mitigate and less likely to accelerate the escalation of crises to genocide and mass atrocities whereas the opposite is true of authoritarian regimes. While most state failures that occurred between 1955 and 1996 did not result in genocide and mass atrocities, one decisive factor that heightened the risk of them doing so was the existence of a non-democratic political elite with an 'exclusionary ideology'.[27] A democratic system of government contains institutional and ideational deterrents that impede political elites from attacking on their own populations. Even semi-democracies – regimes in the process of developing a democratic political system – are less likely to commit genocide or other mass atrocity crimes than autocratic regimes.

That is not to say that the process of transition from authoritarian rule automatically ensures an absence of conflict and identity-based violence. Indeed, some atrocities have been committed in nascent democratic states, or states in the process of democratizing. There is no doubt that the process of democratic transition can exacerbate risk associated with mass atrocities. Indeed, when transitions take place in poorer countries (less than US$2,750 of per capita GDP), the risk of rebellion (and, consequently, the risk of mass atrocities) increases considerably.[28] Michael Mann argues that 'murderous ethnic cleansing' is particularly 'a hazard in the age of democracy', particularly young democracies. This is especially the case when democracies allow 'ethnicity' to become 'the main form of social stratification'.[29] According to Jack Snyder, the risk of 'nationalist conflict' is particularly acute when there is international pressure to democratize when state institutions are still weak. This, he argues, facilitated conflict and atrocities in both Rwanda and Burundi.[30]

Yet even this heightened risk is overshadowed by the menace inherent in autocratic regimes. Although transitions to, and away from, democracy can often result in political instability – such that transitions themselves are the principal contexts in which atrocities occur[31] – autocratic states that fail are three and a half times more likely to result in genocides than democratic or semi-democratic states that experience failure.[32] However, 'rollback' in new democracies is not uncommon, and a number of state-sponsored mass killings have occurred when former or fledgling democracies have experienced a reversion to autocracy, usually during political or economic upheaval.[33]

Non-democratic government may be related to the risk of atrocity crimes in two ways. Various types of autocratic regimes might advocate genocide and other atrocities as a matter of policy, either by denying a particular group's right to exist or by arguing that groups that oppose particular policy programmes act illegitimately and make themselves targets. The types of regimes that have harboured anti-civilian ideologies,[34] which provide the justificatory logic of mass killing, include Marxist-Leninist regimes; extreme anti-communist regimes; rulers presiding over Shari'a law in Islamic states; avowedly racist regimes; and extreme nationalist regimes.[35] Where there is non-democratic government, especially when coupled with weak rule of law, it is often the case that the executive branch is able to exercise arbitrary power, increasing the likelihood of its using extreme violence to protect itself or achieve its goals and the likelihood of armed opposition to it.

These sorts of underlying preconditions might increase the risk of genocide and mass atrocities – indeed, such crimes may be impossible in their absence – but they do not make atrocities inevitable. Far from it. Most countries exhibit signs of these sorts of tensions and weaknesses. At least three additional things are needed. First, there needs to be a *reason* to commit mass atrocities. Typically, perpetrators select mass atrocities as a rational strategy for pursuing their objectives, such as countering a serious existential threat, when there are either no viable alternatives or when the costs of alternative strategies are prohibitively high.[36] Whether committed as part of an armed struggle, to suppress a challenge to the regime, or to realize a programme of radical social transformation, atrocities are a means to an end, not an end in themselves. Unless there is reason to think that their use might serve some purpose, even actors that are strongly predisposed towards committing atrocities will be unlikely to do so. This reason is usually provided by an acute crisis but it can also be generated by an elite's ideology, the many functions of which were ably detailed by Jonathan Maynard Leader.[37] Second, potential perpetrators require the *means* to commit mass atrocities. At the very least, they require a sufficient number of people who are prepared to commit atrocities. Third, they require the *opportunity* to commit mass atrocities whether through the limiting of institutional restraints or the support and/or acquiescence of external actors.

Most episodes of genocide or mass atrocity are directly preceded by a crisis of one form or other. Usually this takes the form of a political crisis but economic or natural crises can also play an important role. A crisis often provides actors with the *reasons* to commit mass atrocities. Without a crisis even actors predisposed towards mass atrocities would have little reason to commit these crimes. This partly explains why some highly authoritarian states prove relatively stable – with opposition unable to mount a credible challenge, they have no reason to resort to atrocities. Should, however, opponents mount a threat such regimes are quite likely to resort to atrocities to protect themselves.

In his landmark book, *Final Solutions*, Benjamin Valentino argued that 'mass killing usually is driven by instrumental, strategic calculations. Perpetrators see mass killing as a means to an end, not an end in itself.'[38] But they only see mass killing as a viable response to *particular kinds* of circumstance. While not always a last resort, mass atrocities are rarely a first resort. As Valentino explained, '[l]eaders adopted mass killing in frustration, only after they came to believe, although often mistakenly, that other strategies for achieving their goals were impossible or impractical'.[39] It is these specific circumstances, therefore, that create powerful incentives to engage in mass killing. The specific motivations, Valentino found, could be divided into two broad types. First, when the pursuit of a political objective requires the 'near-complete material disenfranchisement of large groups of people'.[40] Second, where mass killing is used as a means of coercion when combatants lack the capability to defeat their opponents with conventional armed force. Typically, this strategy is adopted as a counter-insurgency tactic by regimes that face a serious threat from a guerrilla campaign that cannot be mitigated by conventional warfare, by actors in high attrition wars in order to spread terror and coerce the enemy's civilian population, and by imperial powers as an inexpensive way of prevailing.[41]

Although these scenarios create powerful incentives for mass atrocities, they do not invariably 'cause' them. According to Valentino, a number of intervening variables increase or decrease leaders' incentives and capabilities for mass killing, affecting the likelihood that mass killing will occur. These include the value placed on the objective at hand; the physical capabilities for mass killing; the extent of the perceived threat; the availability of other plausible strategies; the extent of the victims' capacity for flight or safety; the victims' capacity for retaliation; and the likelihood of provoking external intervention.[42]

Similar ideas are evident in Alexander Downes' account of 'civilian victimization' in war. Like Valentino, Downes argued that mass atrocities are employed for rational and strategic purposes and are not driven by irrational hatreds or emotions. Also like Valentino, Downes maintained that states are generally cautious about employing mass atrocities because they fear retribution against their own non-combatants or third-party intervention, and only turn to targeting non-combatants when other strategies have failed or proven prohibitively expensive.[43] He maintained that two factors were primarily responsible for decisions to target civilians. First, desperation to win and to save lives on one's own side: 'desperation overrides moral inhibitions against killing noncombatants.'[44] Second, an appetite for territorial conquest. Armed groups sometimes use genocide and mass atrocities to overrun territory inhabited by enemy civilians. In this situation, perpetrators attack enemy civilians in order to prevent future rebellions, deny potential assistance to enemy armed forces, and generate living space for the perpetrator's own civilians.

The only substantive issues on which Downes and Valentino disagreed were the questions of ideology and regime type. Valentino, recall, argued that certain types of regime used mass killing to accomplish ideological goals. Downes, however, insists that regime type and ideology had no discernible effects on a state's proclivity to select mass atrocities. All we need to know, Downes argued, is that the state wants to win.[45] But for our purposes, the most important point to take from these studies is that actors typically use genocide and mass atrocities as a rational means to get what they want – either because their political programme calls for the extermination of a particular group or, much more frequently, because they offer a relatively inexpensive and effective way of countering a challenge or pursuing an ambition. Given the innate rationality that underpins them, therefore, it is unsurprising that mass atrocities almost always occur within the context or immediate aftermath of a major political crisis, which may be augmented by an economic or natural crisis (or both). These crises provide the catalyst for the commission of genocide and mass atrocities by giving the perpetrators a reason to commit them.

What often pushes states and societies towards atrocities are political crises, especially those caused by armed contests, unconstitutional regime changes, state incapacity, and revolutionary government.[46] The most common of these is, of course, armed contests. The use of force to settle political disputes creates an obvious incentive for the commission of genocide and mass atrocities. Weaker parties may be tempted to counter their enemy's superiority by targeting the civilian population, which is unable to defend itself. Alternatively, rebel groups might victimize the civilian population for economic gain or to secure their acquiescence and loyalty by instilling fear.[47] Meanwhile, stronger parties might be tempted to employ violence against the civilian population in order to suppress insurgencies that hide among civilians, weaken, or eliminate opposition groups, or assert their authority. Armed contests typically involve internal rebellion and civil war, external invasion and domestic resistance, or the collapse of a peace process.

In many cases, internal rebellion provides the catalyst for genocide and mass atrocities. Among others, this was the case in Bangladesh, Burundi, Ethiopia (Ogaden), Guatemala, El Salvador, Rwanda (in the 1960s), Biafra, East Timor, South Sudan, former Yugoslavia, and Darfur. Most recently, Syria stands out as an example of a civil war characterized by atrocities that began life as a peaceful rebellion against authoritarian government.[48] In all of these cases, governments and their supporters responded to armed rebellion by minority groups seeking independence or autonomy from a discriminatory, abusive, and/or failed state with campaigns of genocide or mass atrocities. Drawing on Mao's dictum that guerrillas should move among the people as a fish in water, insurgent movements often draw support from the civilian population and use civilians as cover, making it difficult for the enemies to defeat them by conventional means. Lacking the capacity to conduct sophisticated counter-insurgency operations, their opponents target the 'fish' by draining the 'water' – that is, targeting the civilian population.[49] Democratic secession can also heighten the risk of genocide and mass atrocities if the elite chooses to oppose the outcome of elections (as the Indonesian-backed militia did in East Timor) or if the new government carries forth an extremist exclusionary ideology and begins to consolidate power by moving towards autocracy, as in Eritrea.

It is not only civil war, however, that can provide the trigger for mass atrocities. *Intervention by an external power* can have precisely the same effects in some cases. Where intervention forces regime change, the ousted regime and its supporters may resort to insurgency tactics targeting both the invading forces and its supporters among the civilian populations. As in civil wars, where the external forces are unable to respond to insurgency tactics in a sophisticated and effective fashion, they may resort to targeting elements of the civilian population thought sympathetic to the insurgents. The fragmentation of society into those who support the invaders and those who oppose them may also cause domestic groups to target one another. These patterns of violence were in evidence after the Ethiopian invasion of Somalia in 2006, which triggered an escalation of violence and atrocities against civilians, in Iraq after the US-led invasion in 2003, culminating in the rise of the Islamic State (IS) in 2014, and in the Democratic Republic of Congo (DRC) following Rwanda's invasion, which plunged the country into almost a decade of civil war that drew in seven other countries, countless militia groups, and claimed the lives of between 2 million and 5 million people.[50] Sometimes, the trigger may not be the emergence of a new armed contest, but the reigniting of an old one caused by the collapse of a peace process. According to a research team associated with the World Bank, the single most important factor in determining a country's risk of descending into war is whether it has endured war in the previous five years.[51]

Another common source of crisis that can give rise to genocide and mass atrocities are unconstitutional regime changes. The eruption of these episodes can catch the world genuinely by surprise – such as in the cases of the 1965–6 massacre of some 600,000 suspected communists in Indonesia, triggered by a foiled coup; state-led violence in Pinochet's Chile, enabled by a military coup; and the 1997–9 civil war in Congo-Brazzaville which accounted for the death of some 50,000 civilians and was precipitated by an attempted coup. Besides, coups tend to reduce the quality of governance and fragment national elites.[52]

Elections held in countries with high or extreme risk can also serve as triggers for violence, as elites coerce support, fix the results, and then squabble over them.[53] This is precisely what happened in Kenya in 2008–9, leading to the killing of over 1000 civilians before Kofi Annan, serving as a joint UN–African Union envoy, negotiated a peace settlement.[54] Without such significant external engagement and protection for civilians, elections in deeply divided countries with limited histories of democracy are unlikely to be democratic experiences and can often result in violence. Because they serve as a basis for distributing political power, which usually also comes with economic power, elites and the wider social groups they lead have a major interest in the result of elections. In fragmented societies, especially those characterized by an abusive state apparatus, poor rule of law, poverty, and horizontal inequalities, failure to acquire political power can have dire consequences for whole groups, entrenching inequalities that persist for many generations.[55] As such, the stakes tend to be high and the institutional checks and balances extremely weak, creating powerful incentives to use violence to coerce voters, manipulate the results, or to dispute them.

Sometimes, the crisis that triggers atrocities is simply the inability of a state to govern or provide security. Incapacity helps produce a type of state formation that creates grievances and presents opportunities for those prepared to employ violence. The problems caused here are exacerbated in some places by the presence of lootable natural resources that can be used to finance non-state armed groups, as with diamonds in West Africa and oil in Syria. Sometimes, the state itself operates in a fashion not too dissimilar from rebel groups. In some postcolonial settings where states suffered legitimacy problems owing to the poor fit between the state and other forms of identity and where regimes are non-democratic, political leaders are more likely to use violence and other forms of intimidation to manage the economy for their own economic and political gain. Described as 'shadow states', 'kleptocracies', and 'protection racket states', these regimes try to compensate for legitimacy deficits and satisfy the interests of key groups, which are often drawn from a single region, ethnic group, or tribe, by siphoning off state resources to elevate the personal wealth of their leaders and establish patronage networks to protect their position.[56] Clearly, when the state behaves in this manner, it loses legitimacy and establishes grievances. Patronage and corruption work by granting special favours to certain groups, marginalizing others. Marginalized groups are likely to face hardship and have few opportunities to change these facts by peaceful means. In such circumstances, groups are more likely to employ violence to seize power and resources and protect their sectional interests.

Historically, this problem has manifested itself in different ways. New states with low legitimacy may struggle to assert their authority over the whole of their territory. Several new states have found that upon gaining independence they lacked the legitimacy needed to govern throughout their territory. There may be armed or other forms of opposition to the state and the government may only be able to exert its will through the use of force. This sometimes resulted in the instrumental use of genocide and mass atrocities by weak states for purposes of regime establishment or consolidation (as discussed above). Good examples of this type of crisis are Africa's two largest states – Zaire/DRC and Sudan – which have faced a perpetual crisis of legitimacy since independence, giving rise to multiple episodes of mass atrocities, and the country exposed to the most 'conflict years' of all since 1945, Myanmar. Myanmar was confronted by no fewer than twelve secessionist armed groups. The state's inability to impose its authority in some areas creates space for non-state actors to secure political and economic wealth, sometimes by using violence against the civilian population.[57] For instance, highly brutal strategic violence by rebel groups against civilians in Sierra Leone and Liberia was intended, among other things, to secure their acquiescence, their labour, and their resources through fear. It established patterns of shame and disgust that fuelled further rounds of violence and atrocity.[58]

Political crises are not always produced by competition for power. Sometimes they are deliberately provoked by an ideologically driven regime bent on dramatically reshaping society. Revolution and civil war preceded genocide in Cambodia between 1975 and 1979.[59] When the Khmer Rouge seized power, the urban population was sent to the countryside, and anyone who was part of the old urban elite was murdered. Around 2 million people, or a quarter of Cambodia's population, died at the hands of the Khmer Rouge. The Russian Revolution was the catalyst for a large number of atrocities committed in the 1930s and 1940s under Joseph Stalin, some genocidal in nature. At least 9 million people died in Stalin's purges. In an attempt to radically transform the social order and weaken the national identity of different Soviet republics, entire nations were deported from their homelands and, if they survived at all, most never returned.[60]

Sometimes, the path from crisis to atrocities might take only days or even hours. In other cases, atrocities may take longer to actualize. Typically, mobilization involves the organization of hate groups; purging the armed forces of minority groups and those thought disloyal and expanding recruitment among dominant groups; the establishment, arming, and training of militias; and the publication of hate propaganda. Often there are moves to marginalize minority groups through segregation, displacement, the setting up of camps or ghettos, and exclusion from schools and employment. Of course, elements of mobilization are likely to be evident prior to the emergence of a crisis, especially in high- or extreme-risk countries but when crises erupt we can expect to see the acceleration of mobilization if mass atrocities are imminent. Four particularly significant aspects of mobilization are military reorganization, the establishment of militia intended to conduct the killing, the accelerated spread of hate propaganda, and the marginalization of moderates including those in the governing elite.

The point of this is to show that the causes of genocide and mass atrocities, the practices that create moral outrage around the globe and demands for armed intervention to protect vulnerable peoples from their oppressors, are many, varied, and usually deeply ingrained in local politics and societies. They tend to be the products of deep-seated grievances and existential conflicts between groups and as such are often not readily amenable to outside intervention. To be sure, foreign armed intervention can make a significant difference in such cases, as we will show in later chapters, and comprehensive engagement can help societies forge more peaceable futures for themselves. But we need to be modest in our expectations and fully cognizant of the political complexities at play. The factors described above contribute to what the nineteenth-century strategist Carl von Clausewitz labelled the 'fog of war', a problem that confronts all those who would contemplate military intervention. They also remind us that the military component is only one element of these tragedies and should not be understood in isolation of the political, social, historical, and humanitarian components.

How atrocities end

To understand how humanitarian intervention fits into the broader spectrum of responses to atrocity crimes, we need to understand how – historically – episodes of atrocity crimes have actually ended. Understanding what actually happens lays bare the fantasy of humanitarian intervention – the conceit that foreign powers are a people's principal saviours from atrocity crimes. The hard reality is that foreign powers have rarely saved strangers from atrocity crimes. It is much more likely that the strangers will be utterly devastated or that they will save themselves. Thus, understanding how atrocities actually end provides much-needed guidance on which strategies international society can realistically pursue in the face of atrocities. In other words, it helps avoid what de Waal and Conley-Zilkic describe as the 'best of all worlds trap' whereby analysts,[61] advocates, and officials refuse to advocate the most realistic response to genocide and mass atrocities because it is not the perfect response.[62] At the same time, it is important to pay attention to how atrocities end because the manner of its ending influences the durability of the peace.[63] What is more, understanding the termination of atrocity crimes gives us a clearer sense of the precise processes involved which can also amplify understanding of the patterns and causes of killing.

To date, the only substantive attempt to address this question was a 2006 Social Science Research Council colloquium organized by Alex de Waal and Bridget Conley-Zilkic and a study of the role of military intervention in ending genocidal killings.[64] Both accounts were 'preliminary studies' based on relatively loose guidelines for case selection and analysis. De Waal and Conley-Zilkic reviewed the ending of nineteen twentieth-century episodes of mass killing.[65] Across these cases, they found that there were four primary reasons for the de-escalation of mass killing. First, de-escalation occurred when the perpetrators achieved their goals.[66] Second, they found that successful resistance dampened the rate of killing. This effect, they noted, depended on the extent to which the victim group could mount an effective military campaign.[67] The third reason was elite dissension. In several cases, elites disagreed about the most appropriate strategy and militaries were more reluctant to carry out killings than their civilian superiors. This could have a significant dampening effect on the level of killing. The fourth reason was external military intervention for primarily self-interested purposes. Primarily self-interested interventions, they found, tended to be both more likely and more effective than interventions inspired by humanitarian concerns.

These findings were supplemented by an earlier study investigating the role of military intervention in ending twelve cases of genocidal violence from the early twentieth century to 2008.[68] In this study, it was revealed that, with few exceptions, once begun, genocidal killing ends either because perpetrators choose to end it or because they have been defeated militarily. Another finding, however, was that external military intervention to end genocidal killing was quite rare. Where the perpetrators suffered military setbacks this was usually due to either local resistance or primarily self-interested intervention not directly responding to the genocidal killing. Third, the study found that to be effective in halting the killing, external intervention must target the perpetrators and bring about their military defeat. Other forms of intervention, such as impartial peacekeeping or observation missions, do not usually succeed in ending mass killing.[69] These two studies, using slightly different case samples, agreed on the main types of endings and their frequency.[70] Hugo Slim put forth a similar menu of potential endings: (1) success for the perpetrator; (2) internal dissension; (3) sufficient armed resistance; and (4) external military intervention. Military intervention, Slim argued, 'is extremely rare and routinely comes very late, always after the first wave of massacres'.[71]

Another dataset on how atrocities end improved on these findings.[72] The cases identified in the dataset were selected based on lower-end estimates, finding that 5,000 civilians were intentionally killed by the military or other armed groups controlled by the government of the country in which the attacks occurred. Excluded from this dataset are killings by non-state actors and those by states outside their own borders. Episodes were identified in as specific a form as possible (with perpetrators and victims), but in some cases they were so interlinked as to make it almost impossible to disentangle from broader patterns of conflict or mass killing. The subjective judgements required to draw precise lines between and within cases mean that we should not place too much emphasis on the precise breakdown of results, for these could be altered by relatively minor changes to the coding.[73] Instead, what we are looking for are the major observable patterns that could withstand minor changes to how individual episodes are identified and coded. 'Intentional killing' refers to the killing of non-combatant members of the targeted group, which was specifically intended whether as a matter of policy, strategy, or operational requirement. Once cases were selected, a simple inductive analysis was conducted, involving the use of secondary literature to devise a short description of the ending and to identify the principal pathway through which the ending was brought about. In most cases, the pathway to ending was opened by several interrelated factors. Understanding how these factors relate to produce endings requires more detailed examination of individual cases than is possible here. For heuristic purposes, the cases were clustered according to the principal mode of ending categorized by the degree of perpetrator volition in the selection of the ending. At one end of the scale are cases ended by the perpetrators once they have achieved their objectives. At the other end of the spectrum are episodes of atrocities ended by regime change of various types (induced by internal or domestic opponents, complete or 'partial'). In between these polls are endings induced by the perpetrators changing their strategic goals and negotiated endings. The dataset identified sixty-five discrete cases of atrocities perpetrated by states since 1945.

The first key finding was that a majority of cases of mass killing since 1945 perpetrated by states against sections of their own population were ended by the perpetrators themselves – either because they judged that they had achieved their goals or because they decided to change their goals. Indeed, these types of ending are twice as common as the next most common type – regime change. Overall, the perpetrators themselves ended close to half of all the identified cases, once they perceived that they had achieved their goals. However, the proportion of episodes ended by the free will of the perpetrators has declined significantly since the end of the Cold War. During the Cold War, state perpetrators confronting major existential challenges could reasonably expect that the use of mass atrocities would help them achieve their goals because in a majority of cases it seemed to do so. Since the end of the Cold War, however, complete success has become quite rare.

This general finding lends strong support to the view that state perpetrators employ mass atrocities when they believe that it can help them to achieve their objectives at a reasonable cost. If we also accept the view that the perpetrators tend only to use atrocities as a last resort when the stakes are high and other options apparently exhausted,[74] then there are good grounds for thinking that there are circumstances in which a regime may conclude that its interests are best served by committing mass atrocities. This is certainly borne out by the cases themselves, which include episodes where states employed mass atrocities as a tactical response to armed insurgency (as in the Iraqi campaign against the Kurds, the Russian campaign in Chechnya and the Sudanese campaign in Darfur). The other principal type of case that fall into this category involved relatively new regimes employing mass killing as a means of protecting itself from actual or potential enemies or supporting state consolidation – as with the new communist regimes of Eastern Europe and the anti-communist pogroms in South Korea (1950) and Indonesia (1965–6).

Key to the ability of these states to 'get away' with perpetrating atrocity crimes to achieve their goals was their ability to overpower domestic armed resistance (to the extent that any was offered) and avoid excessive external interference. With regards to the latter, great power support to the perpetrators (or the identity of the perpetrators as great powers); their international legitimacy as states and the right to non-interference associated with sovereignty; and their capacity to limit and obscure the flow of information about the commission of atrocities have been identified as key contributing factors.[75] The decline of this type of ending since the end of the Cold War can therefore be explained in part by the withdrawal of great power patronage, the refashioning of sovereignty to include elements of responsibility, and the extension of global media capacity, which have made more scarce the resources typically associated with the successful avoidance of international reaction to mass killing.

But although it has become more difficult for state perpetrators to achieve their goals by committing atrocity crimes, it is not yet impossible for them to do so. In the mid-1990s, the Taliban successfully employed mass killing, among other things, to eliminate opponents, as did Iraq in crushing the Shi'ite rebellion in the south (despite the imposition of an international 'no-fly zone'). In 1999,

Russia successfully employed massive doses of indiscriminate force to destroy its opposition in Chechnya, and Sri Lanka did likewise in defeating the Liberation Tigers of Tamil Eelam (LTTE) in 2009. In each of these cases, the above-mentioned factors – relative weakness of the opposition, connection to great power, state legitimacy, and flow of information –helped contribute to the achievement of relatively successful outcomes for state perpetrators. More recently, indiscriminate violence (and Russian intervention) helped the Syrian government avoid defeat.

One step removed from episodes that end only once the perpetrators themselves have determined that they have achieved their objectives are those where the perpetrators revised their goals in such a way as to negate the need to continue to employ mass atrocities. Domestic resistance and international pressure, both of which may have the effect of increasing the costs associated with using mass killing and/or reducing the perceived likelihood of success, can persuade perpetrators to terminate or reduce the scale of violence earlier than they otherwise would have done. While it is difficult in a survey such as this to provide a full account of the factors that influenced perpetrators' decision-making in complex situations like this, it is worth observing that external pressure played an obvious and direct role in influencing local elites in only a relatively small number of these cases. In the majority of cases, such as when the Chinese Communist Party decided to terminate the Great Leap Forward and suppress the Cultural Revolution or when, in 1988, the Burundian president ordered a halt to the killing of Hutu, the principal impetus for changes comes from domestic sources. In these cases, elites sometimes judge that the strategic goal was misconceived or had become less significant as a result of other changes, that the tactics utilized had proven ineffective, or that resistance had proven stiffer than anticipated. Although international pressure is sometimes a contributing factor – for example, quiet US criticism of Pinochet's tactics likely contributed to the regime's decision to moderate its actions in 1973, and it was a combination of international pressure and local armed resistance that forced Yugoslavia/Serbia to reach terms with Croatia in early 1992 – historically speaking, international society's will and capacity to directly influence perpetrators' decision-making has not proven to be as great as might have been thought.

The second key finding reinforces this sobering point about the relatively limited role that international society has played historically in ending atrocities because it shows that negotiated endings are rare. Although international hopes are often pinned on the power of persuasion and diplomacy – a tendency that became especially prominent in the wake of Kofi Annan's successful mediation in Kenya in 2009 and helped give rise to diplomatic efforts to end the civil war in Syria led first by Annan and then Lakhdar Brahimi – the historical record suggests that when states employ mass killing against sections of their own population, they are rarely open to negotiated settlements. While international negotiations are quite common at the end of an episode of mass killing and are necessary to manage the practical arrangements of whatever order will come afterwards, they are very rarely the primary mechanism for terminating the killing. What is more, even when endings are negotiated, governments are pushed to the negotiations by *other* significant factors. Negotiated endings are likely, therefore, only when certain other conditions exist. Historically, negotiated endings have tended to arise at the end of episodes of mass killing perpetrated within the context of a protracted civil war. Thus, historically speaking, negotiated endings to mass killing have occurred only after local armed resistance has succeeded in preventing governments from accomplishing their objectives through mass killing but has proven insufficiently strong to defeat the perpetrators and effect regime change (whether complete or partial). This has tended to manifest itself most obviously in stalemated civil wars characterized by episodic mass killing, as in Angola, El Salvador, or Guatemala, or in situations such as that in East Timor when government efforts succeeded in holding ground but not in terminating insurgency activities that continued to extract political and financial costs.

The third key finding is that atrocities not ended by the perpetrators are most often terminated with some degree of regime change. As perpetrator-initiated endings have declined since the end of the Cold War, the proportion of episodes terminated by regime change has increased to the extent that regime change endings are now more common than perpetrated-initiated endings. We can further classify regime change endings in two ways: by the nature of the regime change itself and by the nature of the actors responsible. In terms of the nature of regime change, it is useful to distinguish between 'complete' regime change – atrocities that end when the government in question was removed from power wholesale – and 'partial' regime change where the perpetrating regime remained in power in its national capital but lost control over part of its formerly held territory. The former includes the ending of the 1994 Rwandan genocide by the Rwandan Patriotic Front (RPF) and of the Khmer Rouge's reign of terror in Cambodia by Vietnam in 1979. Endings precipitated by partial regime change include the termination of atrocities in Kosovo by NATO intervention in 1999 and in East Pakistan in 1971 by Indian intervention. However difficult the politics associated with regime change may be, the historical record suggests that some form of change is often necessary to end atrocities, especially when this is against the wishes of the perpetrating state. To be clear, since 1945 the principal alternative to regime change of one form or other in situations where states commit atrocities against sections of their own populations has been for the perpetrators themselves to decide when and how to stop the killing.

We should not make the mistake, however, of equating regime change with foreign armed intervention. Regime change can also be induced by domestic actors through one of three principal modes: domestic armed opposition, military coups, and popular uprisings or revolutions. As a means of ending atrocities, domestic-led regime change has proven much more reliable than internationally forced change. Almost three-quarters of all the mass atrocity endings produced by regime change were achieved by principally *domestic* opponents through one of these three pathways.

This means that regime change brought about by foreign military intervention endings is among the rarest of ways in which atrocities perpetrated by states against their own population ends. Overall, since 1945 fewer than one in ten episodes of state-perpetrated atrocities has been terminated by foreign armed intervention. What is more, the frequency of foreign-induced regime change has not changed significantly, in line with the general decline of perpetrator-induced endings since the end of the Cold War, as discussed. In the post-Cold War era, atrocities are still more likely to end when the perpetrators choose to end them or at the hands of domestic opponents than they are to be ended by foreign armed intervention. If, as proponents of the 'moral hazard' approach to humanitarian intervention suggest,[76] rebel groups believe that they can entice foreign intervention on their behalf by provoking governments into perpetrating mass atrocities, the historical record suggests that it is deeply misguided. Even since the end of the Cold War, defeat at the hands of state perpetrators has proven much more common than victory through foreign armed intervention for the victims of atrocity crimes. In earlier decades the odds were stacked against them even more heavily, raising significant questions about the source of the expectations of foreign interference that are so central to moral hazard theorizing. For 'moral hazard' to be correct, its proponents would need to explain why rebel groups behave so consistently in a manner that is obviously contrary to their fundamental interests.

The most likely explanation is that 'moral hazard' theorizing is misguided – that rebel groups do not employ violence to provoke atrocities against them in the (almost always forlorn) hope that this will attract foreign armed intervention; they do so because they believe this is the best way of furthering their interests and – in the context of state-perpetrated mass atrocities – bringing the killing to an end. That perspective hews more closely to the historical record given the frequency with which state-perpetrated mass killing is ended by regime change induced by domestic opposition, primarily domestic armed opposition. Typical of this was the termination of the Rwandan genocide in 1994, brought about not by foreign armed intervention but by the use of force by the RPF. In other cases, determined domestic armed opposition has forced governments to adjust their strategic goals, resulting in a termination of mass killing – as in the cases of the first Chechen war and the war in Croatia – or has forced them to the negotiating table prior to the achievement of their initially stated goals, as in Sudan (1972), El Salvador (1992), and Guatemala (1996).

Given that a significant degree of local armed opposition appears to be necessary in order to induce governments to negotiate an end to atrocities, it seems apparent that the use of force by domestic actors is significantly more likely to end or limit mass atrocities than foreign armed intervention. To return to the moral hazard issue, the historical record suggests that rebel armed groups are much more likely to deliver their own populations from atrocities than they are to attract foreign interveners to do it for them. This would suggest that the former objective (protecting their own interests and advancing their cause) is a more likely motivating consideration than the latter (provoking foreign intervention). It is certainly more consistent with past experience. And, returning to the question of regime change, while regime change is a common form of termination, it is achieved in different ways and most commonly by domestic forces. If the early termination of atrocities is international society's primary goal, therefore, it stands to reason that more attention be paid to these domestic forces than to the prospects of foreign intervention.

While outside states and external activists might be satisfied emotionally by endings that facilitate the perpetrators' downfall, it is not necessarily the case that these sorts of endings are the most peaceable or durable, or that forcing an ending against the wishes of the perpetrators results in lives saved. Understandably, the duration of an episode seems to be important in influencing the overall number of estimated casualties. From the data presented here, it appears that episodes that end with regime change (and remember that most of these are produced by domestic forces) tend to be much longer in duration (more than twice as long based on a simple average of years) than those ended voluntarily by the perpetrating regime. Episodes that end with regime change tend also to be deadlier. This seems to be primarily a function of the longer duration because there is little discernible difference in the average intensity of the killing (i.e. average rate of killing over time) associated with different types of endings. The most likely explanation for the longer average duration associated with regime change endings is that determined domestic opposition prevents a state perpetrator from achieving its goals quickly and pushes it into a protracted campaign of atrocities. Only quite rarely are domestic armed opponents able to defeat regimes quickly. This suggests that the worst of all worlds in terms of an episode's duration and lethality is not when the state perpetrators are confronted by armed opposition per se, but when they are confronted by forces incapable of inflicting a decisive defeat upon them. When this happens, countries enter protracted civil wars characterized by mass killing. For example, once, towards the end of 2011, the conflict in Syria transitioned from street protests to a civil war characterized by atrocities, it entered precisely this scenario: a determined regime facing an existential threat confronts a series of domestic armed groups which are sufficiently strong to resist but insufficiently strong to prevail. The historical record suggests that absent of significant international involvement or a dramatic breakthrough on the ground, the conflict and atrocities in Syria were likely to persist for a little over a decade. And while analysis that is focused on one-sided intervention during mass atrocities suggests that intervention reduces the duration of episodes,[77] studies of civil war suggests that third-party intervention prolongs armed conflict, especially when external parties intervene on both sides.[78] In Syria, while Russia, Iran, and Hezbollah have rallied behind the state, Turkey, Saudi Arabia, Qatar, and the West have provided support to the opposition. As a result, Syria's civilians have confronted the worst of all worlds.

The durability of endings is also important. It is well established that in the first five years after civil war there is a significant chance of a recurrence of armed conflict.[79] With that in mind, it is worth asking which type of atrocity ending is likely to produce the most durable peace. To do this, the cases listed in the dataset on atrocity endings were cross-referenced with the Uppsala Conflict Data Program's data on one-sided violence and armed conflict more generally.[80] Comparing the different types of ending by reference to the frequency of the recurrence of either mass killing or armed conflict within the first five years after the termination of an episode, it appears that negotiated settlements provide the most stable form of ending – though because there are relatively few cases of negotiated endings we should be careful not to read too much into this finding. Behind that, the voluntary termination of mass killing by the state perpetrators also tends to establish a relatively stable peace less likely than other types to produce recurrence.

Regime change endings tend to be the least stable.[81] Indeed, almost half of the countries that experienced state-perpetrated atrocities followed by regime change experienced a further episode of atrocities within five years of the termination of the previous episode. This is significantly higher than the general risk of relapse into civil war noted earlier. What is more, an even higher proportion (nearly three-quarters) of cases ended by regime change experienced a recurrence of armed conflict in that same five-year period. To explain the apparent instability of regime change endings, it is important to understand that the presence or absence of civil war is more important than the mode of ending as an influence on the likelihood of recurrence. Among the cases identified, when atrocities were perpetrated in a context of civil war, this has been associated with higher rates of recurrence than any of the individual modes of ending. Irrespective of the type of ending, atrocities are less likely to recur if they occur outside of a context of civil war. This suggests that it is the presence or resolution of underlying conflict – whether by the destruction of the opposition's capacity to perpetrate violence, negotiation, or foreign imposition – rather than the precise mode of ending that is the critical determinant of recurrence. We might label this the 'decisive resolution' thesis: atrocities that produce decisive results one way or another are less likely to recur than those that do not.

This would also help explain why the small number of negotiated endings have proven more stable than other types of ending. Before reaching a negotiated settlement, the parties presumably reached a 'mutually hurting stalemate'[82] in which they recognized that they could not prevail at a reasonable cost through violence. Having failed to prevail through force of arms, the negotiating process helped them to find an accommodation that at least mitigated the underlying sources of conflict or offered a pathway for its management. The 'decisive resolution' thesis might also explain why successful state perpetrators are less likely to reoffend than their less successful peers. Having eliminated sources of opposition, victorious state perpetrators simply have no need to resort once more to mass atrocities, creating what we might term the 'perpetrator's peace'. Perhaps the clearest example of this tendency in practice are the two Chechen wars, both of which were characterized by the massive use of indiscriminate violence by Russia. The first Chechen war ended in a stalemate when the Russian regime failed to impose its will on Chechnya and was forced to withdraw its forces from Grozny. The indecisive nature of the ending helped precipitate a second round of violence, which did result in a decisive victory for Russia and the dismembering of Chechnya's capacity to resist Russian rule. This 'decisive resolution' was not followed by recurrence.

Although regime change endings tend to be the least stable of all the various kinds examined in this chapter, regime change induced by foreign intervention is less unstable than regime change engineered by domestic forces.[83] Matthew Krain, for example, has shown that this effect is strongest when the intervention is robust and decisively targeted against the perpetrators of atrocities, though there is also a positive effect, albeit less pronounced, associated with the deployment of traditional and multidimensional peacekeeping operations.[84] This suggests that any form of international deployment on the ground may be expected to have some mitigating effect on the likelihood of recurrence.

Implications

Although every case is different and international responses need to be tailored to the individual circumstances of each, several implications flow from the above.

First, however politically uncomfortable it may be, the reality seems to be that, of those cases where perpetrators terminate the violence prior to achieving their goals, regime change of one form or another has proven to be the principal means by which conflict is ended. Such regime change is usually affected by domestic actors rather than through international militarily intervention, which remains relatively rare. The sting in the tail, however, and a caution to those who would advocate arming rebel armed groups as a matter of course, is that protracted domestic armed opposition to state-perpetrated atrocities tends to lengthen the duration of an episode, increasing the death toll above the average across all cases, as well as increasing the chances of recurrence within five years above other sorts of endings and civil war in general. This is the case especially when, as in Syria, the armed opponents are able to prevent the state achieving its goals, but lack the capacity to inflict a decisive defeat on it.

The implication for international policy-makers is that supporting domestic armed opposition by, for example, supplying them with arms, is an option that should be entered into cautiously and as part of a broader strategy. Arming rebels to get them to the point at which they can resist but not defeat state perpetrators can sometimes set the groundwork for negotiations, but can be expected to prolong an episode significantly and lead to more deaths than otherwise would have been the case were the state perpetrators allowed simply to impose their will through atrocities. This presents third parties with a difficult moral choice: is it better to let the perpetrating state prevail or to facilitate armed opposition which will help regime change but at the cost of more lives lost and a greater chance of recurrence? Of course, there is an alternative to this apparently Faustian bargain, which would be to provide assistance to the rebels on such a massive scale that it allows them to score a rapid and decisive victory. This might entail a combination of measures designed to choke the government's ability to perpetrate violence (tight sanctions and embargoes, asset freezes, indictments, etc.) with a massive flow of arms and training support to the rebels. Armed intervention on the rebels' behalf would lend further assistance. Assuming that this latter course of action is off the table, as it has most often proved to be, the supply of direct support to rebels remains a high-risk strategy, given the lack of certainty about their capacity to absorb assistance effectively and translate external support into effective military operations, the likelihood of escalation from the government side that this would provoke, the high degree of international coordination that this strategy would require, and the possibility that rebel armed groups themselves might perpetrate atrocity crimes. There are, of course, other alternative policies that might contribute to this same effect. For example, international society might apply pressure and incentives to encourage a change of regime from within, so that the elite itself removes the direct leadership and appoints a new set of leaders, but we need to be cautious about the capacity of outsiders to directly influence domestic affairs when the stakes are so high.

In these conditions, where international society faces an apparently Faustian choice between minimizing the expected death toll (by allowing the perpetrators to prevail quickly) and enforcing shared standards of behaviour (by acting, short of force, to oppose the perpetrators), a more prudent course of action might be to forgo interference aimed at shaping how the episode is terminated and instead focus on saving as many civilian lives as possible while the mass killing continues. The underlying rationale for this approach is that unless there is sufficient will and consensus for external military intervention (which, for good reason, remains rare), there is relatively little that international society can do to end the conflict until the parties themselves are prepared to do so. As the experiences of Bosnia and Syria demonstrate only too well, diplomacy and negotiations are likely to prove fruitless until the parties reach a mutually hurting stalemate and come, of their own accord, to accept that their interests are better served by talking than by fighting. It can often take many years for them to arrive at this judgement. In the meantime, there may be grounds for thinking that doing whatever can be done to protect civilians from direct harm may be the best available course of action.

There exist a variety of measures that provide direct and indirect protection to civilian populations. Many have already been canvassed in relation to the situation in Syria, but several could be combined into a coherent strategy. Options include facilitating the flight of civilians by opening borders and caring for refugees; delivering humanitarian assistance into affected regions; bearing witness of atrocities and gathering evidence for future prosecutions and referring the situation to the International Criminal Court; adopting specific humanitarian measures such as humanitarian corridors, safe areas, and 'peace days' to facilitate medical treatment and evacuations; the provision of assistance to civilian protection committees or other evident means of self-protection; making life more difficult for the perpetrators by radio jamming; and reducing availability of weapons and ammunition. We will return to the question of peaceful measures in Chapter 3.

The second implication is that although it is difficult and dangerous, decisive international military intervention can have strongly positive effects. These include the early termination of atrocities, reducing the number of lives likely to be lost, and reducing the likelihood of recurrence within five years. Further, the more decisive the intervention, the greater these positive effects are likely to be. However, decisive foreign military intervention is very rare, primarily because it requires third parties to assume significant risks (of military casualties and political backlash) and costs (decisive intervention is expensive). Thanks to the 'fog of war', military intervention can also sometimes prove counter-productive, causing more disorder than it aims to stem, or can produce indecisive and uncertain outcomes, as in Libya. These are challenges that are not likely to change any time soon.

Assuming that military intervention is likely to remain rare, and therefore not an option that will be available in the great majority of cases, it would seem wise to refrain from investing hopes and energies in this direction. The principal way of preventing the apparent Faustian choice between the pursuit of regime change and allowing the perpetrators to prevail through atrocities is to prevent the escalation of killing in the first place. Once the number of civilian deaths escalates, the number of viable options available to international society is significantly reduced. Early action, probably using measures short of force, is therefore imperative – both in terms of saving lives and in terms of reducing the risk that regime change will become the principal means of saving lives. There is an emerging body of work on how this might be achieved.[85] In 2014, the UN Secretary-General issued a report on how the international community might assist states to prevent mass killing and other atrocity crimes.[86]

It is to this question – of how international society's response to the problem of atrocity crimes has evolved over the past few decades – that we now turn.

Notes

1. On the mixed record see Oliver Richmond, *Failed Statebuilding: Intervention, the State and the Dynamics of Peace Formation* (New Haven, CT: Yale University Press, 2014).

2. See Scott Straus, *The Order of Genocide: Race, Power and War in Rwanda* (Ithaca, NY: Cornell University Press, 2008).

3. See Paul Collier, *Wars, Guns & Votes: Democracy in Dangerous Places* (London: The Bodley Head, 2009); Roland Paris, 'The "Responsibility to Protect" and the Structural Problems of Preventive Intervention', *International Peacekeeping*, 21, no. 5 (2014), pp. 569–603.

4. Scott Straus, *Making and Unmaking Nations: War, Leadership and Genocide in Modern Africa* (Ithaca, NY: Cornell University Press, 2015), p. 326.

5. Stephen McLoughlin and Deborah Mayersen, 'Reconsidering Root Causes: A New Framework for the Structural Prevention of Genocide and Mass Atrocities', in Bert Ingelaere, Stephan Parmentier, Jacques Haers, and Barbara Segaert (eds), *Genocide, Risk and Resilience: An Interdisciplinary Approach* (Basingstoke: Palgrave, 2013); Stephen McLoughlin, *The Structural Prevention of Mass Atrocities: Understanding Risk and Resilience* (London: Routledge, 2014).

6. Michael Gilligan and Stephen John Stedman, 'Where Do Peacekeepers Go?', *International Studies Review*, 5, no. 4 (2003), pp. 37–54; Kyle Beardsley and Holger Schmidt, 'Following the Flag or Following the Charter? Examining the Determinants of UN Involvement in International Crises 1945–2002', *International Studies Quarterly*, 65, no. 1 (2012), pp. 33–49.

7. A point well made by James Waller, *Confronting Evil: Engaging our Responsibility to Prevent Genocide* (Oxford: Oxford University Press, 2016).

8. Thomas Cushman, 'Is Genocide Preventable? Some Theoretical Considerations', *Journal of Genocide Research*, 5, no. 4 (2003), pp. 523–542.

9. See, for example, Ban Ki-moon (2013), *The Responsibility to Protect: State Responsibility and Prevention*, Report of the Secretary-General, A/67/9290S/2013/399, 9 July.

10. See Ben Kiernan, *Blood and Soil: A World History of Genocide and Extermination from Sparta to Darfur* (New Haven, CT: Yale University Press, 2007).

11. Barbara Harff, 'No Lessons Learned from the Holocaust? Assessing Risks of Genocide and Political Mass Murder since 1955', *American Political Science Review*, 97, no. 1 (2003), pp. 57–73: 63–66.

12. Manus Midlarsky, *The Killing Trap: Genocide in the Twentieth Century* (Cambridge: Cambridge University Press, 2005), pp. 43, 62.

13. Martin Shaw, *War and Genocide: Organized Killing in Modern Society* (Oxford: Polity, 2003).

14. Straus, *Making and Unmaking Nations*.

15. See Alex J. Bellamy, *Massacres and Morality: Mass Killing in an Age of Civilian Immunity* (Oxford: Oxford University Press, 2012).

16. Kenneth J. Campbell, *Genocide and the Global Village* (New York: Palgrave, 2001), p. 34.
17. Shaw, *War and Genocide.*
18. Neil J. Kressel, *Mass Hate: The Global Rise of Genocide and Terror* (Cambridge, MA: Westview Press, 2002), p. 171.
19. Catherine Barnes, 'The Functional Utility of Genocide: Towards a Framework for Understanding the Connection between Genocide and Regime Consolidation, Expansion and Maintenance', *Journal of Genocide Research*, 7, no. 3 (2005), pp. 309–330: 320–325.
20. Helen Fein, *Accounting for Genocide: National Response and Jewish Victimization During the Holocaust* (New York: The Free Press, 1979), p. 8.
21. Leo Kuper, *Genocide: Its Political Use in the Twentieth Century* (New Haven, CT: Yale University Press, 1982), p. 50.
22. Kuper, *Genocide*, p. 57; Fein, *Accounting for Genocide*, p. 9.
23. Harff, 'No Lessons Learned', p. 67.
24. Bernd Simon and Bert Kalndermans, 'Politicized Collective Identity: A Social Psychological Analysis', *American Psychologist*, April 2001, p. 319.
25. See Frances Stewart (ed.), *Horizontal Inequalities and Conflict: Understanding Group Violence in Multiethnic Societies* (London: Palgrave, 2008).
26. Gerard Prunier, *Darfur: The Ambiguous Genocide* (London: Hirst, 2005), pp. 3–4; Julie Flint and Alex de Waal, *Darfur: A New History of a Long War* (London and New York: Zed Books, 2008), p. 19.
27. Harff, 'No Lessons Learned', p. 63.
28. Paul Collier and Dominic Rohner, 'Democracy, Development and Conflict', *Journal of the European Economic Association*, 6, nos. 2–3 (2008), pp. 531–540: 534.
29. Michael Mann, *The Dark Side of Democracy: Explaining Ethnic Cleansing* (Cambridge: Cambridge University Press, 2005), pp. 1–2, 5.
30. Jack Snyder, *From Voting to Violence: Democratization and Nationalist Conflict* (New York: W.W. Norton and Company, 2000), p. 16.
31. Frances Stewart, 'The Causes of Civil War and Genocide: A Comparison', in Adam Lupel and Ernesto Verdaja (eds), *Responding to Genocide: The Politics of International Action* (Boulder, CO: Lynne Rienner, 2013), pp. 47–84.
32. Harff, 'No Lessons Learned', p. 66.
33. Matthew Krain, 'Democracy, Internal War, and State-Sponsored Mass Murder', *Human Rights Review*, 1, no. 3 (2000), pp. 40–48.
34. Hugo Slim, *Killing Civilians: Method, Madness and Morality in War* (London: Hurst and Co., 2007).
35. Harff, 'No Lessons Learned', p. 66.

36. Benjamin A. Valentino, *Final Solutions: Mass Killing and Genocide in the Twentieth Century* (Ithaca, NY: Cornell University Press, 2004).
37. Jonathan Maynard Leader, 'Rethinking the Role of Ideology in Mass Atrocities', *Terrorism and Political Violence,* 26, no. 5 (2014), pp. 821–841.
38. Valentino, *Final Solutions,* p. 235.
39. Valentino, *Final Solutions,* p. 235.
40. Valentino, *Final Solutions,* p. 69.
41. Valentino, *Final Solutions,* pp. 68–90.
42. Valentino, *Final Solutions,* pp. 68–90.
43. Alexander B. Downes, *Targeting Civilians in War* (Ithaca, NY: Cornell University Press, 2008), p. 10.
44. Downes, *Targeting Civilians,* pp. 3–4.
45. Downes, *Targeting Civilians,* p. 11.
46. What we mean by 'regime change' is described in further detail in Chapter 5.
47. Jeremy M. Weinstein, *Inside Rebellion: The Politics of Insurgent Violence* (Cambridge: Cambridge University Press, 2007); Mary Kaldor, *New and Old Wars: Organized Violence in a Global Age* (Cambridge: Polity, 1997).
48. Samer M Abboud, *Syria* (Cambridge: Polity); and David W. Lesch (2013), *Syria: The Fall of the House of Assad* (New Haven, CT: Yale University Press, 2016).
49. See Valentino, *Final Solutions.*
50. Gerard Prunier, *Africa's World War: Congo, the Rwandan Genocide and the Making of a Continental Catastrophe* (Oxford: Oxford University Press, 2008).
51. Paul Collier, V. Elliott, H. Havard, A. Hoeffler, A. Reynal-Querol, and N. Sambanis, *Breaking the Conflict Trap: Civil War and Development Policy* (Oxford: Oxford University Press for the World Bank, 2003).
52. Collier, *Wars, Guns & Votes,* p. 153; Barbara Harff, 'The Etiology of Genocides', in Isidor Wallimann and Michael N. Dobkowski (eds), *Genocide and the Modern Age: Etiology and Case Studies of Modern Death* (Syracuse, NY: Syracuse University Press, 1987).
53. Collier, *Wars, Guns & Votes.*
54. See Kofi Annan, *Interventions: A Life in War and Peace* (New York: Penguin, 2012).
55. Frances Stewart and Armin Langer, 'Horizontal Inequalities: Explaining Persistence and Change', in Stewart (ed.), *Horizontal Inequalities,* (2008), pp. 54–83.
56. See William Reno, *Warfare in Independent Africa* (Cambridge: Cambridge University Press, 2011).

57. See Mary P. Callahan, *Making Enemies: War and State-Building in Burma* (Ithaca, NY: Cornell University Press, 2003); and Thant Myint-U, *The River of Lost Footsteps: Histories of Burma* (New York: Farar, Straus and Giroux, 2006).
58. Kieran Mitton, *Rebels in a Rotten State: Understanding Atrocity in the Sierra Leone Civil War* (Oxford: Oxford University Press, 2015).
59. Ben Kiernan, *The Pol Pot Regime: Race, Power, and Genocide in Cambodia Under the Khmer Rouge, 1975–1979*, 3rd edn (New Haven, CT: Yale University Press, 2008).
60. Norman Naimark, *Stalin's Genocides* (Princeton, NJ: Princeton University Press, 2011).
61. Alex de Waal and Bridget Conley-Zilkic, 'Reflections on How Genocidal Killings are Brought to an End', *Social Science Research Council* (Berlin: Nomos, 2006), p. 11.
62. This is precisely the charge levelled against the UN in Darfur by Flint and de Waal, Darfur.
63. For example, as Prunier, *Africa's World War*, has convincingly demonstrated, the manner in which the Rwandan genocide ended (RPF victory, with the world then turning a blind eye to its abuses and massacres) was a direct cause of the subsequent, and much deadlier, war in the DRC.
64. Alex J. Bellamy, 'Military Intervention' in D. Bloxham and D. Moses (eds), *Oxford Handbook of Genocide Studies* (Oxford: Oxford University Press, 2009).
65. The Hercro genocide in Namibia (1904); the Armenian genocide; Stalinist genocide; Nazi Holocaust; Mao's China; massacre of communists in Indonesia (1965–6); Biafran war (1967–70); Bangladesh (1970); Red Terror in Ethiopia; Cambodia; Guatemala; Uganda (1983–4); Iraq – Anfal; Somalia (1991–2); Nuba genocide; Rwanda; Bosnia; Kosovo.
66. De Waal and Conley-Zilkic, 'Reflections', p. 9.
67. De Waal and Conley-Zilkic, 'Reflections', p. 10.
68. Bellamy, 'Military Intervention'. Cases were selected according to the proclivity of genocide studies scholars to refer to them as relatively controversial cases: Herero, Armenia, Ethiopia (Italy), Soviet Union, Japan in East Asia, Nazi Holocaust, Bangladesh, Cambodia, Guatemala, Bosnia, Rwanda, and Darfur.
69. See also Matthew Krain, 'International Intervention and the Severity of Genocides and Politicides', *International Studies Quarterly*, 49, no. 2 (2005), pp. 363–387.
70. De Waal and Conley-Zilkic, 'Reflections'; Bellamy, 'Military Intervention'.
71. Hugo Slim, 'Using What We Know: Politicizing Knowledge and Scholarship to Stop Group Violence', *Social Science Research Council*, (2006), 22 December.

72. See Alex J. Bellamy, 'When States Go Bad: The Termination of State Perpetrated Mass Killing', *Journal of Peace Research,* 52, no. 5 (2015), pp. 565–576.
73. See Laurie Nathan, 'Correspondence: Civil War Settlements and the Prospects for Peace', *International Security,* 36, no. 1 (2011), pp. 202–210.
74. Daniel Chirot and Clark McCauley, *Why Not Kill Them All? The Logic and Prevention of Mass Political Murder* (Princeton, NJ: Princeton University Press, 2006).
75. Alex J. Bellamy, *Massacres and Morality.*
76. For example, Alan J. Kuperman, 'The Moral Hazard of Humanitarian Intervention: Lessons from the Balkans', *International Studies Quarterly,* 52, no. 1 (2008), pp. 49–80.
77. See, for example, Krain, 'International Intervention'; Taylor Seybolt, *Protection of Civilians in Armed Conflict: Cross Cutting Report,* Security Council Report, New York, 2007.
78. See, for example, Dylan Balch-Lindsay and Andrew Enterline, 'Killing Time: The World Politics of Civil War Duration, 1820–1992', *International Studies Quarterly,* 44, no. 4 (2000), pp. 615–542; Patrick Regan, 'Third-Party Interventions and the Duration of Intrastate Conflict', *Journal of Conflict Resolution,* 46, no. 1 (2002), pp. 55–73.
79. Charles T. Call and Elizabeth M. Cousens, 'Ending Wars and Building Peace: International Responses to War-Torn Societies', *International Studies Perspectives,* 9, no. 1 (2008), pp. 1–21.
80. L. Themner and Peter Wallensteen, 'Armed Conflict: 1946–2013', *Journal of Peace Research,* 51, no. 4 (2014), pp. 315–527.
81. For an exception to this claim, see Monica Duffy Toft, 'Ending Civil Wars: A Case for Rebel Victory?' *International Security,* 34, no. 4 (2010), pp. 7–36.
82. See, for example, William I. Zartman, 'The Timing of Peace Initiatives: Hurting Stalemates and Ripe Moments', *Global Review of Ethnopolitics,* 1, no. 1 (2001), pp. 8–18.
83. On the general problems associated with foreign-induced regime change see Alexander B. Downes and Jonathan Monten, 'Forced to be Free? Why Foreign Imposed Regime Change Rarely Leads to Democratization', *International Security,* 37, no. 4 (2013), pp. 90–131.
84. Krain, 'International Intervention'.
85. See, for example, David Hamburg, *Preventing Genocide* (Boulder, CO: Paradigm, 2008) Adam Lupel and Ernesto Verdeja (eds), *Responding to Genocide: The Politics of International Action* (Boulder, CO: Lynne Rienner, 2013); I. William Zartman, M. Anstey and P. Merts (eds), *The Slippery Slope to Genocide* (Oxford: Oxford University Press, 2012).
86. Ban Ki-moon (2014), *Fulfilling our Collective Responsibility: International Assistance and the Responsibility to Protect,* Report of the Secretary-General, A/68/947-S/2014/449, 11 July.

2

Towards Human Protection

Despite the challenges described in the previous chapter, over the past few decades the frequency and lethality of atrocity crimes has declined. Meanwhile, international responses to such violence have become more widespread and more sophisticated. What explains these two phenomena and are they connected? If we accept Steven Pinker's thesis, this decrease in atrocities may not be surprising, as it could be construed simply as part of a broader historical trend of social change that has prioritized cooperation over war, our 'better angels' over our 'inner demons'.[1] Others claim that more immediate conditions have led to this recent decline in violence, such as the end of the Cold War, an increase in global activism and peacekeeping, and the decrease in civil wars.[2] And there are others still who doubt whether global violence has declined at all.[3]

In this chapter we propose that there is compelling evidence to demonstrate that atrocities have declined over the past few decades and that international activism against them is increasing. Moreover, we claim that these two trends are linked by an emerging international regime focused on human protection.[4] As we argue in the rest of the book, this regime has had a profound impact on the politics of humanitarian intervention. Human protection, as stated by UN Secretary-General Ban Ki-moon, is a 'subset of the encompassing concept of human security', and is related to the 'more immediate threats to the survival of individuals and groups'. We argue that over the past few decades an international human protection regime has emerged, consisting of 'principles, norms, rules, and decision-making procedures' aimed at protecting individuals and groups from systematic and targeted violence. Although it has its roots in the legacy of Nuremberg, not until the 1990s did the regime begin to fully take shape. Best understood as an 'overlapping' regime, the international human protection regime has developed unevenly over time but it has had significant effects on how international society thinks about, and responds to, atrocity crimes: constraining the actions of armed combatants; and building commitments, norms, and decision-making processes that shape how international society acts in response to mass violence. It can be seen as an 'International Protection Regime' similar to the kind identified by Bruce Cronin in that it protects 'clearly defined classes of people within sovereign states',[5] though not by design, but rather through an evolution of juridical, diplomatic, and other practices.[6]

In order to sustain this argument – that an international human protection regime has emerged which has contributed to the decline of atrocities – this chapter unfolds in four parts. It first presents evidence supporting our core assertions that armed conflict and atrocities have declined, while international activism against atrocity crimes has grown. Second, it charts the emergence of the international human protection regime, and examines its scope and limitations. Third, it examines the extent to which this regime has impacted the changing behaviour of third parties to mass violence – that is, whether it has changed how international society reacts to atrocity crimes. Finally, it considers alternative explanations for the changes we describe, focusing on four principal theses (the decline of communism thesis, the economic development thesis, the improvement of technology thesis, and the swinging pendulum thesis) as well as the null hypothesis (that nothing has changed). It argues that none of these alternative theses explain changing behaviour as well as the international human protection regime does.

Declining atrocities, rising activism

Has there really been a decline in atrocities and a corresponding rise in international activism in relation to such violence? Given the unfolding crises across the world – including those arising from the Arab Spring, and entrenched conflicts in sub-Saharan Africa – one may be forgiven for doubting that the world is becoming more peaceful and for thinking that international efforts to confront such crises have had negligible impact. This is indeed what some prominent thinkers have concluded. Thus, Michael Ignatieff cautioned that a 'new world disorder' heralding the rise of 'violence and hate' was emerging; Louise Arbour, former chief prosecutor of the International Criminal Tribunal for the former Yugoslavia, claimed that international society's approach to the atrocity problem 'just doesn't work'.[7] But such pessimism is ill-founded. Although there has been a global spike in violence since 2011, a spike which has tapered off since 2015, numerous studies, each deploying different datasets and definitions, all reach similar conclusions – that over the longer term there is a clear downwards trend in atrocity crimes. The *peaks* of violence experienced in 2013–14 were lower than the *average* levels of global violence experienced in the 1990s, which were in turn lower than the levels experienced throughout the Cold War and before it. The arrested decline of atrocity crimes has created a sense of crisis within the international human protection regime – one we will return to in Chapter 8 – but it has not reversed the underlying trends.

The case for a decline in violence is relatively easy to substantiate. For instance, R. J. Rummel's surveys on 'democide' – the killing of people by their own government – shows a strong trend of decline from a peak during the Second World War.[8] This is despite Rummel's tendency towards high estimates of casualties. The Political Instability Task Force's (PITF) more recent datasets – which incorporate the first decade or more of the twenty-first century – also show this general trend. They show that government-sponsored mass killings have been steadily declining since 1993.[9] The Uppsala Conflict Data Program also drew similar conclusions. They compiled data on one-sided violence for the 2013 Human Security Report that showed a decline in both the number of cases and the number of casualties after peaking in 2001. Although they showed a small upwards movement owing to the conflict in Syria, it was not enough to alter the overall pattern. The report also broke down the data according to region, which showed significant declines in Central and South Asia, East Asia and Oceania, Europe, the Americas, and sub-Saharan Africa, as well as an increase in the Middle East and North Africa.[10] Pinker himself, meanwhile, aggregated the data from these sources and controlled for population growth to demonstrate a distinct pattern of declining violence over the period of the twentieth and twenty-first centuries.[11] Other smaller datasets draw similar conclusions, pointing to a decrease in both the frequency of violent episodes against civilians and the overall number of casualties.[12]

Even more recently than this, leading analyst for forecasting mass violence Jay Ulfelder identified this clear downwards trend: 'the spell of global political instability that began in the late 2000s has not yet produced a significant increase in the severity of one-sided violence around the world, at least as of the end of 2013.'[13] This was also picked up by the PITF, which has been charting a gradual decline between 1950 and 2011. While it too has charted an increase in violence since 2011, it has not (as yet) changed this overall downwards trend over the longer term.[14]

What all these datasets point to is consistent evidence demonstrating the fact that there has been a sustained decline in atrocity crimes over the past few decades. The trend appears to have started prior to the end of the Cold War, but became more pronounced since the early late 1990s. The decline ceased around 2011, however, and there was an upturn in atrocities between 2011 and 2015 and a levelling off thereafter. However, despite this increased violence, which we discuss in greater detail in Chapter 8, the overall levels of violence remained significantly lower than during the 1990s and the Cold War decades prior to that. Thus, disagreement among those who take the data seriously today mostly stems from the *causes* of this downwards trend, rather than the *fact* of a general decline in mass violence.[15] That does not mean that the data does not have limits – it is important to acknowledge that these represent our best approximations, and a number of studies point out that there are patterns within specific cases that show that mass violence is complex and inconsistent.[16] Moreover, as some feminist scholars have rightly pointed out, these datasets do not sufficiently pick up gender-based violence.[17] Yet, overall, and across multiple datasets employing different methods, it is clear that there has been a sustained decline in atrocity crimes.

The claim that there has been a corresponding rise of international activism against atrocity crimes is more difficult to establish, because 'activism' is much more difficult to measure. Indeed, some claim that there has been no change in this sense, and that the practice of international politics continues much the same as it did in the 1990s and earlier – rare moments of decisiveness where great power interests are peaked, set against longer periods of disengagement.[18] Yet it is possible to demonstrate empirically that two important things have changed over time: that international society, acting through the UN Security Council, has become more likely to respond to atrocities than it once was; and that, on average, these responses have grown in scale and complexity, and have become more explicitly focused on protecting populations from atrocities. We can ascertain both of these things by examining the totality of the UN Security Council's response to atrocity crimes over time. To do this, we used a dataset of atrocity crimes and asked whether the UN Security Council adopted resolutions and whether those resolutions included the clear objective of human protection. We then compared the results over time.[19]

Table 2.1 shows the raw numbers, and Figure 2.1 shows change over time. Clearly, prior to the Cold War ending, international society was profoundly constrained in what it was willing or able to do in response to atrocities against civilians. Indeed, in the majority of cases, the Security Council simply did not respond at all. Limited or non-existent responses were also the norm beyond the Security Council, primarily owing to the protection that superpower politics afforded perpetrators, as well as the weakness of relevant norms and institutions.[20] Consequently, most actors that committed atrocities during the Cold War were able to fulfil their intended objectives.[21] This began to change after the end of the Cold War, when international society became more involved in trying to bring an end to civil wars and other complex emergencies, as well as to prioritize the protection of civilians. The immediate post-Cold War years saw the Security Council increase its activism, principally (though not exclusively) through its growing utilization of peacekeeping. During this time, military interventions were sometimes considered but rarely employed. Even though this period has been characterized by some as the 'golden age' of humanitarianism,[22] international responses to atrocities remained far from consistent and comprehensive. As Table 2.1 shows, the Security Council responded to fewer

Table 2.1   International responses to mass killing (1970–2015)

Decade	New onsets	UNSC* action	Protection
1970s	23	3	0
1980s	15	4	0
1990s	19	12	3
2000s	5	3	2
2010s	6	6	6

* United Nations Security Council

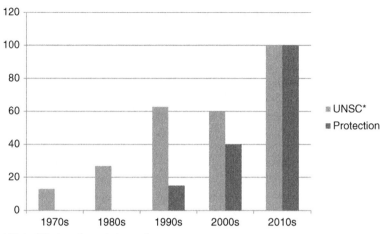

Figure 2.1 International responses to mass killing: 1970–2015

* United Nations Security Council

than two-thirds of cases, and even when it did authorize action, protecting populations was rarely a strong priority, if even considered at all. Thus, in most cases, the effective protection of populations from atrocities was a peripheral concern. This was the decade when UN peacekeepers failed to protect civilians from atrocities in Angola, Bosnia, and Rwanda, because they had neither the mandate nor adequate capacity to do so. Moreover, there continued to be much conjecture within the Security Council as to whether atrocity crimes were something that fell under its mandated purview of 'international peace and security', especially if committed within a state's borders.[23] We can see the beginnings of international society prioritizing human protection in the 1990s, but it was not until the end of the decade that international activism began to look anything like consistent.

It is fair to say, then, that practices of human protection did not emerge suddenly, or out of nowhere. They emerged gradually and fitfully during the 1990s, in a decade that concluded with the highly controversial NATO intervention in Kosovo, in 1999, and the more broadly supported Australia-led intervention in East Timor in the same year. The end of the decade was also accompanied by Kofi Annan's challenge for international society to find a way to better overcome the tension between sovereignty and human rights, which was borne out of both a failure to respond to tragedies like Rwanda and the controversies that surrounded action like Kosovo. Annan lamented the tendency for this tension to often marginalize international concerns for human protection.[24] The 2000s saw a gradual improvement, with protection receiving greater emphasis in Security Council responses, and the likelihood of such responses going up, as Figure 2.1 shows.

The real turning point came in early 2011, following the adoption of a number of landmark Security Council resolutions in response to crises in Libya (Resolutions 1970 and 1973) and Côte d'Ivoire (Resolution 1975). Indeed, the Council has responded to all six of the new cases involving atrocity crimes since that time, such that responding to such cases is becoming a matter of routine. Furthermore, in all of these cases, the response has contained a deliberate focus on the protection of civilians. Of course, there have been times when the response has not lived up to what was needed, particularly obvious with respect to international society's response to the unfolding crisis in Syria, a failure that was mainly the product of disagreements between the great powers. Yet even in the difficult and highly contentious case of Syria, the Council has found sufficient consensus to occasionally respond to the protection issues there by condemning the targeting of civilians, and demanding the conflicting parties comply with International Humanitarian Law (IHL), calling for the disarming of Syria's chemical weapons, and mandating the provision of humanitarian aid without the Syrian government's consent.[25]

Debates around what cases to include and exclude and how one might code responses notwithstanding, there is a clearly observable pattern towards greater international activism on atrocity crimes.[26] In 2015, the non-governmental organization (NGO) Security Council Report, which closely monitors the Council's deliberations, resolutions, and overall performance, published a report that reviewed the Council's work on human protection. Taking into account the full Council agenda, the report concluded that protection concerns were present in 'nearly all' of the Council's resolutions and presidential statements.[27] The fact that the Security Council is now more likely to respond to mass violence than it has done in the past did not happen by chance. It provides good grounds for claiming international protection norms have become more prevalent over the last few decades. With changed norms come changed practices.

Of course, looking at Security Council practices highlights only one aspect of a broader set of responses to atrocity crimes by international society. There is evidence to suggest that patterns emerging in the Council are also reflected in other sectors. For instance, regional organizations are becoming more active in their own peacekeeping operations as those operations become larger and more complex.[28] The African Union Mission in Somalia (AMISOM) and Central African Republic Mission (MISCA), as well as NATO and European Union (EU) missions in the former Yugoslavia have all appointed protection advisers, providing an illustration of this increased priority to civilian protection. Beyond this, it is becoming widely acknowledged that there is a growing commitment to providing mediation in violent conflict and cases of one-sided violence. Such mediation comes from both regional organizations and the UN, sometimes both at the same time, as was the case in Kenya in 2007–8, and presently in Syria.[29] In turn, the demands surfacing from mediated settlements have contributed to the expansion both in breadth and depth to international peacebuilding;[30] and, in spite of obstacles, there has been an expansion of international human rights mechanisms as well as a number of other processes including international criminal justice, transitional justice and truth commissions, and regional processes in the global South.[31] In addition, widespread or systematic sexual and gender-based violence has gained much greater attention in recent years due to more frequent UN reporting, various regional programmes, targeted collective actions, and a UK-led initiative to specifically prevent sexual violence.[32] Clearly, activities related to human protection are broadening and incorporate a wide range of actors beyond the Security Council. However one measures the reach of human protection, it extends further today than it did twenty, forty, or sixty years ago.

Taken together, evidence of these practices indicates that, overall, international society is becoming more committed to the protection of populations from atrocity crimes. At the very least there appears to be a *prima facie* case for thinking that the coinciding of the decline in atrocities charted earlier and the increase in international activism are indeed linked in such a way that this increased activism is making a contribution to lowering levels of violence. If nothing else, this coincidence is informative in terms of debunking the idea that this increase in international activism is demand-driven, as global 'demand' for such responses has, if anything, diminished. In order to get a better sense of the relationship between these two trends, we need to consider 'supply-side' accounts for why it is that states now appear to be more willing to commit time and resources to responding to atrocity crimes and protecting vulnerable populations. The next section proposes as explanation – the emergence of an international human protection regime – that has replaced the narrow politics of humanitarian intervention with the much broader, and more comprehensive, field of human protection.

The international human protection regime

According to Steven Krasner, international regimes are collections of interconnected 'principles, norms, rules, and decision-making procedures' that impact the behaviour of states in specific issue-based areas.[33] They are examples of rules-based cooperation in international politics. As we pointed out earlier, international *protection* regimes are regimes that are committed to the protection of 'defined classes of people within sovereign states'.[34] While it is broadly accepted that regimes have an influence over the way states behave, exactly how they influence behaviour remains open to debate. Neoliberals, for example, would understand the international human protection regime as a manifestation of cooperation with the goal of supporting stability in world politics through the management of some of its most lethal conflicts. In this way, international regimes would be a way of resolving inefficiencies arising out of uncertainty, misinformation, and collective action problems. Thus, the promotion and regulation of cooperation would be a way to mitigate this. As Robert Keohane argues, such regimes are state-initiated instruments that help them meet their interests. That there is a common underlying interest among states means that acting together helps them to achieve their interests, and it is this that is the basis of their capacity to influence behaviour. Recognition of and adherence to a common set of rules, therefore, become the most effective ways of serving their interests, rather than by any short-term advantages that might be gained from acting alone.[35] Incentives for compliance are then compounded by the fact that once such institutions are established, it is not easy to alter them.[36] While this explanation is fairly convincing, particularly in the way it highlights how new institutions and practices arise out of problems with coordination and collective action, what it is less adept in explaining is how and why shared interests in protecting vulnerable populations from mass violence spur states to action, given that such interests are difficult to explain on the basis of rational self-interest alone.

One possible perception of the international human protection regime is that it is simply a symptom of Western hegemony. For instance, a typical realist/neorealist account of regimes holds that they are established by hegemonic powers to serve their own interests,[37] to consolidate existing power structures, or to reduce transaction costs.[38] This is also a perspective that some 'critical' scholars share,[39] arguing that movements related to the international human protection regime are no more than the West exerting hegemonic influence over the non-Western world, as a part of a design to control the periphery and possibly propagate Western liberalism. However, the blind spot in this perspective is that the international human protection regime gained momentum without much great power support. Indeed, some aspects of the regime were openly opposed by Western powers, most obviously with US opposition to the International Criminal Court (ICC). Meanwhile, some aspects of the regime were championed by states from the global South, such as Guatemala, Rwanda, and South Africa.

Constructivists, who view international society as a principally social space, claim that social structures contribute to the constituting of actors' identities, which then inform the actors of who they are, what they want, and what they are willing to do to attain it. This then forms the bedrock of how such actors form societies that are regulated by certain norms, which then in turn create patterns of appropriate behaviours, conditioning which types of actors and actions are regarded as legitimate. Legitimacy breeds support, while illegitimacy attracts condemnation and opposition, which means that behaviours that complement existing shared norms are more likely to influence behaviour, and will induce fewer consequences than those that do not. Regimes, then, come about from shared *ideas* about the world (one example being that civilians should not be prone to mass violence). Consequently, they function by helping to influence beliefs about identities, correct behaviour, and acceptable responses to non-compliance.[40] The focus on ideas allows the connecting of the international human protection regime to ideas about the prohibition of targeting civilians during war, and provides an explanation for how it is that great powers become tied to a framework that influenced their own behaviour, despite their not having created it.

Yet the coming about of the international human protection regime has, to some degree, defied explanations from all of these theoretical perspectives, largely because the regime was not consciously developed by any state or group of states. Rather, it arose from at least eight different interconnected streams of rules, norms, institutional developments, and practices that came into being in a diversified way, in response to different levels of civilian suffering during war. These streams include (1) IHL; (2) the UN Security Council's increasing tendency to prioritize civilian protection and the integration of this protection into the peace operation mandates; (3) the strengthening of international regimes focused on specific challenges in relation to civilian vulnerability, such as those endured by refugees, displaced persons, women, and children; (4) the promotion of global human rights; (5) the establishment and strengthening of institutions dealing with international criminal justice; (6) a strengthening focus on protection among humanitarians; (7) a growing tendency for regional organizations to engage in protection commitments; and (8) the international commitment to the Responsibility to Protect (R2P) in 2005 and its ensuing implementation.

Each of these streams developed in their own ways, without regard for the whole human protection regime, and as such their development was a reflection of the diverse priorities and concerns of a wide range of norm entrepreneurs, each putting emphasis on different aspects of human protection. Some of the streams have roots extending much further into history than the Cold War period – IHL being a notable example here. However varied and separately these individual streams developed, it was not until after the Cold War – and indeed more acutely in the early twenty-first century – that their collective power emerged. The character of this development has produced, on the one hand, a broad regime focused on different forms of vulnerability and measures for their amelioration (legal, political, judicial, etc.), but on the other hand, a regime that still contains significant gaps and blind spots, owing to an absence of overall orchestration.

The first stream – IHL – ostensibly established the foundation for others.[41] IHL – as is well known – originated in the mid to late nineteenth century with the Red Cross movement inspired by Henry Dunant and the establishment of the US government's Lieber code, or 'General Orders No. 100'.[42] It was further refined and codified after the Second World War through the establishment of a number of international treaties, such as the Genocide Convention in 1947, which defined and prohibited the crime of genocide and directed all states to prevent and punish perpetrators.[43] More recently, the International Court of Justice (ICJ) ruled that because of this convention, there exists a responsibility among all states that they do what they can, in order to prevent genocide, within the law as it currently exists. This included the responsibility to take preventive action when prior knowledge about the imminence of such violence exists, along with the capacity for states to influence the behaviour of would-be perpetrators.

In addition to this, four Geneva conventions (1949) along with two additional protocols (1977) added further codification to the laws of wars, including a range of protocols that cover the use of Certain Conventional Weapons (1980, 1995, 1996, 2008). Of particular relevance here is Common Article 3 in the 1949 Geneva Conventions, which declared that committed parties respect the human rights of all those in combat, as well as the Convention on the Protection of Civilian Persons (Convention IV), which established legal protection to all non-combatants who were located in occupied territories.[44] This legal protection was extended by the Geneva Protocols (1977) to include instances of non-international armed conflict. The Protocols also declared that armed attacks would be rigidly confined to military goals (Article 52, Protocol I), prohibiting attacks on both non-combatants and their property. The Protocol also established the principle of discrimination,[45] which created both a legal and a moral foundation for later advocacy in relation to conventions to ban weapons such as cluster munitions and landmines, which were regarded as indiscriminate. This is now a key part of both international criminal law and the UN Security Council's agenda for the protection of civilians. These developments in IHL have established a strong normative standard for the protection of civilians – a standard which not only proscribes the targeting of non combatants and the use of some weapons, but also requires the prevention of particular crimes (such as genocide) and calls for the punishment of those who commit them.

The second stream concerns the UN Security Council's commitment to the broad agenda of the protection of civilians in armed conflict, and how this has materialized into protection mandates for UN peacekeeping operations. Starting in 1998, the UN Security Council has taken on this agenda, which incorporates demands to adhere to IHL, operational matters in relation to peace operations and humanitarian missions, the manner of international responses to humanitarian emergencies, peacebuilding, and issues around disarmament.[46] Following a request from Canada – at the time a non-permanent member – the Security Council issued a presidential statement inviting the Secretary-General to provide periodic reports on how the UN could improve the protection of civilians.[47] Thereafter the Council has conducted open meetings on the protection of civilians, at least annually, and through this protection has emerged as one of the Council's key thematic priorities. Through this process, the Council has built a common understanding that protecting civilians from atrocity crimes is crucial to international peace and security, and as such a matter for international society's system of collective security. This was reflected in the Council's unanimously adopted Resolution 1265 (1999), which declared a 'willingness' to adopt 'appropriate measures' in relation 'to situations of armed conflict where civilians are being targeted or where humanitarian assistance to civilians is being deliberately obstructed'. It also articulated a readiness to consider ways in which peacekeeping mandates might be reassessed to ensure that civilians receive better protection. Protection of civilians was evoked once again in Resolution 1674 (2006), which called for belligerent parties in armed conflict to allow for unconditional humanitarian access to civilians, reiterating the Council's commitment to respond in cases where civilians are deliberately targeted. This resolution also reaffirmed R2P.

In addition to the development of thematic interest in the civilian protection, the Council also made its *practices* of protection more robust, setting precedents along the way. As we noted earlier, for the first time in its history, the Council authorized the use of force against the consent of a *de jure* government when Resolution 1973 (2011) mandated the use of force for the purpose of protecting civilians in Libya without the permission of the Libyan government.[48] Resolution 1973, and the preceding Resolution 1970, authorized a broad range of collective security powers available to the Council through the UN Charter. In 2014, the Council once again authorized action without seeking the consent of a host state when it mandated humanitarian assistance in Syria, in Resolution 2165. This marked the first time that the Council had authorized such action, which provided further evidence as to how far it would be willing to go to assist in the protection of civilians.

One of the key ways the Council has advanced the agenda of civilian protection is through its peacekeeping operations. While peacekeeping operations have historically included human rights provisions,[49] it was not until the turn of the twenty-first century that civilian protection was regarded as a central part of peacekeeping. One turning point was the so-called 'Brahimi Report', published in 2000, which pronounced that peacekeepers should operate under the presumption that they be authorized to stop any violence against civilians (within their means) that they witness.[50] From 1999, with the UN mission in Sierra Leone (UNAMSIL), the Security Council has, with increasing regularity, authorized peacekeepers to use 'all necessary means' (i.e. force) for the purpose of protecting civilians.[51] Nowadays, the protection of civilians and the authorization to use 'all means necessary' for that purpose are central components of UN peacekeeping, particularly in many of the newest mandates, including those for Mali (MINUSMA), South Sudan (UNMISS), and the Central African Republic (MISCA). In one case – the Democratic Republic of Congo (DRC) – the Security Council went beyond this by authorizing the creation of a 'Force Intervention Brigade' to proactively seek out and eliminate non-state armed groups that had perpetrated atrocities against civilians.

The third stream is the emergence of international regimes that are committed to addressing specific vulnerabilities, especially those confronted by refugees, the displaced, women, and children. International society has, since the end of the Second World War, acknowledged groups that have faced specific dangers, and in response has created a range of mechanisms designed to reduce those dangers. Most prominent among these is the international refugee regime, as set out in the 1951 Refugee Convention and 1967 Protocol, whose terms are overseen by the UN High Commissioner for Refugees (UNHCR). People who face persecution are accorded the right to claim asylum and attain settlement in third countries. The UNHCR is also mandated to ensure that refugees are given due protection, and that they are able to access workable solutions to their imposed displacement.[52] As the 1990s unfolded, it became increasingly evident that this regime was not able to deal with a new displacement challenge – that of people being forced from their homes, but remaining within their country's borders (otherwise known as *internal* displacement). At the time there was little enthusiasm for an international convention that would provide protection for the displaced, as it was regarded as a 'domestic' issue. Instead, the UNHCR altered its mandate in order to incorporate protection for all displaced persons, and, correspondingly, UN officials drafted 'guiding principles' for their treatment based on the human rights that already covered them.[53]

Other vulnerable groups also become subject to focused protection regimes. For example, the gendered effects of atrocities, including but not limited to sexual and gender-based violence, became particularly apparent in Bosnia and other conflicts. Helped by strong advocacy from women's groups around the world, this realization spurred the UN Security Council to ensure that the protection of women and girls would be one of the key components of its 'Women, Peace and Security' agenda as articulated in Resolution 1325 (2001).[54] Following this resolution, the UN went on to set up numerous mandates that have prioritized the prevention of sexual and gender-based violence, including establishing the position of Special Representative of the Secretary-General in relation to the issue, and instituting a number of internal reports that put a spotlight on where such violence is committed and provide expert advice on how best to respond. The protection of women and girls is also being mainstreamed in the UN with the deployment of women's protection advisers.[55] Initiatives are also emerging elsewhere. The British government, for example, established a Prevention of Sexual Violence Initiative (PSVI), which assisted in winning the backing of two-thirds of the world's states to lend support to a 'Declaration of Commitment to End Sexual Violence in Conflict'. At the same time, initiatives with a focus on protecting children in armed conflict are also emerging. A Special Representative on the protection of children has been established in the UN, whose mandate is to report on the particular challenges that children face in the context of conflict, including the recruitment of child soldiers. In 2016, Gordon Brown, the UN's ambassador for promoting education, declared an international initiative to create a contingency fund that supports the provision of education to children caught up in humanitarian crises, regardless of whether they are human-induced or natural. Another UN Working Group is currently working on the issue of enforced disappearances.[56]

A fourth stream relates to the global human rights system. Although human rights can be regarded as having established its own regime, which far surpasses the parameters of the international human protection regime, the two overlap significantly, particularly through norms, principles, and decision-making mechanisms.[57] There are two areas that are especially illustrative of the connection between human rights and the international human protection regime, although the overlap between the two regimes goes well beyond this. The first is the emergence of a number of principles and practices among peers that are becoming instrumental in developing expectations about the kinds of measures that states should be adopting to shield their populations from human rights abuses, including mass violence. Despite the immovability of some states, the evidence points towards the positive effects of peer review processes, such as the UN's Universal Peer Review process, as well as other less widespread regional processes, leading states towards greater compliance in relation to their human rights obligations.[58] Such processes strengthen norms that lie at the core of the international human protection regime, and in doing so spur international society to influence the domestic practices of states in order to have an impact on protection outcomes far in advance of the manifestation of mass violence, at which time it becomes an international issue of peace and security. The second area concerns the practice of human rights investigations, which helps influence decision-making within the international human protection regime. Since the late 1990s, such practices, in the form of both permanent and ad hoc human rights monitoring and reporting arrangements, have become increasingly important with regards to international society's decision-making in relation to mass violence. There is a wide range of mechanisms available for the purposes of monitoring and preventing mass violence. Examples include independent commissions and inquiries, the designation of special rapporteurs to provide reports on particular issues within countries, and fact-finding missions, particularly those established by the UN Secretary-General. Such reporting contributes towards decision-making in relation to atrocities by providing the relevant agencies and institutions with timely and relevant information. It also supports norm compliance by publicizing human rights practices at the domestic level.[59]

A fifth stream is the establishment and evolution of international criminal justice mechanisms, principally through the ICC, but also through several special and ad hoc tribunals (for example, the International Criminal Tribunal for Rwanda (ICTR), the International Criminal Tribunal for the former Yugoslavia (ICTY), the Extraordinary Chambers in the Courts of Cambodia (ECCC), and the Special Court for Sierra Leone (SCSL)). Having grown considerably in number since the mid-1990s, these institutions support protection by providing accountability for individual perpetrators. Some argue that withdrawing impunity helps to deter potential perpetrators, and provides some legal protection for the victims.[60] This marks the first time that efforts to internationalize and institutionalize individual criminal action were not blocked by political disagreements, as they were after the Nuremberg and Tokyo trials. The genesis for this came in the mid-1990s when the Security Council authorized the establishment of ad hoc tribunals in Bosnia and Rwanda, in the wake of atrocity crimes committed in those places.[61] Then, in 1998, the Rome Statute established the ICC. The Statute determined that the ICC's jurisdiction would be activated in the event that a state party was either unwilling or unable to gather evidence related to the perpetration of widespread and systematic crimes against humanity, war crimes, and genocide. To this end, the ICC prosecutor would be able to commence case proceedings when he or she could convince a panel of judges that a case would indeed fall under the court's jurisdiction. This usually occurred in the event of a complaint made by a signatory state, or through a referral to the prosecutor from the Security Council, which also had the power to defer investigations by up to twelve months. So far, the Security Council has referred several cases to the ICC, including situations in Darfur and Libya, though Council referrals remain far from common and a draft resolution to refer Syria to the Court was vetoed by China and Russia. More common are self-referrals by state parties. The DRC, Uganda, and the Central African Republic have all made formal requests for investigations into crimes committed in those countries. The ICC also launched an investigation into atrocities committed in Kenya in 2007–8, its jurisdiction invoked by the fact that Kenya is a state party.

Although it is too soon to make a judgement on how effective the court has been as a deterrence to mass violence, early indicators suggest that some potential perpetrators have been stalled.[62] Beyond the court, emerging evidence suggests that processes of transitional justice, whereby perpetrators are held to account for human rights abuses, indeed does make reoffending less likely, improving human rights in the process, while also deterring would-be perpetrators from committing such abuses in other countries. As Kim and Sikkink argue, this is the product of two factors – the pressure for compliance that arises from these mechanisms and the effects of punishment.[63] That is not to say that there is no tension between criminal proceedings and political processes – at times criminal proceedings do work against leaders negotiating an end to violence, as well as facilitating regime transition and peacebuilding processes, for fear of prosecution.[64] This is an illustration of one of the ways that different aspects of the international human protection regime can sometimes clash, resulting in protection gaps.

The sixth stream concerns the principles of humanitarian relief to civilians in times of need. While this stream may appear to be on the periphery of human protection, given the strong role played by NGOs and intergovernmental bodies, what is important here is the fact that the rules and processes related to humanitarian relief have had an influence on state behaviour and have been developed by international society. A core aspect of the development of humanitarianism that dates back to the nineteenth century was the idea that civilians should be provided with humanitarian assistance during wartime. This was incorporated into IHL, with its reach gradually extended. In the 1990s, the UN Security Council started to mandate peacekeeping missions whose tasks included supporting the delivery of humanitarian aid. Indeed, in Somalia and Bosnia, this included authorizing the use of force to that end. Subsequently, the Council's authorization of the use of force for humanitarian relief has become common practice. Moreover, in a number of resolutions on the Protection of Civilians, the Council has demanded that access to humanitarian agencies be forthcoming from warring parties. It even went one step further in Resolution 2165 (2014) when it authorized the delivery of humanitarian aid into Syria without the consent of the Syrian government.

The seventh stream is the promotion of the human protection agenda at the regional level. This agenda has made its way into the principles and practices of various regional organizations in different ways. In Europe, for example, the idea of civilian protection first found form with the Helsinki Accords of the 1970s, which in time became the foundation for the Conference on Security and Co-operation in Europe (CSCE). By the 1990s, the CSCE had internationalized references to protection-related matters, including protection against torture and the protection of children.[65] In 1995, the CSCE became the Organization for Security and Co-operation in Europe (OSCE), at which time it adopted greater capacities and responsibilities in order to assist in protecting human rights. To that end, the post of High Commissioner for National Minorities was established.[66] Around the same time, NATO also began placing more importance on its protection of civilians dimension of crisis management, as it did during the Bosnian conflict.[67] The EU also developed a civilian protection aspect to its work within its Common Foreign and Security Policy, as seen in the French-led multinational force in eastern DRC (Operation *Artemis*, 2003), among other operations. The African Union (AU) has also incorporated a strong focus on civilian protection from mass violence into its comprehensive regional system for crisis management and response. Indeed, the AU has gone further, by enshrining the right to intervene in member states' domestic affairs in cases where genocide or other mass atrocities are unfolding, as seen in Article 4(h) of the Constitutive Act. While this particular article has never been invoked, the AU-led peacekeeping operation in Darfur (AMIS) and its missions in Mali, Somalia, and the Central African Republic have all included a civilian protection mandate.[68] In Latin America also, states have moved to create a regional human rights mechanism, and within the non-interference culture of the Association of Southeast Asian Nations (ASEAN) a mechanism for promoting and protecting human rights has been set up through the organization's Intergovernmental Commission on Human Rights.

The eighth stream has emerged through the international commitment to the R2P principle. This was cemented in September 2005, when world leaders unanimously supported the adoption of R2P within the World Summit Outcome Document (paras 138–140). This pledge was subsequently reaffirmed by the UN Security Council and the General Assembly, and included a commitment to considering how to implement the principle. R2P, as endorsed by member states, is premised on three pillars.[69] Pillar One entails the responsibility of each state to protect populations from genocide, war crimes, ethnic cleansing, and crimes against humanity, and from their incitement. Pillar Two affirms the commitment of the 'international community' to assist states to carry out this responsibility. Pillar Three endorses the international community's responsibility to respond in a timely manner to situations where states are manifestly failing to protect their populations from the aforementioned atrocity crimes. Secretary-General Ban Ki-moon declared that R2P's implementation would be one of his key priorities, and to that end has overseen much of its institutional development within the UN. Since 2005, R2P has become very much a key element of the working language that articulates international responses to political crises. An example includes the way that it was utilized to inform diplomatic efforts that were initiated to help resolve the conflict in Kenya, following contested elections in late 2007.[70] Since then, the Security Council has referred to R2P in more than fifty resolutions, and has used the principle in a variety of ways, such as to remind some governments of their responsibility to protect their populations (e.g. Resolution 2014 (2011) regarding Yemen and Resolution 2165 (2014) on Syria), and demanding that parties engaged in violent conflict take action to protect civilians (one example includes Resolution 2139 (2014) on Syria). Resolutions such as 1996 (2011) on South Sudan and 2085 (2012) on Mali exemplify the way in which the principle was used to mandate peacekeepers to help governments to protect their populations. Other resolutions have called for the perpetrators of mass violence to be held accountable in a legal sense for crimes committed. Resolution 2211 (2015) on DRC exemplifies this. The Security Council has also made links between R2P and its work on conflict prevention and preventive diplomacy, genocide prevention, counter-terrorism, international policing, and the control of small arms and light weapons.

The emergence of the international human protection regime was a product of these eight streams that unfolded alongside each other. They each developed their own individual trajectories, and were championed by different sets of actors. Taken together, the regime increases the chances that there will be international responses to mass violence, ensuring at the same time that protection concerns remain a core part of such responses, both motivating the involvement of international society and guiding the manner of their involvement. Indeed, the rise of the international human protection regime contributes to the decline of mass violence – as discussed earlier – by regulating behaviour through normative pressure, and by increasing the likelihood of response.

How do these streams sit together within the international human protection regime? To gain a better understanding of this, it is valuable to refer to Krasner's definition of an international regime, considering all the elements he associates with it. We use Krasner's basic definition of a regime (consisting of principles, norms, rules, and decision-making processes) for illustrative purposes, while also acknowledging the robust criticisms of his definition as being conceptually thin (largely owing to its inability to distinguish between different elements),[71] without delving into a detailed and intricate explanation of the regime, which would require a much longer analysis that goes beyond the scope of this book.

The first element refers to *principles*, defined by Krasner as 'beliefs of fact, causation and rectitude'.[72] We could posit that the international human protection regime is premised on four such principles. The first is a normative principle, almost universally acknowledged by the world's major religions and ethical frameworks – that is, that non-combatants should not be subjected to mass violence.[73] The second is a causal principle, which draws links between mass violence against unarmed civilians and increased levels of international disorder. The third principle is one that acknowledges that international peace and security is characterized not only by positive relations between states, but also by what goes on within individual states. The fourth principle concerns collective action – in other words, that the problem of mass violence can be addressed through cooperation between states.

The second element of a regime is its *norms*, which here are defined as shared expectations about acceptable behaviour for an actor with an established identity.[74] The norms contained within the international human protection regime are many and varied, which both limit and promote different types of action for a range of different actors. They include norms that serve to place constraints on the behaviour of combatants, including the proscription of targeting non-combatants (the principles of discrimination and non-combatant immunity) and the condemnation of disproportionate force (the principle of proportionality); norms that prohibit the use of certain weapons; norms prohibiting other forms of violence and abuse other than killing in combat (such as sexual violence, forced displacement, and torture); and norms that prohibit the violent targeting of particular groups, such as children, humanitarians, and peacekeepers. A second set of norms requires positive actions from combatants. These include allowing humanitarians access to peoples in need, the honouring of safe places and ceasefires, and the cooperation with certain international actors. Another set of norms establishes expectations about acceptable international responses by a range of different third parties. This includes, for instance, the legal obligations we outlined in the introduction as well as the UN Security Council's responsibility to engage in 'timely and decisive action' in response to mass violence. It also entails the responsibility of the ICC to conduct investigations and to punish those who commit atrocities, where it has the power to do so. In addition, it includes the responsibility for humanitarian actors to secure the provision of aid to civilians. Beyond this there is the responsibility of peacekeepers to protect civilians from violence within their purview, the responsibility of human rights organizations to investigate and provide information about unfolding abuses, and the responsibility of regional organizations to assist in the management and amelioration of conflict within their regions of concern. It is worth pointing out that these norms also operate within a wider set of norms that are connected to the UN system and its framing of international security. The international human protection regime itself was nurtured within this system of collective security and as such remains solidly and self-consciously part of that order.

The third component of a regime is its *rules*. This refers to specific authorizations and prohibitions that govern how states (along with other actors) should behave so as to satisfy the regime's norms. With the international human protection regime, we can see that different parts are subject to different clusters of rules, yet at the same time each of the eight streams entails particular rules that counsel particular types of behaviour. Some are intricate and complex, like the rules upon which the ICC's criminal prosecutions are based, or the agreements and rules of engagement to which peacekeepers are subject. Others are opaque, sometimes deliberately so. An example here is the flexibility with which the UN Security Council operates – both by the UN Charter and by relevant parts of the international human protection regime, which in turn allow it much discretion in determining when and by what means it will operate to fulfil shared norms.

Trying to account for all the *decision-making* structures connected to the international human protection regime is beyond the scope of this book, which is focused more narrowly on humanitarian intervention. Because the international human protection regime developed out of the UN's collective security system, and remains a part of it, it shares some of these decision-making procedures and, to use Krasner's words, 'prevailing practices for making and complementing collective choice' with that same order.[75] The UN Security Council, for instance, through the utilization of powers to maintain international peace and order, as given to it by the 1945 UN Charter, is the body that makes crucial decisions about whether or not to authorize international forces, bring in sanctions in response to non-compliance, order the delivery of humanitarian aid, or to set up an ad hoc international tribunal. There are other separate decision-making structures that deal with other aspects of the regime, but they sometimes overlap with the Security Council's authority. One can see this with the way the Rome Statute underpins the decision-making of the ICC, yet the Security Council still has the power to impose the ICC's jurisdiction on non-signatories of the Statute. Other decision-making structures exist independently of the Security Council, such as the UN's human rights mechanism and regional organizations.

Because the international human protection regime's development was subconscious and fragmented – the individual streams giving little regard for the whole – inevitably there are gaps in what it covers. One example is the gap between *expectations* and *capabilities.* Expectations regarding human protection have continued to progress, yet the capacity of international society to meet these expectations has not grown in a corresponding manner. There are some states that simply do not have the capacity to protect their populations, while others are lacking in the will to do so. At the same time, international actors are able to improve protection, but limitations in their capacity to do so (not to mention the complexities involved in providing comprehensive protection) mean that they are not able to apply the same level of protection that exists in stable states and societies. A second example involves blind spots in *geographic coverage.* The international human protection regime has an uneven spread throughout the world, partly owing to variations in regional arrangements, and also to the fact that some states are not signatories to all parts of the IHL, or to the ICC's Rome Statute. A third example concerns *agency* gaps. As the regime is better positioned to reach out to states, but less so to non-state actors, this tends to result in a clarity deficit in terms of what the protection responsibilities of non-state armed actors are, but also impinges on activities of self-protection by targeted communities and the role of the private sector. Fourth, *substantive* gaps continue to prevail. An example here is the fact that while some indiscriminate weapons – such as landmines and cluster bombs – have been banned in some places, others – like nuclear weapons – have not. There have also been gaps in the codification and enforcements of some protective practices, such as the protection responsibilities that occupying powers have.[76] Finally, there exist *coherence* gaps. Such gaps in both coherence and coordination result in inefficiencies across different streams of protection, and, in some cases, might result in situations where action in one stream may have a negative effect on action in other streams.[77] A better comprehension of these gaps should comprise the future research agenda of the international human protection regime, as bridging them will surely be part of its future political agenda.

Human protection and the decline in mass violence

To this point, we have argued that there has been a decline in atrocity crimes over the last few decades, an increase in international society's responsiveness to such crimes, and the surfacing of an international regime for human protection comprised of at least eight interconnected streams of practice. But the fact that these three patterns have coincided does not on its own prove that they are connected. For one thing, some writers have claimed that these streams of practice – in particular those concerned with R2P and the ICC – have exerted negligible influence over behaviour in these 'endtimes' of human rights.[78] In order to establish whether or not the international human protection regime has had a substantive and positive impact, we need to first contemplate how and why the international human protection regime may be linked to the decline in atrocities, while also assessing potential alternative explanations.

To evaluate the connection between the international human protection regime and the decline in atrocity crimes, we can ask two questions. The first is whether or not the international norms, rules, institutions, and practices that comprise the regime have had a positive impact on global patterns of violence. The second is how much the regime itself has influenced participation in these actions. If both answers are positive, then there would be a strong case for asserting the association between the regime and the decreasing levels of mass violence.

The first question is relatively easy to answer given a plethora of studies (some of which we have already cited) that show the positive effects of many parts of the international human protection regime. There are too many examples to identify here, but they include a finding that the presence of a peace operation decreases the chances of a conflict reigniting in that country;[79] deploying peacekeepers with a civilian protection included in their mandates decreases the chances that civilians will be attacked within the areas of operations;[80] armed interventions which specifically target perpetrators decrease the severity of genocide,[81] and impartial third-party interventions reduce mass killing in the long term;[82] well-run humanitarian missions can contribute to decreased casualty numbers through the provision of life-sustaining relief and sanctuary for displaced persons; publicizing the names of perpetrators of serious human rights abuses has a tendency to lead to better human rights practices, particularly in conjunction with pressure applied by third parties;[83] and transitional justice processes that promise accountability for past crimes committed by perpetrators have been proven to improve human protection within the relevant country, as well as deterring further violations by other potential perpetrators.[84] While there have been fewer broad-based studies that investigated the effectiveness of measures designed to protect women and girls from sexual and gender-based violence, the studies that have been done suggest that well-organized initiatives involving multiple actors can have a positive effect on reducing the incidence of such violence. In addition, the *absence* of such measures has been associated with increased risk.[85]

Taken together, these studies suggest that the regime as a whole asserts strong downwards pressure on atrocities. This occurs in three key ways. First, by upping the costs that are likely to be imposed on potential perpetrators, as manifested by the costs of 'naming and shaming', the costs of criminal persecution, and the increased potential for third-party intervention. The second way is by making it harder for perpetrators to actually commit atrocities through the deployment of peacekeepers and humanitarians, and reporting through human rights monitors. The third way is by adding to the protection given to vulnerable groups through the stationing of peacekeepers, through humanitarian action, or through providing opportunities for flight.

However, even if it is clear that such practices put downwards pressure on atrocities, it does not necessarily mean that the international human protection regime itself is having an impact. For all we know, such effects may well simply be unintended results of actions undertaken for other reasons, or simply the product of chance. So how can we know the reasons for third parties committing particular courses of action? First, we can eliminate chance. We know that these effects are the product of deliberate choices that states make, and not merely the cumulative effect of random decisions. We know, for instance, that the UN Security Council is more likely to authorize a peacekeeping mission in the event of a civil war when parties to that conflict are targeting civilians, as Lisa Hultman has pointed out.[86] Hultman showed that this pattern – although evident across the whole period between 1989 and 2006 – became particularly acute after 1999. Such conclusions are backed up by earlier investigations which demonstrated that the more severe a crisis, and the greater the risk of escalation, the more likely the Security Council would become involved.[87] Thus, it would seem reasonable to assert that third-party activism in response to mass violence is on the increase because of deliberate choices on the part of states to be involved.

In order to effectively ascertain *why* states are making such choices more regularly is by looking at the ways they justify such choices. In recent years, a broad diversity of states (not only Western liberal states) have repeatedly accounted for their practices in a range of settings as being motivated by concerns of human protection. States have certainly declared their own support for these norms. R2P, for instance, is one of the most controversial of the norms associated with the international human protection regime, yet the vast majority of states endorsed it. During the September 2014 General Assembly dialogue on R2P, China referred to it as a 'prudential norm', and posited that in order to implement it 'states should establish relevant policies and mechanisms', also pointing out the appropriateness of international measures to support R2P, which included, 'as a last resort', the use of force. In the dialogue India also voiced its support for the norm, pointing out that R2P 'was agreed [upon] by all'; Indonesia also declared strong support, noting that it 'fully subscribes to the finest purposes and objectives of the concept of R2P'; Nigeria voiced strong support, declaring that 'R2P is apt, based on humanitarian and human rights law, representing a global conceptual and policy shift in the notion of sovereignty and security'; Iran posited that 'we cannot agree more with the Secretary-General' and the way that he had approached the norm; the Philippines pointed out that 'we subscribe to our shared responsibility' with regards to R2P; and Argentina emphasized that 'since the beginning, Argentina supports the concept of R2P'.[88] All coming from states in the global South, these statements reveal overwhelming support for the notion that states do indeed recognize norms that are associated with the international human protection regime.

But while committing to a principle is one thing, allowing the principle to have an impact on behaviour is another thing entirely. What evidence is there that suggests that state *practices* are the product of factors relating to the international human protection regime? There is actually considerable evidence of compliant practices and corresponding rhetoric, which appear in statements made by numerous states in their justifications of decisions to take collective action in a range of crises, including the Central African Republic, DRC, South Sudan, Somalia, Mali, and Darfur. Moreover, there is evidence that suggests that in the most challenging cases, where countervailing norms and geopolitical interests are particularly strong, the international human protection regime will sometimes convince states to commit to actions they would not ordinary commit to.

Illustrating this is the UN Security Council's unprecedented swift reaction to Libya in 2011. Within days of violence escalating there, the Security Council unanimously agreed on the imposition of a range of coercive measures, including arms and financial embargoes and an ICC referral, without the consent of the Libyan government. Even Russia and China, typically opposed to such measures so soon, supported Resolution 1970. Why was this the case? Russia was candid and direct in its formal explanation:

> The Russian Federation supported Security Council resolution 1970 (2011) because of our serious concern over the events taking place in Libya. We sincerely regret the many lives lost among the civilian population. We condemn the use of military force against peaceful demonstrators and all other manifestations of violence and consider them absolutely unacceptable. We call for an immediate end to such actions. We exhort the Libyan authorities to comply with the demands of the international community.[89]

Similarly, China justified its vote by pointing out that 'it is of the greatest urgency to secure the immediate cessation of violence, avoid further bloodshed and civilian casualties, restore stability and normal order as soon as possible'.[90] While other factors also had an influence on the final decision (states are rarely moved by single motivating factors), what these statements demonstrate is that both states understood the crisis in Libya clearly in terms of the international human protection regime. The same concerns were apparent three weeks later when both states took the unprecedented step of abstaining on a draft resolution that authorized the use of force in Libya. Here again, while acknowledging the fact that other considerations also impinged on their decisions, it is impossible to explain their choice to allow armed intervention in Libya without having a sense of the normative influence that the international human protection regime had.

Russia's justification of its decision to abstain is framed strongly in human protection terms:

I underscore yet again that we are consistent and firm advocates of the protection of the civilian population. Guided by this basic principle as well as by the common humanitarian values that we share with both the sponsors and other Council members, Russia did not prevent the adoption of this resolution.[91]

China did make the observation that it is 'always against the use of force in international relations' but opted to abstain as a result of the 'special circumstances' in Libya:

China is gravely concerned by the continuing deterioration of the situation in Libya. We support the Security Council's adoption of appropriate and necessary action to stabilize the situation in Libya as soon as possible and to halt acts of violence against civilians.[92]

While the Security Council's actions in Libya were unprecedented, looking carefully at international society's response to Syria provides us with evidence that Libya was not a one-off. The crisis in Syria is distinct in many ways, but from an international perspective it is a situation where some of the core interests of great powers have clashed. Despite the divisions arising from nearly every aspect of the conflict, human protection concerns have remained at the fore of international deliberations and important concessions have been made. While such concerns have not been sufficient to change state behaviour fundamentally, amid countervailing pressures, even here there have been times when human protection concerns have overridden self-interest. One example can be seen in Security Council Resolution 2165 (2014), when member states voted to relinquish Syria of its chemical weapons and override Syria's sovereignty by authorizing the delivery of humanitarian assistance without the government's consent. Key Syrian ally Russia explained its support for the resolution by positing that:

The Russian federation participated actively in the negotiation of this resolution, given the need to improve the humanitarian situation in Syria, alleviate the plight of the civilian population in the country and improve conditions for the work of humanitarian agencies. We were able to support the resolution after sponsors took into account our key priorities.[93]

In order words, Russia acknowledged the need to relieve civilian suffering in a context of mass violence, and it is this imperative which is a central component of the international human protection regime. This is not to claim that that the international human protection regime 'caused' Russia's choosing to allow action in the absence of the consent of its close ally, but there is a case to be made that Russia would not have supported Resolution 2165 without the imperative of the international human protection regime.

In light of this compelling evidence, we can advance two arguments with confidence. The first is that the *practices* of human protection have applied strong downwards pressure on mass violence. The second is that the *justifications* states make for such practices point compellingly towards the principles and norms connected to international human protection regime. Thus, the regime is strongly associated not just with the norms and principles to which states appeal to justify their actions, but also with the practices themselves. By shifting the balance of likely costs and payoffs associated with atrocity crimes, the regime has placed downwards pressure on them, contributing to declining levels of violence. But are there any alternative explanations that accounts for this decline and the increased response?

Alternative explanations

There are three possible alternative explanations worth examining here: the *general decline thesis,* the *end of communism thesis*, and the *swinging pendulum* thesis. Here, we suggest that although each makes good points about a part of the puzzle, none of them provide convincing alternative explanations that account for the decrease of mass violence and increase of international activism.

The *general decline thesis* posits that the decline of mass atrocities is part of a long-term historical process, thus not connected to the relatively recent emergence of the international human protection regime. Steven Pinker, for example, argues that the overall decline in mass violence is a product of an evolutionary downwards trend in violence more generally, dating back to 10,000 BCE.[94] This seems to question the role of the international human protection regime in spurring the decline of mass violence. Yet this thesis does not contradict our own, much narrower, argument. Unpacking Pinker's claim further, we find that this broader long-duration decline in violence can be observed in five discrete stages, the most recent of which he calls the 'new peace', which emerged out of the Cold War, and is marked by the diminishing of great power rivalry, but also by international cooperation to confront violent conflict. From this angle, the international human protection regime is the latest expression of a broader historical trend. Furthermore, the international human protection regime is a manifestation that looks like it has accelerated these historical trends. As Human Security Report points out, it has been 'remarkably effective in driving down the number and deadliness of armed conflicts'.[95] The overall decline in violence is not a self-fulfilling phenomenon, but rather one that is shaped and reshaped by historically specific forces. In the period following the end of the Cold War, Pinker argues that it is international activism that is the key driver of this recent decline. Such activism is closely associated with the international human protection regime.

The second alternative explanation is the *end of communism thesis.* This thesis, advanced by analysts such as Benjamin Valentino and Chad Hazlett, contends that the recent decline in mass violence was because of the collapse of communism at the end of the Cold War.[96] This was largely due to the diminishing of radical ideologies that justified the mass killings of collectives, but also because it marked an end to the global armed struggle between capitalism and communism. While there is no dispute that communist regimes were behind some of the worst episodes of mass violence in the twentieth century, or that rivalry between capitalism and communism encouraged atrocities, the collapse of communism and the end of the Cold War cannot alone account for this decline in violence. For one thing, it does not account for the decline of mass violence in East Asia, where many communist regimes continue to prevail (such as in China, North Korea, and Vietnam).[97] In addition, there are trends of violence in other volatile regions, such as the Middle East and sub-Saharan Africa, where violence was not principally driven by ideological clashes between capitalism and communism. This argument also cannot account for why this downwards pressure on mass violence increased in Eastern Europe, well beyond the collapse of communism.

Verging closely toward a null hypothesis argument is the third explanation, the *swinging pendulum thesis*.[98] The principal suggestion here is that the key drivers that account for trends towards and away from atrocities are deep and historical, thus not easily dislodged by direct human intervention. In other words, international history is cyclical, with peaks and troughs of violence but few fundamental changes. Therefore, any variation in patterns of violence is nothing more than history's swinging pendulum. A decline in mass violence, then, is a result of chance more than anything else, and any such decline is bound to be temporary. We can put to one side the question of whether the decline is temporary, since there is no claim that it might not be. The thesis is premised on unreliable empirical grounds, given the long historical decline in violence charted by Pinker. If as a species, humans are genetically driven towards violence, even the most recent pattern of accelerated decline would be difficult to account for. In addition, while there are no doubt inconsistencies across cases, there are clear patterns of increased commitment by international society to address mass violence, with a number of studies showing the downwards pressure that this commitment exerts.

Finally, we should also – of course – acknowledge that the decline of atrocities is also connected to the decline in civil wars more generally. Yet the decline in the number and severity of civil wars cannot be completely accounted for without factors connected to the international human protection regime. And nor is the decline of civil wars an adequate explanation on its own for the decline in atrocity crimes, as mass violence also occurs both in situations outside of armed conflict, as well as in interstate war.

Conclusion

In this chapter we have argued that the downwards trend in mass violence and the increasing levels of international activism in response to mass violence, as has been observed since the early 1990s, appear to have a strong correlation with the emergence of a fragmented international human protection regime. This regime – through eight individual but interrelated streams of practice – has helped to codify norms of appropriate behaviour, and created responsibilities for international institutions and third party states. Consequently, cases of mass violence today are often met with complex – and not always coherent or effective – responses initiated by a broad range of actors whose objective is to place constraints on the behaviour of warring parties in order to limit or nullify their ability to harm civilians, and to also provide assistance to vulnerable civilian populations. A large number of practices that fall under the rubric of the international human protection regime have had demonstrably positive effects. Taken together, then, these practices can be said to display a strong downward pressure on mass violence. Looking at the declared justifications of some non-Western states for their decision-making provide evidence for thinking that it is indeed principles, norms, rule and decision-making structures associate with the regime that is spurring them to action.

Notes

1. Pinker's thesis is that the world is much more peaceful today than it has ever been, and that there is evidence to support the claim that we are experiencing a long-term downward trajectory in levels of societal violence. See Steven Pinker, *The Better Angels of Our Nature: The Decline of Violence in History and its Causes* (New York: Allen Lane, 2011). See also Azar Gat, *The Causes of War and the Spread of Peace: But Will War Rebound?* (Oxford: Oxford University Press, 2017), who ascribes the same decline to 'modernization'.
2. See, for example, Joshua Goldstein, *Winning the War on War: The Decline of Armed Conflict Worldwide* (New York: Dutton, 2011); and Gary Goertz, Paul F. Diehl, and Alexandru Balas, *The Puzzle of Peace: The Evolution of Peace in the International System* (Oxford: Oxford University Press, 2016).
3. Ronald Wright, *A Short History of Progress* (Toronto: House of Anansi Press, 2004).
4. To claim that the two are connected is not new, see Goldstein, *Winning the War on War*.
5. Bruce Cronin, *Institutions for the Common Good: International Protection Regimes in International Society* (Cambridge: Cambridge University Press, 2003).
6. Emmanuel Adler and Vincent Pouliot, 'International Practices: Introduction and Framework' in Emmanuel Adler and Vincent Pouliot (eds), *International Practices* (Cambridge: Cambridge University Press, 2011).
7. Doug Saunders, 'Why Louise Arbour is Thinking Twice', *The Globe and Mail*, 28 March 2015, Available at: http://www.theglobeandmail.

com/globe-debate/why-louise-arbour-is-thinking-twice/article 23667013/.

8. Rudolph J. Rummel, *Death by Government* (Piscataway, NJ: Transaction 1994); Rudolph J. Rummel, *Statistics of Democide* (Piscataway, NJ: Transaction, 1997).

9. See Benjamin A. Valentino, 'Why We Kill: The Political Science of Political Violence against Civilians', *Annual Review of Political Science*, 17 (2014), pp. 89–103.

10. Human Security Report, *Human Security Report 2013: The Decline in Global Violence: Evidence, Explanation and Contestation* (Burnaby: Simon Fraser University, 2013), pp. 107–113.

11. Pinker, *The Better Angels of our Nature*, pp. 338–343.

12. See Alex J. Bellamy, *Mass Atrocities and Armed Conflict: Links, Distinctions and Implications for the Responsibility to Protect*, Policy Analysis Brief for the Stanley Foundation, February 2011; Alex J. Bellamy, *Massacres and Morality: Mass Killing in an Age of Civilian Immunity* (Oxford: Oxford University Press, 2012); Benjamin A. Valentino and Paul Huth, 'Mass Killing of Civilians in Time of War', in Emmanuel Adler and Vincent Pouliot (eds), *Peace and Conflict* (Boulder, CO: Paradigm, 2004); For a dataset focused on Africa, see Scott Straus, *Making and Unmaking Nations: War, Leadership and Genocide in Modern Africa* (Ithaca, NY: Cornell University Press, 2015), pp. 96–97. Though Straus does not, himself, draw inferences about change over time, we can extrapolate this from his dataset (Table 4.2).

13. Jay Ulfelder, 'Genocide is Going Out of Fashion', *Foreign Policy*, 14 May 2015.

14. Monty G. Marshall and Benjamin R. Cole, *Global Report 2014: Conflict, Governance and State Fragility* (Vienna, VA: Center for Systemic Peace, 2014), pp. 18–19.

15. See, for example, Bradley A. Thayer, 'Humans, Not Angels: Reasons to Doubt the Decline of War Thesis', *International Studies Review*, 15, no. 3 (2013), pp. 411–416; Jack S. Levy and William R. Thompson, 'The Decline of War? Multiple Trajectories and Diverging Trends', *International Studies Review*, 15, no. 3 (2013), pp. 405–411. Debate does persist on the fact of the decline too, however. Fry (2013) and his collaborators suggest that human life prior to 10,000 bce was largely warfare-free.

16. Gerald Schneider and Margit Bussmann, 'Accounting for the Dynamics of One-Sided Violence: Introducing KOSVED', *Journal of Peace Research*, 50, no. 5 (2013), pp. 635–644.

17. Sara Davies and Jacqui True, 'Reframing Conflict-Related Sexual and Gender Based Violence: Bringing Gender Analysis Back In', *Security Dialogue*, 46, no. 6 (2015), pp. 495–512.

18. See, for example, Justin Morris, 'Libya and Syria: R2P and the Spectre of the Swinging Pendulum', *International Affairs*, 89, no. 5 (2013), pp. 1265–1283.

19. Cases based on Bellamy, 'Mass Atrocities and Armed Conflict' appendix, and updated to take account of the most recent cases.

20. See Bellamy, *Massacres and Morality*; Nicholas J. Wheeler, *Saving Strangers: Humanitarian Intervention in International Society* (Oxford: Oxford University Press, 2000).

21. Alex J. Bellamy, 'When States Go Bad: The Termination of State Based Mass Atrocities', *Journal of Peace Research*, 52, no. 4 (2015); Alex de Waal and Bridget Conley-Zilkic, 'Reflections on How Genocidal Killings are Brought to an End', *Social Science Research Council,* 22 December 2006.

22. Thomas G. Weiss, 'The Sunset of Humanitarian Intervention? The Responsibility to Protect in a Unipolar Era', *Security Dialogue*, 25, no. 2 (2004), pp. 135–153: p. 135.

23. Wheeler, *Saving Strangers,* pp. 143–144.

24. See Kofi Annan, *Interventions: A Life in War and Peace* (New York: Penguin, 2012), pp. 81–134.

25. For the best a-ccount see Christopher Roberts, *The Battle for Syria: International Rivalry in the New Middle East* (New Haven, CT: Yale University Press, 2016).

26. For example, we coded the UN's response to the conflict in Bosnia as including protection because of the peacekeeping mission's title (UN Protection Force – UNPROFOR) and its mandate to deter attacks of civilians and support the delivery of humanitarian aid. It could, however, be argued that because UN forces were not specifically mandated to protect civilians, protection was not in fact a core priority. However, making that judgement does little to the general trends identified besides moderately sharpening the acceleration of human protection post-2000.

27. Security Council Report, *Protection of Civilians in Armed Conflict: Cross Cutting Report* (New York: Security Council Report, 2015), p. 28.

28. See, for example, Arthur Boutellis and Paul D. Williams, 'Peace Operations, the African Union and the United Nations: Toward More Effective Partnership' (New York: International Peace Institute, 2013); Paul F. Diehl and Alexandru Balas, *Peace Operations,* 2nd edition (Oxford: Polity, 2014), pp. 74–75.

29. Informal sources have also been involved in such mediation. See Peter Wallensteen and Isak Svensson, 'Talking Peace: International Mediation in Armed Conflicts', *Journal of Peace Research*, 51, no. 2 (2014), pp. 315–327.

30. Alexandru Balas, Andrew P. Owsiak, and Paul F. Diehl, 'Demanding Peace: The Impact of Prevailing Conflict on the Shift from Peace-keeping to Peacebuilding', *Peace and Change*, 37, no. 2 (2012), pp. 195–226.
31. See, for example, Kathryn Sikkink, *The Justice Cascade: How Human Rights Prosecutions are Changing the World* (New York: Norton, 2011).
32. Sara Davies, Kimberley Nackers, and Sarah Teitt, 'Women, Peace and Security as an ASEAN Priority', *Australian Journal of International Affairs*, 68, no. 3 (2014), pp. 333–355.
33. Stephen D. Krasner, 'Structural Causes and Regime Consequences: Regimes as Intervening Variables', in *International Regimes,* ed. Stephen D. Krasner (Ithaca, NY: Cornell University Press, 1999), pp. 1–21: p. 2.
34. Bruce Cronin, *Institutions for the Common Good: International Protection Regimes in International Society* (Cambridge: Cambridge University Press, 2003), p. 3.
35. Robert Keohane, *After Hegemony: Cooperation and Discord in the World Political Economy* (Princeton, NJ: Princeton University Press, 1984), pp. 80–81.
36. See Oran Young, 'International Regimes: Toward a New Theory of Institutions', *World Politics*, 39, no. 1 (1989), pp. 104–122.
37. See, for example, Stephen D. Krasner, *Sovereignty: Organized Hypocrisy* (Princeton, NJ: Princeton University Press, 1999).
38. Robert Gilpin, *War and Change* (Cambridge: Cambridge University Press, 1981).
39. For example, Mahmood Mamdani, *Saviors and Survivors: Darfur, Politics and the War on Terror* (New York: Bantam Doubleday Dell, 2009).
40. See, for example, Peter Haas, 'Do Regimes Matter? Epistemic Communities and Mediterranean Pollution Control', *International Organization,* 43, no. 3 (1989), pp. 377–403; Emmanuel Adler and Peter Haas, 'Conclusion: Epistemic Communities, World Order and the Creation of a Reflective Research Program', *International Organization,* 46, no. 1 (1992), pp. 367–390. For an example of the application of this type of thinking to a related regime see Nuket Kardam, 'The Emerging Global Gender Equality Regime from Neoliberal and Constructivist Perspectives in International Relations', *International Feminist Journal of Politics,* 6, no. 1 (2004), pp. 85–109.
41. Alex J. Bellamy and Paul D. Williams, 'Protecting Civilians in Uncivil Wars', in Sara E. Davies and Luke Glanville (eds), *Protecting the Displaced: Deepening the Responsibility to Protect* (The Hague: Martinus Nijhoff, 2010), pp. 127–162: p. 142.

42. The General Orders No. 100 are reproduced in full and discussed in Richard Shelly Hartigan, *Lieber's Code and the Laws of War* (New York: Transaction, 1983); on Dunant and the Red Cross see David P. Forsythe, *The Humanitarians: The International Committee of the Red Cross* (Cambridge: Cambridge University Press, 2005); and Caroline Moorehead, *Dunant's Dream: War, Switzerland and the History of the Red Cross* (New York: Carroll and Graf, 1998).
43. See Samantha Power, *A Problem from Hell: America and the Age of Genocide* (New York: Basic Books, 2002).
44. See Alwyn V. Freeman, 'War Crimes by Enemy Nationals Administering Justice in Occupied Territory', *American Journal of International Law,* 41, no. 3 (1947), pp. 579–610: p. 581; and Olivier Durr, 'Humanitarian Law of Armed Conflict: Problems of Applicability', *Journal of Peace Research,* 24, no. 3 (1987), pp. 263–273: p. 268.
45. Louise Doswald-Beck, 'The Civilian in the Crossfire', *Journal of Peace Research*, 24, no. 3 (1987), pp. 251–262: p. 253.
46. For a recent overview see Security Council Report, *Protection of Armed Civilians.*
47. See UN doc. S/1998/318, 13 April 1998.
48. Alex J. Bellamy and Paul D. Williams, 'The New Politics of Protection? Côte d'Ivoire, Libya and the Responsibility to Protect', *International Affairs,* 87, no. 4 (2011), pp. 825–850.
49. Katarina Månsson, 'Use of Force and Civilian Protection: Peace Operations in the Congo', *International Peacekeeping*, 12, no. 4 (2005), pp. 503–519; Katarina Månsson, 'Integration of Human Rights in Peace Operations: Is There an Ideal Model?', *International Peacekeeping*, 13, no. 4 (2006), pp. 547–563.
50. Lakhdar Brahimi, 'Report of the Panel on UN Peace Operations', A/55/303 – S/2000/804, 21 August 2000, p. x.
51. Kofi Nsia-Pepra, *UN Robust Peacekeeping: Civilian Protection in Violent Civil Wars* (London: Palgrave, 2014); Benjamin de Carvalho and Ole Jacob Sending, *The Protection of Civilians in UN Peacekeeping: Concept, Implementation and Practice* (Berlin: Nomos, 2012); Siobhan Wills, *Protecting Civilians: The Obligations of Peacekeepers* (Oxford: Oxford University Press, 2009).
52. Gil Loescher, Alexander Betts, and James Milner, *The United Nations High Commissioner for Refugees (UNHCR): The Politics and Practice of Refugee Protection into the Twenty-First Century* (London: Routledge, 2008), pp. 203.
53. Roberta Cohen, 'Developing an International System for Internally Displaced Persons', *International Studies Perspectives,* 7, no. 2 (2006), pp. 87–101.
54. Janie L. Leatherman, *Sexual Violence and Armed Conflict* (Oxford: Polity, 2011).

55. See Louise Olsson and Theodora-Iseme Gizelis, *Gender, Peace and Security: Implementing UN Security Council Resolution 1325* (London: Routledge, 2015); Sara Davies, Sarah Teitt, Eli Stamnes, and Zim Nwokora (eds), *Responsibility to Protect and Women, Peace and Security: Aligning the Protection Agendas* (The Hague: Brill, 2013).
56. Emilie M. Hafner-Burton, *Making Human Rights a Reality* (Princeton, NJ: Princeton University Press, 2013), p. 101.
57. For a compelling account of the liberal human rights regime see John Charvet and Elisa Kaczynska-Nay, *The Liberal Project and Human Rights: The Theory and Practice of a New World Order* (Cambridge: Cambridge University Press, 2008). The international human protection regime overlaps, but is distinct from, this regime since it relates to a narrower sphere of rights and also encompasses elements of collective security, international humanitarianism, and other regimes beyond human rights.
58. Roland Chauville, 'The Universal Periodic Review's First Cycle: Successes and Failures', in Hilary Charlesworth and Emma Larking (eds), *Human Rights and Universal Periodic Review: Rituals and Ritualism* (Cambridge: Cambridge University Press, 2014), pp. 87–108.
59. According to Risse and Ropp, the gathering of information is key for applying pressure on governments and mobilizing action: Thomas Risse and Stephen Ropp, 'Introduction and Overview', in Thomas Risse, Stephen Ropp, and Kathryn Sikkink (eds). *The Persistent Power of Human Rights: From Persistence to Compliance* (Cambridge: Cambridge University Press, 2013).
60. See, for example, William Schabas, *An Introduction to the International Criminal Court* (Cambridge: Cambridge University Press, 2008), p. 57.
61. Gary J. Bass, *Stay the Hand of Vengeance* (Princeton, NJ: Princeton University Press, 2000); Richard J. Goldstone, *For Humanity: Reflections of a War Crimes Investigator* (New Haven, CT: Yale University Press, 2000).
62. Hyeran Jo and Beth A. Simmons, 'Can the International Criminal Court Deter Atrocity?' *Social Science Research Network,* 2014.
63. Hunjoon Kim and Kathryn Sikkink, 'Explaining the Deterrence Effects for Human Rights Prosecutions in Transitional Countries', *International Studies Quarterly,* 54, no. 4 (2010), pp. 939–963.
64. See, for example, Jack Snyder and L. Vinjanmuri, 'Trials and Errors: Principle and Pragmatism in Strategies of International Justice', *International Security,* 28, no, 3 (2003–4), pp. 5–44; Daniel Sutter, 'The Deterrent Effects of the International Criminal Court', *New Political Economy,* 23, no. 1 (2006), pp. 9–24.
65. S. Neil MacFarlane and Yuen Foong Khon, *Human Security and the UN: A Critical History* (Bloomington, IN: Indiana University Press, 2006), p. 183.

66. Walter A. Kemp, *The OSCE in a New Context* (London: Royal Institute of International Affairs, 1996).

67. S. Neil Macfarlane and Yun Foong Khong, *Human Security and the UN: A Critical History* (Bloomington, IN: Indiana University Press, 2006), p. 174.

68. See Paul D. Williams, 'From Non-Intervention to Non-Indifference: The Origins and Development of the African Union's Security Culture', *African Affairs*, 106, no. 423 (2007), pp. 253–279; Arthur Boutellis and Paul D. Williams, 'Peace Operations, the African Union and the United Nations: Toward More Effective Partnership' (New York: International Peace Institute, 2013).

69. Ban Ki-moon (2009), *Implementing the Responsibility to Protect: Report of the Secretary-General*, A/63/677, 12 January.

70. Kofi Annan, *Interventions: A Life in War and Peace* (New York: Penguin, 2013).

71. See, for example, Oran Young, 'International Regimes: Toward a New Theory of Institutions', *World Politics*, 39, no. 1 (1986), pp. 104–122: p. 106. Young rightly points out that it offers little explanation on how to identify and make distinctions between the four elements of any given regime.

72. Krasner, 'Structural Causes and Regime Consequences', p. 2.

73. See Bellamy, *Massacres and Morality*.

74. See, for example, Martha Finnemore, *National Interests in International Security* (Ithaca, NY: Cornell University Press, 1996), p. 22.

75. Krasner, 'Structural Causes and Regime Consequences', p. 2.

76. Thakur, 'R2P after Libya and Syria', p. 331. These responsibilities have not progressed beyond their original positions, as set out in the 1949 Geneva Conventions.

77. Sarah Kenyon Lischer, 'Military Intervention and the Humanitarian "Force Multiplier"', *Global Governance*, 13, no. 1 (2007), pp. 99–118.

78. See, for example, Stephen Hopgood, *The End Times of Human Rights* (Ithaca, NY: Cornell University Press, 2013).

79. Virginia Page Fortna, *Does Peacekeeping Work? Shaping Belligerents' Choices After Civil War* (Princeton, NJ: Princeton University Press, 2005).

80. Lisa Hultman, Jacob Kathman, and Megan Shannon, 'United Nations Peacekeeping and Civilian Protection in Civil War', *American Journal of Political Science*, 57, no. 4 (2013), pp. 875–891.

81. Matthew Krain, 'International Intervention and the Severity of Genocides and Politicides', *International Studies Quarterly*, 49, no. 2 (2005), pp. 363–387.

82. Jacob Kathman and Reed Wood, 'Managing Threat, Cost, and Incentive to Kill: The Short- and Long-Term Effects of Intervention in Mass Killing', *Journal of Conflict Resolution*, 55, no. 5, (2011), pp. 735–760.

83. Amanda M. Murdie and David R. Davis, 'Shaming and Blaming: Using Events Data to Assess the Impact of Human Rights INGOS', *International Studies Quarterly,* 56, no. 1, (2011), pp. 1–16.

84. Hunjoon Kim and Kathryn Sikkink, 'Explaining the Deterrence Effects for Human Rights Prosecutions in Transitional Countries', *International Studies Quarterly,* 54, no. 4, (2010), pp. 939–963.

85. Jo Spangaro, Chinelo Adogu, Geetha Ranmuthugala, Gawaine Powell Davies, Léa Steinacker, and Anthony Zwi, 'What Evidence Exists for Initiatives to Reduce Risk and Incidence of Sexual Violence in Armed Conflict and Other Humanitarian Crises? A Systematic Review', *PLos ONE,* 8, no. 5, (2013).

86. Lisa Hultman, 'UN Peace Operations and the Protection of Civilians: Cheap Talk or Norm Implementation?', *Journal of Peace Research,* 50, no. 1, (2013), pp. 59–73.

87. Kyle Beardsley and Holger Schmidt, 'Following the Flag or Following the Charter? Examining the Determinants of UN Involvement in International Crises 1945–2002', *International Studies Quarterly,* 56, no. 1, (2012), pp. 33–49.

88. All cited in Alex J. Bellamy, 'The Responsibility to Protect Turns Ten', *Ethics and International Affairs,* vol. 29, no. 2 (2015), pp. 161–185.

89. UN Doc. S/PV.6491, 26 February 2011, p. 4.

90. S/PV.6491, p. 4.

91. UN Doc. S/PV.6498, 17 March 2011, p. 8.

92. S/PV.6498, p. 10.

93. UN Doc. S/PV.7216, 14 July 2014, p. 5.

94. Pinker, *The Better Angels of our Nature.*

95. Human Security Report, *Human Security Report,* p. 3.

96. For more on this see Ulfelder, 'Genocide is Going Out of Fashion'.

97. Alex J. Bellamy, *East Asia's Other Miracle: Explaining the Decline of Mass Atrocities* (Oxford: Oxford University Press, 2017).

98. Morris, 'Swinging Pendulum'.

3
Protection without Force

Humanitarian intervention remains a rarely used option in the repository of measures adopted by international society to prevent, halt, or minimize the perpetration of mass atrocities. Indeed, as we pointed out in Chapter 2, there is growing evidence to suggest that the steady decline in atrocities witnessed in the past few decades resulted in part from the transformation of a narrowly focused politics of humanitarian intervention into a broader (albeit fragmented) international human protection regime comprising a wider range of norms, rules, institutions, and practices. Within this context, the place of humanitarian intervention itself has moved from the centre of attention, displaced by the primacy of vulnerable individuals and groups and questions about the best way of protecting them from harm – questions to which the non-consensual use of force are rarely the best answer. Thanks to the emergence of the international human protection regime, humanitarian intervention is now best understood as existing at one end of a spectrum of measures for human protection, most of which are peaceful and non-coercive because humanitarian intervention entails the use of force without the consent of the sovereign state, it is the most intrusive and most controversial of these measures. And because of this, forcible intervention is employed only very rarely. To understand precisely how international society responds to atrocity crimes, and the place of armed intervention within the broader politics of protection, we need to understand these other, less intrusive, measures. That is the purpose of this chapter.

This chapter examines the peaceful measures that might be used to protect individuals and groups from atrocity crimes. First, we show that R2P's third pillar – the element most commonly associated with armed intervention – makes explicit reference to the use of peaceful measures to protect populations from genocide and mass atrocities and to explore the conceptual possibilities of peaceful responses to mass atrocities, as laid out in Paragraphs 138 and 139 of the 2005 World Summit Outcome.[1] Following this, we examine the types of actors that could initiate peaceful strategies to protect populations. Third, we propose some of the policies, tools, and strategies associated with the peaceful application of pillar three, focusing on eleven such approaches. Finally, we assess the practicality of these measures. In doing so, we also identify a number of limitations, as well as the conditions that seem to make their use more effective, and the international community's capacity to employ these measures.

The peaceful dimension of human protection

This chapter focuses on peaceful means of responding to genocide and mass atrocities, and specifically the peaceful dimension of the third pillar of the Responsibility to Protect (R2P). Paragraph 139 of the World Summit Outcome document outlines what it incorporates, asserting that: 'The international community, through the United Nations, also has the responsibility to use appropriate diplomatic, humanitarian, and other peaceful means, in accordance with Chapters VI and VIII of the Charter, to help to protect populations from genocide, war crimes, ethnic cleansing, and crimes against humanity.' As the UN Secretary-General has emphasized, this articulation speaks to the notion that pillar three is 'integral' to R2P. As he pointed out in 2009, the peaceful dimension of pillar three was 'an ongoing, generic responsibility that employs the kind of peaceful, pacific measures specified in Chapter VI and in Article 52, Chapter VIII' of the UN Charter.[2]

Paragraph 139 goes on to stress that coercive and enforcement measures, as identified by Chapter VII of the UN Charter, should only be considered after two conditions are present: when peaceful means have proven to be inadequate, and when national authorities are 'manifestly failing' in their responsibility to protect their populations from atrocity crimes. Moreover, utilizing such measures should only be considered by the UN Security Council 'on a case-by-case' basis, as well as in consultation with regional organizations, wherever possible and appropriate. Despite this, it is often assumed that military action and the third pillar are one and the same, and that the third pillar itself should only be considered after a state has 'manifestly failed'.[3] Such misconceptions have the effect of obfuscating the peaceful dimension of R2P's third pillar. Consequently, this blurs the crucial distinction between first response and last resort that was built into the R2P principle in 2005.

Thus, R2P's third pillar is properly understood to have two components: the responsibility to use lawful and peaceful measures, in line with Chapters VI and VIII of the UN Charter; and the responsibility to take 'timely and decisive action' through the Security Council, when such measures are deemed to be insufficient. The peaceful dimension of R2P's third pillar should be understood to be the first response of the international community. In articulating this transition from peaceful to coercive measures, the language used by Paragraph 139 resonates with Article 42 of the UN Charter, which bestows authority on the UN Security Council to take military or other types of actions when peaceful measures 'would be inadequate or have proved to be inadequate'.

Yet the articulation of this peaceful dimension of R2P's third pillar remains broad in at least three ways. The first is in its identification of actors who might be engaged in protection. Paragraph 139 identifies the international community – this arguably refers principally to UN member states and regional arrangements, but it might also include other actors like civil society organizations, the private sector, and individuals.[4] While the agreement stipulates that action be taken 'through the UN' Chapters VI and VIII of the UN Charter allow for the involvement of a broad range of actors. The implication is that all members of the international community share the collective responsibility but just precisely how this responsibility is played out will vary from case to case.

Second, the type of potential activities that such actors could initiate are broadly construed, including 'diplomatic, humanitarian and other peaceful means in accordance with Chapters VI and VIII of the UN Charter'. The UN Charter, through Articles 33 and 52, also defines broadly the range of measures that could be utilized.

Third is the broad temporal scope. There is no specified limit in relation to either how soon such measures could be adopted, or how long they could be in place. For instance, the initiation of enforcement measures does not assume that peaceful measures have been entirely depleted – peaceful measures could feasibly continue while the threat to populations remain, and while their usefulness endures.

There is indeed much overlap between the peaceful dimension of the third pillar and the second pillar (which entails international assistance). The second pillar, for instance, includes helping governments in their capacity to protect populations, assisting them during periods of stress and encouraging them to comply with their responsibilities. Measures around compliance, for example, could see such overlap – between 'assisting states under stress before a crisis breaks out' (the second pillar) and 'diplomatic' measures to protect populations (the third pillar). What matters here, then, is that efforts to protect populations from atrocity crimes remain broad in scope, are contextually specific and are not limited to a narrow scope of coercive options. Often the most effective response is one that utilizes a range of peaceful measures, rather than one which considers only coercive measures.

Peaceful protection actors

As pointed out in the previous section, the range of actors that can engage in the peaceful protection of populations is broad, contingent on the nature of the situation at hand. There are four broad types of actors with responsibilities for protecting populations.

States are primary bearers of responsibility. The international community, as stated in Paragraph 139, refers principally to the community of UN member states. While the UN itself is the vehicle for action, it is the community of states that holds the responsibility to commit to action. The question of which states bear the most responsibility depends on how much knowledge and influence over a particular situation they might have.

As every situation involving the perpetration of mass atrocities is different, just how individual states should act on this responsibility will also vary. In general terms, three types of action are worth considering. The first is on the basis of existing bilateral relations. In the event of ongoing or imminent atrocities, governments could reconsider, or reconfigure, such bilateral relations to align with the protection of populations. Priorities such as diplomatic relations, foreign aid, and refugee policy could be altered in response to unfolding situations. Second, informal groups such as 'groups of friends' could be utilized to bolster protection efforts. States can use informal networks in various ways: to put pressure on would-be or actual perpetrators, to facilitate processes of conflict resolution, or to facilitate greater protection of vulnerable populations. Third, states can utilize formal institutions (such as the UN) to pursue their established commitments to R2P or other principles associated with human rights and non-indifference. This includes making arrangements that ensure the full implementation of collective decisions that these institutions make in response to atrocity crimes.

The next group of actors fall under the banner of the UN. The UN is central, principally because it is identified as the global institution 'through' which action is taken, according to Paragraph 139. Within the UN system, key actors include its Principal Organs (especially the UN Security Council and General Assembly) as well as secondary bodies such as the Human Rights Council (HRC) and the Peacebuilding Commission. Other bodies, not specifically charged with protection action could also be used. The Secretary-General, for example, has the ability to devote resources to preventive diplomacy, the use of good offices, as well as fact-finding and reporting, not to mention offices within the Secretariat that are charged with relevant mandates, such as the Special Advisers on Genocide Prevention and R2P, the Special Representatives on the Prevention of Sexual Violence and Protection of Internally Displaced Persons, and the High Commissioners on Human Rights and Refugees. Beyond this, action taken by various programmes, funds, and departments within the broader UN system (such as Office for the Coordination of Humanitarian Affairs (OCHA), Office of the High Commissioner for Human Rights (OHCHR), United Nations High Commissioner for Refugees (UNHCR), United Nations Development Programme (UNDP), United Nations Children's Fund (UNICEF)) could also undertake protection responsibilities under the terms of their own mandates. Indeed, the Charter contains no constraint on the work that can be carried out by such actors, provided that they are adopted with the consent of the state in question.

Regional and sub-regional arrangements (hereafter 'regional arrangements') are another set of actors who play crucial protection roles. Since 2005, it is clear that protection efforts have worked most effectively when there has been an alignment of states, the UN and regional arrangements. Although there will be variation in the roles that regional arrangements play, due to the case-by-case nature of these situations, there is no doubt that cooperation between the UN and regional arrangements produces the best results when it comes to responding to genocide and mass atrocities. Not least, it is helpful in cultivating regional ownership, and in facilitating local ownership along the lines of existing regional norms. This in turn enhances cooperation between the UN and regions, and provides a strong regional voice in deliberations on how to respond to genocide and mass atrocities.

Finally, it is worth considering how non-state actors – international non-governmental organizations (NGOs), domestic civil society groups, private sector actors, researchers and analysts, activists, and other individuals – contribute to protection. Broadly construed, their roles are threefold. First, they contribute to diplomacy, by holding governments to account. If a government is violating its protection responsibilities, often it is brought to light by international and domestic NGOs. The second role is as agents of humanitarian relief, often providing vulnerable populations with life-saving relief. Third, non-state actors such as civil society groups, private sector actors and prominent individuals can be instrumental in protecting vulnerable groups on the ground, as well as reducing tensions that often trigger atrocity crimes.

Peaceful measures

There is no single viable approach to addressing impending or ongoing atrocity crimes. Just as the range of protection actors are diverse, so too are the tools, strategies, and policies that they might adopt. Just which course, or courses of action, might be put into practice depends on a complex range of factors present in any given situation. To advocate coercive tactics for every situation would be tantamount to ignoring the contextual factors at play, risking the possibility of doing more harm than good. The important thing here is to bring together the responses of different agents, ensuring that the most effective action is one that arises when these actors work in conjunction with each other. There are three distinct approaches worth considering here: actions that seek to persuade or deter perpetrators; actions which make the perpetration of atrocities more difficult, and actions that provide shelter and protection for vulnerable populations. Addressing these broad approaches are eleven key measures, outlined below.

The gathering of information through fact-finding missions or other investigations on the ground are important for determining whether atrocities crimes are being perpetrated, and by whom. Such information can act as a deterrent, while also raising the possibility that perpetrators will be held accountable. The authority to gather information is attributed to numerous bodies. Article 34 of the Charter allows the Security Council to 'investigate any dispute, or any situation that might lead to international friction or give rise to a dispute'. Articles 11, 12, 13, and 14 give the General Assembly similar authority. The HRC also has the power to initiate a range of information gathering measures, such as authorizing fact-finding missions, or appointing special rapporteurs. Regional bodies, such as the Organization for Security and Co-operation in Europe's (OSCE's) High Commissioner on National Minorities, or the African Union's Peace and Security Council, have their own capacity for fact-finding, as do a number of NGOs, including Human Rights Watch and the International Crisis Group.

Diplomacy is one of the key peaceful strategies that can be deployed in crisis situations, both to pressure perpetrators to stop atrocities that have started and to prevent tense situations from escalating to the perpetration of such violence. This type of action has been used by a wide range of actors, not least through the UN Secretary-General's 'good offices', as well as by UN-appointed envoys, regional arrangements, ad hoc groupings and individuals. Indeed, it is not unusual for a combination of such measures to be adopted. Diplomacy entails efforts to persuade leaders to opt for negotiation and peacemaking over the perpetration of atrocities, which includes reminding leaders of their protection responsibilities. It is a reminder that such action attracts international attention, and in doing so signals public pressure for restraint and mediation. Diplomacy in crisis situations is crucial because words often matter when it comes to persuading leaders to adopt or refrain from particular courses of action.

Another form of persuasion is public advocacy, which involves calling publicly on leaders to act in line with their protection responsibilities. Recent examples of public advocacy include the work of the UN Secretary-General, his Special Advisers on Genocide Prevention and R2P, and the UN's High Commissioner for Human Rights. All have invoked R2P in public statements in their calls for states to fulfil protection commitments and to comply with international legal obligations. Côte d'Ivoire, Libya, Yemen, South Sudan, Sudan, Syria, and Iraq have all been the focus of such statements in recent years. Resolutions passed by the Security Council and the General Assembly fulfil the same function but with greater influence. Indeed, as we noted in Chapter 2, the Security Council has become more frequent in voicing its concern about atrocity crimes. Likewise, the

General Assembly has called on the governments of Syria and North Korea to fulfil their legal obligations when it comes to protection. Prominent individuals are also becoming more vocal in their public statements, with examples including Kofi Annan's public diplomacy in relation to Kenya; Surin Pitsuwan's public diplomacy on the Rohingya crisis in Southeast Asia; and Michael Kirby's use of R2P in the UN Human Rights Council's Commission of Inquiry's report into human rights in North Korea.

Facilitating the peaceful resolution of disputes can be achieved through a range of options. The UN Secretary-General's good offices, the AU's Panel of the Wise, the OSCE and the Council of Europe, as well as ad hoc mediation efforts (such as Malaysia's mediation of the Mindanao crisis in the Philippines) are all examples of dispute resolution. Non-state actors also engage in arbitration and dispute resolution – the Geneva-based Centre for Humanitarian Dialogue or the global Elders network have both been engaged in such work. The types of measures that such actors adopt, as well as which actors are involved, are contingent upon the specific circumstances of each case, but are necessarily premised on the extent to which specific actors are accepted and trusted by the parties to a conflict. Such work can go ahead without Security Council or General Assembly authorization,[5] and local processes of mediation and negotiation can be – and often are – initiated without the presence of national or international processes. There are also judicial paths of settlement – national constitutions and legal mechanisms, the International Court of Justice, and the International Criminal Court have varying roles to play, from issuing advisory opinions to investigating and prosecuting alleged atrocity crimes.

Human rights mechanisms can fulfil a range of functions that help bolster the protection of populations from atrocity crimes. There are three levels where such mechanisms can have effect – the international, the regional and the state. At the international level, the UN primary human rights body is the HRC, which is tasked with the promotion of human rights and freedoms for all people. The range of powers that the HRC has can, as the UN Secretary-General observed in 2012, 'play a vital role in any comprehensive response' to atrocity crimes.[6]

Regional human rights mechanisms include Latin America's Commission on Human Rights and regional Court of Human Rights. The Commission has a range of functions, including investigating alleged human rights violations, monitoring human rights situations in member states, engaging in fact-finding missions, and making recommendations. It also has the power to refer situations to the regional Court. While narrower in scope, Africa's Commission on Human and Peoples' Rights is tasked with promoting human rights throughout the region, as well as conducting information gathering through special rapporteurs or commissions. It also has the power to refer situations to the African Court of Human and Peoples' Rights, as occurred in the case of Libya in 2011. Other regional mechanisms include the EU's European Court of Human Rights, the OSCE's Council of Europe, and ASEAN's Intergovernmental Commission on Human Rights (AICHR).

At the state level, the tasks of National Human Rights Institutions and nationally based human rights defenders can also play significant roles in providing early warning for atrocity crimes, through the collection and analysis of information. They are often the first actors to hold governments or other armed groups to account, as well as providing an important conduit for cooperation with regional and international actors.

Humanitarian action can be deployed in order to mitigate some of the most damaging outcomes that affect civilian populations during armed conflict and one-sided violence. It does this through the provision of necessities such as food, shelter and medicine, among other things.[7] In doing this, it can provide support for existing local coping strategies, as well as ensuring access to populations under threat. Where possible, it can also prevent or limit displacement where possible, and provide safe passage to and from stricken areas.[8]

The number of humanitarian organizations that can and have played crucial roles in providing life-saving relief to populations under threat are too numerous to mention here. Often it is these organizations that are on the front line of providing relief when international bodies fail to reach consensus to protect civilians in imminent danger. Syria, CAR and Darfur are recent examples of this kind of work. In Darfur, international humanitarians in conjunction with local organizations provided protection for around 2 million civilians who had been displaced in the first year of the conflict, which began in 2003. Thus, where there may be despair about the failure of international political bodies to find sufficient consensus to effectively protect civilians in imminent danger in placed such as Syria and the CAR, it needs to be understood that agencies like the Red Cross and Red Crescent,

Caritas, and Islamic Relief and the UN's UNHCR, UNICEF, and WFP work every day to protect civilians in their homes (through the provision of humanitarian aid) or wherever they have fled (by providing shelter). Often they are the first international actors on the ground when violence escalates and civilians' lives are at risk.

This crucial role that humanitarian actors play was reiterated in the UN Secretary-General's 2012 report on R2P, emphasizing that humanitarian action plays an important role in protecting populations from atrocity crimes.[9] Yet this should not diminish the challenges that humanitarian actors face. The report goes on to stress that such action should not be seen as an alternative to political action.

Yet, by remaining outside of politics, humanitarian actors are able to gain access to places that are out of bounds for other actors. For instance, Save the Children was able to operate within Taliban-controlled Afghanistan. Médecins Sans Frontières gained access to parts of rebel-controlled northern Mali that Mali's government, along with other international actors, was unable to go to. By not posing a direct political threat, and by maintaining the principles of impartiality, independence and humanity, such humanitarian organizations often gain such access and influence. These principles comprise the humanitarian space in which these organizations work, though aid workers have paid a terrible personal price over the past decade as violent attacks on them have increased.[10]

Economic measures in the form of sanctions are well-known strategies for responding to atrocity crimes. Sanctions can be effective because they raise the costs associated with violent behaviour, which increases the level of difficulty for perpetrators to reach their goals. For this reason, sanctions, along with embargoes, have been used frequently by the UN Security Council.

Inducements, for promoting and rewarding responsible behaviour, are less well known. Such inducements are usually economic in nature, and have been used to great effect in numerous cases in order to encourage a path to dispute resolution. One key example here is inducement of financial assistance to bring about Middle Eastern endorsement of the Camp David Accords. Economic inducements have also been used to convince ex-combatants to disarm and demobilize. Although it can be both politically and ethically challenging to offer inducements to those who have allegedly committed atrocities, it is worth considering them as a possible strategy for encouraging actors to achieve their ends without resorting to atrocities.

One of the greatest protective factors in times of armed conflict is a group's ability to escape from immediate harm. If a vulnerable group has the ability to find refuge from violence, then the casualties are likely to be lower. Seeking refuge also has its challenges – displacement itself can lead to further vulnerability and persecution. The challenge for international actors, then, is to help vulnerable populations flee from violence, and to provide safe haven in the wake of such action.

The most common form of self-protection is indeed the act of leaving an area under threat, whether to a second country or to a camp run by international agencies. Although flight is an effective means of avoiding imminent danger, the displaced face long-term security challenges, particularly in relation to deprivation. Displaced populations often miss out on the essentials of life, such as 'shelter, food, medicine, education, community and a resource base for self-reliant livelihood'.[11] IDPs typically have a higher mortality than any other group, with the possible exception of groups who have not been able to flee.[12]

These problems can be compounded by the fact that IDPs often remain under the authority of the same government that has originally targeted them, or failed to protect them, from other armed groups.[13] These authorities and non-state armed groups that control territory sometimes deny humanitarian agencies the access they need to protect displaced people, intensifying the challenge of operating in an insecure environment. Today, however, the world faces an almost unprecedented crisis of displacement caused by a combination of massive new humanitarian crises, such as that in Syria, caused in part by atrocity crimes and the international community's failure to find long-term resettlement places for those displaced by past crises.

There has always been a strong connection between international responses to genocide and mass atrocities and the protection of refugees. Indeed, R2P arguably arose out of earlier attempts to link responsible sovereignty with the protection of IDPs.[14] The UN Secretary-General has repeatedly stressed that one key way that states fulfil their responsibility to protect was by fully implementing international refugee law. The same has been argued by two of the world's leading thinkers on refugee protection, Brian Barbour and UNHCR's Brian Gorlick: 'there may be no easier way for the international community to meet its responsibility to protect than by providing asylum and other international protection on adequate terms.'[15] This involves implementing the 1951 Convention on the Protection of Refugees and the subsequent 1967 Protocol through the existing mechanisms, including UNHCR, which had already been established to achieve that goal. Asylum ought to be a key element of the international community's repertoire of responses to atrocity crimes.[16]

There are a range of measures that can support the protection of refugees – measures often undertaken by states, with the support of the UNHCR and the IOM. They include ensuring that neighbouring states provide safe haven for those seeking it; supporting such receiving states so they have the adequate resources to provide shelter and other necessities; helping these receiving states by facilitating the movement of refugees to other countries for temporary protection; increasing the options for long-term protection and resettlement worldwide; encouraging states to increase their intake of asylum seekers, especially those who are potential victims of atrocity crimes;[17] addressing the unique concerns of women and girls; and enabling a better understanding of why people are fleeing in the first place.[18]

IDPs themselves face different hurdles because they are not recognized under international refugee law. It was this oversight that led to the development of 'Guiding Principles' for the way displaced people should be treated, taking into account existing human rights law. Despite the legal gap, the idea that the protection of IDPs should be a central part of any response to atrocity crimes is beyond repute.[19]

Another means of reporting atrocity crimes is to send out monitoring, observer and verification missions. Such missions usually have specific objectives, such as monitoring a ceasefire, or verifying the compliance of human rights. In doing so they normally carry out three processes: collecting information, seeking verification of that information, and using the collected information to help carry out their mission's objectives. An example of such a mission is the OSCE's Kosovo Verification Mission, whose task it was to verify the compliance of a ceasefire agreement and associated human rights commitments.

A relatively new course of action is *unarmed civilian protection*, which entails sending unarmed actors into areas of high risk, in order to assist with the protection of populations. This is done through providing a presence, persuading potential aggressors against using violence, and building capacity. The most prominent organization engaged in such activity is an NGO called Non-violent Peaceforce, which runs a number of missions in such places as Ukraine, South Sudan, the Philippines and Myanmar.

Political support and peacebuilding activities provide broader opportunities for civilian engagement in crisis situations, which go beyond the traditional domains of diplomacy, humanitarian action and monitoring and observation. The emergence of these activities is due to a growing realization that a more strategic approach to transitioning away from peacekeeping operations was needed, as well as the belief that the international community's response to such situations needed to be political, given that most of the world's conflicts were political in character.[20] Such activities are a much less expensive option, while allowing the international community to have a ground presence at an earlier stage of a crisis, and can include measures that range from humanitarian assistance and disarmament to promoting democracy, the rule of law and human rights.

These activities may be conducted by the UN, whether through a discrete mission or through bilateral country assistance agreements, or other agencies. The EU in Africa, for example, and Australia, in the Pacific Islands region, have provided extensive support of this type to countries on request. Moreover, bilateral support between states is quite common. In addition, non-state actors can often play important roles here also. For example, the Carter Center is one of several NGOs that provides expertise and technical support to states holding elections as well as monitoring those elections.

While *peacekeeping* missions have become more complex and varied in recent decades, they are commonly understood as a consensual exercise designed to support and oversee a peace process at the invitation of the parties concerned. This entails a wide range of protection responsibilities.[21] Yet peacekeeping can also fall within the peaceful dimension of the third pillar as it often involves the use of peaceful (i.e. consensual) means to protect populations from atrocity crimes. This overlapping of responsibilities is born out in different UNDPKO-managed missions, such as UNMISS South Sudan, whose mandate comprises elements of pillars two (supporting the state to fulfil its protection responsibilities) and three (protecting civilians within its areas of operation). Many other UN and non-UN missions also contain overlaps of these responsibilities, including UNOCI (Côte d'Ivoire), MONUSCO (Democratic Republic of Congo), MINUSCA (Central African Republic), and MINUSMA (Mali). Indeed, most contemporary peacekeeping operations already perform tasks which support protection goals, as has been acknowledged by a recent study conducted by the UN's Office of Internal Oversight Services (OIOS).

They found that the preventive and political work of UN peacekeeping operations has 'notable and positive results' for the protection of civilian populations: 'civilians invariably attach high value to missions' physical presence, which evidence suggests had a huge deterrent impact and avoided violence that otherwise would have occurred ... The value of such deterrence is unquantifiable but enormous.'[22]

The support that peacekeeping can provide to efforts to protect populations from genocide and mass atrocities falls into three main categories. First, missions help vulnerable states to strengthen their own capacity to protect their populations. Many peacekeeping missions contain capacity building in their mandates, typically covering such activities as institution building and capacity development, in partnership with local actors. Second, peacekeeping operations can provide *indirect* protection to endangered civilian populations by supporting work in areas such as security sector reform and the rule of law, which give rise to a more protective social environment. This entails a range of activities, including understanding the extent of threats to civilians through a nuanced appreciation of the prevalence of sexual and gender-based violence and strategies to address those specific risks; and monitoring and promoting basic standards of human rights and protection; as well as a range of other tasks conducted by international police contingents, which can be understood to contribute to indirect protection through deterrence and confidence building. Through presence and patrols, peacekeepers can deter would-be perpetrators quite effectively.[23] Third, peacekeepers often engage in more direct protection measures.[24] Placing troops between at-risk populations and the armed elements that threaten them can have the effect of deterring attacks, as well as restricting the activities of the perpetrator group.

Taking stock of peaceful measures

The repertoire of peaceful measures outlined above provides an indication that the international community is becoming more sophisticated in the measures it can adopt to address the threat of atrocity crimes. However, these strategies do not guarantee success[25] – their effectiveness is contingent on a range of contextually specific factors, including the willingness of conflicting parties to negotiate, the political will of international actors to invest in preventive measures, and the ability to apply the measures at the right time. In this section, we consider, in general terms, factors which inhibit the success of non-violent protection measures. We then outline the general conditions for the effective deployment of protection measures. Finally, we provide an outline of where global capacity and commitment currently exist.

None of the measures outlined in the previous section are without their limitations. Successful diplomacy and mediation are contingent upon conflict parties being willing to negotiate and trust each other. Humanitarian action might provide immediate relief for vulnerable parties, but it cannot stop perpetrators from committing atrocities. Monitoring and early warning might deter the actions of some perpetrators, but only if they value their international reputation. While the application of non-coercive measures are best utilized at an early stage in a conflict, successful early mobilization can be particularly challenging, not least because in the absence of widespread atrocities having already been committed, persuading international actors that such violence is likely or imminent without action can be difficult when the end result is a non-event.

These challenges flag potential structural obstacles to protection strategies. Engaging in early action is highly controversial, and often involves interference in the domestic affairs of states.[26] Likewise, states staunchly defend their sovereignty and rarely seek international assistance, nor do they particularly welcome such offers.[27] This reluctance to cooperate or acknowledge atrocity crimes committed at home can produce a significant obstacle to protection by peaceful means.

It is also unusual for states to commit the resources necessary for human protection in the absence of overwhelming evidence that atrocities are occurring. Moreover, the resources available for peaceful protection are often profoundly limited. Austerity measures in many wealthy states have resulted in shrinking aid and international development budgets. The UN has also made cuts to its budget, by approximately 1 per cent in 2014/15 and another 1 percent in 2016/17.[28] This has had reverberations on the UN's commitment to peaceful measures, particularly its political missions.[29] What this means is that efforts to improve commitments to peaceful measures for human protection will need to be carried out without new resources. This could have an impact on the decision to commit to early action, as the immediate costs are always far more apparent than the long-term benefits of prevention. Why commit to uncertain action, especially when there is no pressure to do so?[30]

Often compounding these obstacles are constraints on global capacity and commitment in relation to the international community's ability to implement peaceful strategies for protection. For instance, diplomacy and mediation at the UN are chronically underfunded, with 20 per cent of the UN Department of Political Affairs' budget, including all of the Mediation Support Unit's funds, acquired through voluntary contributions. This renders such work insecure and places profound limitations on the Department's ability to hire, train and send out experts as needs arise. There is also inconsistency with public advocacy. This worked very effectively in Kenya in 2008 and 2013, but has been tragically ineffective in other places, such as Sri Lanka and Central African Republic.

Humanitarianism and the growing crisis of displacement are two other areas where global capacity falls far short of needs. Indeed, there is a growing gap between humanitarian need and available resources. In 2016, only 25 per cent of the Humanitarian Response Plan compiled by UN OCHA has been funded, according to the 2016 Global Humanitarian Review. In monetary terms, this amounts to $5.5 billion out of $21.6 billion of identified financial requirements.[31] This gap is also starkly apparent in the global response to forced displacement. Global displacement levels reached 65.3 million in 2015, which is the highest it has been since the Second World War. Of this number, 107,100 people were resettled in 2015.[32]

Further compounding these issues is the inadequate global response to help stabilize places that have experienced atrocity crimes. Peacekeeping missions, for example, rarely have adequate resources to help protect populations.[33] This capacity is a product of both host country reticence to welcome peacekeepers on their soil and reluctance by the UN Security Council to authorize and fund large-scale peacekeeping operations, not to mention the issues involved in sourcing peacekeepers from already-stretched contributing countries' militaries.[34]

Nevertheless, there are factors that can facilitate greater success when initiating peaceful strategies for protection. It is far more helpful if leaders – both local and national – are receptive to international efforts to improve protection.[35] While in most crises peaceful measures will most likely not dissuade the actions of leaders who are determined to perpetrate atrocities, committing such violence is rarely their first option of choice, and is usually a last resort.[36] This means that there are opportunities within the unfolding of a crisis to persuade leaders not to commit atrocities.

Timing and a diversity of strategies are also important. As violence escalates, often the opportunities for peaceful measures to be effective diminish considerably. For this reason, it is much more likely that the utilization of peaceful measures will have a greater chance of success at the early stage of a crisis. In addition, a coordinated and multi-levelled international response, involving a range of actors, is more likely to result in success.

It is also important to commit the necessary resources – both political and material – to ensure that peaceful measures have the best chance of working. Any decisions made, or mandates passed, at the international level must be supported with the requisite resources in order for them to be carried out effectively. At the same time, it is important for the international community to declare a commitment to re-assess and intensify its response if needed. This can have the effect of changing the calculations of leaders if they are convinced that the costs of perpetrating atrocity crimes become too high. Thus, while peaceful measures are often aimed at persuading leaders to refrain from such violence, they are likely to be more effective if there is a clear signal from the international community that it will intensify its action should further violence be committed.

Finally, the resilience of societies experiencing crises is important. Domestic resilience can have many sources – through civil society, national institutions, the private sector, religious organizations, as well as other culturally specific means of resolving disputes and dealing with violence. Any international action is likely to have a more positive effect if it can tap into existing sources of resilience. Where resilience is low, there is a greater chance of societal fragmentation, and more likelihood of order being imposed by violent means.

Conclusion

This chapter has identified several different peaceful practices, measures and actors that contribute to the prevention of atrocity crimes and the protection of vulnerable populations. No particular approach is a magic bullet; indeed, no approach is wholly effective on its own – every situation will contain its own contextually specific challenges, and every situation will be met with varying degrees of political will and capacity. Just as the circumstances that lead to atrocities are contextually specific, so should international responses to such cases be tailored to specific situations and the specific time frames that these circumstances provoke. More research is needed on which combinations of measure have been most effective in different risk environments. While international responses to risk escalation – and indeed, the decisions as to who are the most effective actors to respond – will be tailored to the specific challenges of each unique case, it is certainly possible, in a broad sense, to develop a more sophisticated understanding of the calculus of measures that might work best. For the purposes of this chapter, what these measures are illustrative of is the range of options that are available to international actors, short of using force. Indeed, if international society can make better and more comprehensive use of peaceful measures at the early stages of escalation, it is likely that the UN Security Council will have to deal with fewer cases that require the authorization of coercive measures.

While such peaceful measures are being utilized more frequently, and with tangible effects – thanks to the international human protection regime – efforts here still remain ad hoc, piecemeal and under-resourced. Many of the preventive measures that have been championed by the UN – including early warning, diplomacy and mediation – continue to receive well below the funding required to meet current needs. This is in no small part due to the challenge of having to persuade decision-makers that atrocities are likely, or imminent, when casualties have yet to mount. Action is needed to strengthen these capacities across the board, so that they can be utilized more often, more rapidly, and on a greater scale.

There are, however, some situations where peaceful measures do not sway leaders from violent paths – cases where the international community continues to confront questions about the use of force. Traditionally, this is where the politics of humanitarian intervention begins, sharpened by the fact that the UN Security Council's reticence to authorize force has occasionally pushed states and groups of states to step outside the boundaries of international law in order to save strangers in peril. The question of when and under what circumstances – especially in relation to the extent to which peaceful measures have been tried – the use of force for protection purposes should be considered, is the subject of the next chapter. There we suggest that the Security Council's decision to authorize force in the case of Libya marked a significant evolution of the international human protection regime, indicating that the regime itself could authorize and make lawful the use of force against a state for human protection – that it would not rule out such force as a matter of principle as it had done in the past.

Notes

1. On this, see Alex J. Bellamy, *The First Response: Peaceful Means in the Third Pillar of the Responsibility to Protect*, Policy Analysis Brief, The Stanley Foundation, December 2015.
2. Ban Ki-moon (2009), *Implementing the Responsibility to Protect: Report of the Secretary-General*, A/63/677, 12 January, para. 49.
3. See Adrian Gallagher, 'What Constitutes a Manifest Failing? Ambiguous and Inconsistent Terminology and the Responsibility to Protect', *International Politics*, 28, no. 4 (2014), pp. 428–444.
4. On the important but as yet under-recognized *individual* R2P, see Edward C. Luck and Dana Luck, 'The Individual Responsibility to Protect', in Sheri P. Rosenberg, Tibi Galis, and Alex Zucker (eds), *Reconstructing Atrocity Prevention* (Cambridge: Cambridge University Press, 2015).
5. Ban Ki-moon (2012), *Responsibility to Protect: Timely and Decisive Response*, A/66/874, para 22.
6. Ban, *Timely and Decisive Response*, para. 34.
7. Amelia Bookstein, 'Beyond the Headlines: An Agenda for Action to Protect Civilians in Neglected Conflicts', *Humanitarian Exchange Magazine*, no. 25, December 2003, p. 6.
8. Bookstein, 'Beyond the Headlines', pp. 16–17.
9. Ban, *Timely and Decisive Response*, para. 44.
10. See the IRIN News dataset of attacks on aid workers: http://newirin. irinnews.org/aid-worker-attacks-map-methodology/
11. Francis M. Deng, 'Divided Nations: The Paradox of National Protection', *The Annals of the American Academy of Political and Social Science*, 603 (2006), p. 218.
12. Roberta Cohen and Francis M. Deng, *Masses in Flight: The Global Crisis of Internal Displacement* (Washington: The Brookings Institution, 1998), p. 227.
13. Deng, 'Divided Nations', p. 218. Nor are refugees always in a much better position; see K. Morjane, 'The Protection of Refugee and Displaced Persons', in *Human Rights Protection in the Field*, special issue of *International Studies in Human Rights*, 87 (2006), p. 79.
14. See Roberta Cohen and Francis Deng, 'From Sovereignty as Responsibility to R2P', in Alex J. Bellamy and Tim Dunne (eds), *The Oxford Handbook on the Responsibility to Protect* (Oxford: Oxford University Press, 2016).

15. Brian Barbour and Brian Gorlick, 'Embracing the Responsibility to Protect: A Repertoire of Measures Including Asylum for Potential Victims', *International Journal of Refugee Law*, 20, no. 4 (2008), p. 533.
16. See Sara E. Davies and Luke Glanville (eds), *Protecting the Displaced: Deepening the Responsibility to Protect* (The Hague: Martinus Nijhoff, 2010).
17. Barbour and Gorlick, 'Embracing R2P', p. 558.
18. See note 17, above.
19. The best regional example is the AU Convention for the Protection and Assistance of IDPs in Africa, 2009.
20. Jean-Marie Guehenno, *The Fog of Peace: A Memoir of International Peacekeeping in the 21ˢᵗ Century* (Washington DC: Brookings Institution, 2015).
21. See, for example, United Nations, *Fulfilling our Collective Responsibility: International Assistance and the Responsibility to Protect*, Report No. A/68/947-S/2014/449 (New York: United Nations, 2014).
22. United Nations Office of Internal Oversight Services, *Evaluation of the Implementation and Results of Protection of Civilians Mandates in United Nations Peacekeeping Operations*, A/68/787, 7 March 2014, para. 68.
23. Lisa Hultman, 'UN Peace Operations and Protection of Civilians: Cheap Talk or Norm Implementation?', *Journal of Peace Research*, 50, no. 1 (2013), pp. 59–73.
24. Charles Hunt and Alex J. Bellamy, 'Mainstreaming the Responsibility to Protect in Peace Operations,' *Civil Wars*, 3, no. 1 (2011), pp. 1–20.
25. Alex J. Bellamy and Adam Lupel, *Why We Fail: Obstacles to the Effective Prevention of Atrocity Crimes*, Policy Brief, International Peace Institute, New York, 2015.
26. The central argument advanced by Ruben Reike, 'The Responsibility to Prevent: An International Crimes Approach to the Prevention of Mass Atrocities', *Ethics & International Affairs*, 28, no. 4 (2014), pp. 451–476.
27. Reike, 'The Responsibility to Prevent'.
28. Michele Nichols, 'UN General Assembly Approves $5.5 Billion Budget for 2014/2015', *Reuters*, 27 December 2013, Available at: www.reuters.com/article/2013/12/27/us-un-budget-idUSBRE-9BQ0JX20131227; United Nations, *Fifth Committee Recommends $5.4 Billion Budget for 2016–2017 Biennium as it Concludes Main Part of Seventieth Session*, United Nations Meetings Coverage Press Release, Available at: http://www.un.org/press/en/2015/gaab4185.doc.htm.
29. Donald C. F. Daniel, 'Contemporary Patterns in Peace Operations: 2000–2010', in Alex J. Bellamy and Paul D. Williams (eds), *Providing*

Peacekeepers: The Politics, Challenges and Future of United Nations Peacekeeping Contributions (Oxford: Oxford University Press, 2013).

30. A point made by Guehenno, *Fog of Peace*, p. 270.
31. OCHA, *Global Humanitarian Overview 2016* (Geneva: OCHA, 2016).
32. UNHCR, *Global Trends: Forced Displacement in 2014* (Geneva: UNHCR, 2016).
33. See, for example, Alex J. Bellamy and Paul D. Williams, 'Protecting Civilians in Uncivil Wars' in Sara E. Davies and Luke Glanville (eds), *Protecting the Displaced: Deepening the Responsibility to Protect* (Leiden: Martinus Nijhoff, 2010), pp. 127–162.
34. Michael O'Hanlon and Peter W. Singer, 'The Humanitarian Transformation: Expanding Global Intervention Capacity', *Survival*, 46, no. 1 (2004), p. 97, n. 7.
35. Edward C. Luck, *The Responsibility to Protect at Ten: The Challenges Ahead*, Policy Analysis Brief for the Stanley Foundation, 2015, p. 6.
36. See, for example, Benjamin A. Valentino, *Final Solutions: Mass Killing and Genocide in the 20th Century* (Ithaca, NY: Cornell University Press, 2004).

4

Intervention in Libya

On 17 March 2011, the UN Security Council issued Resolution 1973, authorizing the use of all necessary means to protect civilians from imminent attack, imposing a no-fly zone over Libya, and enforcing the establishment of an arms embargo. Two days later, air forces from France, Canada, the UK, and the USA led a joint action, targeting Libya's air defences and army. This initial action was soon followed by a summit held in Paris on 20 March, where plans for a broader operation – *Odyssey Dawn* – were drawn up, bringing in participants from eighteen states and two regional organizations. Renamed Operation *Unified Protection* on 31 March, the continued military operations against Gaddafi's regime in Libya were effective in helping to resist the fall of Benghazi, and in doing so preventing a massacre there that appeared to be very imminent. Over the next few months, as the fighting endured a period of stalemate, the bombing of military targets by NATO and its allies precipitated a shift in the rebels' favour, culminating in forces fighting on behalf of the National Transitional Council (NTC) taking control of Tripoli on 19 August. The last government strongholds fell by October, when Gaddafi himself was captured and killed.

International society's response to the 2011 Libyan crisis, typified by Resolution 1973, represents a significant turning moment in the post-Second World War history of humanitarian intervention and human protection. That is because Resolution 1973 was the first time in its history that the Security Council had authorized military action, *without* the consent of the state in question, with the express purpose of protecting populations from atrocity crimes. Up until then, the Council had not – as a matter of principle – overridden state sovereignty in such a direct way to protect populations. And while the decision itself was enabled by a rare combination of factors unlikely to be often repeated, it represented a significant change to the international politics of protection: no longer would collectively authorized intervention against states be ruled out *as a matter of principle*. That is not to say that such interventions will become common, just that – in principle at least – this last barrier against the privileging of fundamental human rights over sovereign rights has been removed. That is why the significance of Libya extends well beyond Libya itself.

The purpose of this chapter is to demonstrate how the international response to the 2011 crisis in Libya represents a crossing of the Rubicon in terms of the measures that international society is prepared, in principle, to take in order to protect populations from atrocity crimes. Resolution 1973 followed concerted earlier attempts to address Libya's escalating violence through an unusually wide range of non-violent measures. It was the utilization of this range of proximate preventive measures prior to the adoption of Resolution 1973 that set in motion international society's graded and escalating approach to human protection, culminating in military action against a sovereign government that was targeting its own people. The chapter has four sections. The first outlines the combination of circumstances that led up to the passing of Resolution 1973. Second, we explain the resolution and the ensuing humanitarian intervention. Third, we point out why Resolution 1973 represents an in-principle turning point in the way that international society responds to atrocity crimes. Finally, we consider the aftermath of the international action and some of the controversies provoked by the intervention in Libya.

Countdown to Resolution 1973

To understand why Security Council Resolution 1973 was authorized, we must go back to the political upheavals that unfolded across northern Africa in 2011, as part of the Arab Spring. In Tunisia and Egypt, widespread non-violent protests led to the overthrow of authoritarian governments in both countries. In Libya, protests rapidly took a violent turn, with the Libyan regime launching a brutal crackdown, and some dissidents developing an armed opposition group, as part of the NTC. Many members of Libya's armed forces defected to the NTC, boosting their strength and helping the rebels make significant early territorial gains, including the taking of a number of major cities such as Benghazi and Tobruk. By early March, however, Gaddafi's forces had regrouped and started regaining lost territory, which the overstretched rebels were unable to defend. Libya's armed forces threatened to bring on a crushing defeat to the rebel stronghold city of Benghazi.

As the civil war continued, several international actors publicly raised concern about the escalation of violence. Navi Pillay, the UN High Commissioner for Human Rights, and the UN Special Advisers for Genocide Prevention and the Responsibility to Protect (R2P) released public statements reminding Libya of its responsibility to protect populations there, pointing out that violence committed against protestors could amount to crimes against humanity.[1] Both the League of Arab States (LAS) and the African Union (AU), through its Peace and Security Council, condemned Gaddafi's regime for attacking unarmed civilians and the LAS suspended Libya's membership.

The escalating violence and growing chorus of international bodies expressing alarm at the Gaddafi regime prompted the UN Security Council to adopt Resolution 1970, on 26 February. The resolution – itself among the most comprehensive human protection resolutions ever adopted – condemned government-sanctioned violence against civilians, and repeated the suspicion that such violence could amount to crimes against humanity. It demanded a swift end to the violence; referred the situation in Libya to the Prosecutor of the International Criminal Court; set up an arms embargo; issued travel bans on key members of the regime; and urged the Libyan government to allow humanitarian and medical supplies into conflict-affected areas.

In the days and weeks following Resolution 1970, the Libyan government steadfastly refused to comply with the demands or cooperate with outside bodies. Humanitarian access to cities such as Misrata and Ajdabiya was not permitted. Diplomatic efforts continued through the UN Special Envoy and the AU High Level Committee. This was followed by a forty-minute telephone call to Gaddafi from the UN Secretary-General himself, in which the Secretary-General appealed to the Libyan leader to comply with the Security Council's demands and find a peaceful resolution to the crisis. None of these efforts persuaded Gaddafi to change course and his forces continued to brazenly disregard the Security Council's demands. The failure to sway Gaddafi to change course prompted many governments to reach the view that consensual, non-coercive, measures would be insufficient to change the course of events on the ground. In particular, such measures would not be enough to avert a massacre in the event that Benghazi fell to Gaddafi's forces.

Meanwhile, the NTC's declaration that it was the only legitimate authority in Libya was slowly gaining international support. It then called on the international community to carry out its duty to protect the Libyan people from any further atrocities, albeit without committing to a military intervention on Libyan soil. The Gulf Cooperation Council (GCC) added support to this call by releasing its own statement, calling for the international community to enforce a no-fly zone over Libya. On 8 March, the Organisation of Islamic Conference (OIC) also called for a no-fly zone, stressing that this did not include putting troops on the ground.

The turning point came on 12 March, when the LAS issued a resolution urging the UN Security Council to authorize the imposition of a no-fly zone over Libya and establish safe zones in places that were affected by government shelling, so as to ensure the protection of populations living in places under siege. The LAS declared that the Libyan government had lost its legitimacy urged the Council to communicate officially with the NTC.[2]

Other states, however, were more reticent about escalating the situation. The AU's leadership rejected any kind of foreign military intervention and voiced its support for continued negotiation. NATO was also initially divided – the UK and France were in favour of a strong international response, while Germany and the USA were more reluctant about committing to action. Obama himself was initially opposed to committing to any coercive action in Libya. Elected on a promise to withdraw US forces from the Middle East, the president had little interest in opening up yet another US intervention in the region. Yet he was persuaded by a combination of the force of the humanitarian argument and the level of regional support for decisive action.

The catalyst for a debate on the use of force was a French–Lebanese proposal for a resolution imposing a no-fly zone over Libya, itself instigated at the urging of the LAS. At a White House meeting of senior officials on 15 March, many, including Defense Secretary Robert Gates, were against the idea of committing to a military intervention. The president too was cautious. Obama was eventually swayed by Special Assistant and National Security Council Director of Multilateral Affairs Samantha Power, and Secretary of State Hillary Clinton, among others.[3] Crucially, his decision was also influenced by the prospect of such action being the product of a 'unified European-Arab front'.[4] He accepted the need for military action, but worried that a no-fly zone would prove insufficient and could lock the USA into a long-term operation over Libya. His advisers agreed. The USA would need to seek support for a broader mandate authorizing 'all necessary means' to protect civilians, not just a no-fly zone. It was this, much broader, mandate that the USA sought from the Security Council.

It was in this climate of increasing concern about the fate of Benghazi, growing regional and international condemnation of the Libyan regime, and widespread calls for international society to strengthen its response that the Security Council members discussed the possibility of establishing a no-fly zone over Libya.[5] One of the recurring arguments aired behind the scenes was that the Council had already accepted (in Resolution 1970) that the ongoing conflict in Libya represented a threat to international peace and security, and that without decisive action the situation would only get worse, compounding the already growing humanitarian crisis. Gaddafi's reference to protestors as 'cockroaches' and 'rats', and his threat to track them down, 'house by house, alley by alley', heightened the immediacy of the crisis, convincing many that widespread massacres were imminent.[6] Rarely had a political leader issued such a direct threat to commit a massacre. Especially chilling was the fact that some of his rhetoric directly echoed language used by perpetrators of the Rwandan genocide in 1994.

Yet a number of issues were raised by Council members reluctant to cross the sovereignty Rubicon. China questioned the need to resort to the use of force amid concerns that a military response might make a bad situation worse. Brazil raised similar concerns, drawing attention to the possible implications an external intervention would have on a conflict that was domestic in nature. A number of procedural questions were raised, particularly by China, India, and Russia, regarding how a no-fly zone would be policed, who would finance it, and what the end result would be. These concerns led to two competing drafts circulating among members of the Security Council – one drafted by Russia, which proposed more political dialogue; and one by France and Lebanon, now joined as a sponsor by the UK and backed by the USA, proposing the wider mandate sought by Obama – a no-fly zone – but also a broader mandate to protect civilians, among other measures. Because of the mounting evidence coming from both within and beyond the UN Secretariat that atrocities seemed imminent, and a strong diplomatic push from the USA, it was the latter draft that gained the most support.[7]

Resolution 1973 was put to a vote on 17 March, passing with ten positive votes and five abstentions.[8] The resolution followed on from 1970, echoing the concerns about possible crimes against humanity and the growing humanitarian crisis. It made note of calls coming from a number of regional and international organizations to authorize a no-fly zone over Libya, including the statement issued by the LAS. This included a prohibition of all flights over Libyan air space apart from those for the purposes of humanitarian provision. Referring to the situation in Libya as a threat to international peace and security, it reflected the Obama administration's preference for a broad protection that mandated and authorized the use of 'all necessary measures' to protect civilians who were being targeted by the regime and enforce the arms embargo imposed on the country.

Explaining Resolution 1973

There were two main forces that led to the passing of Resolution 1973: international society's growing commitment to civilian protection, particularly over the last decade, encapsulated by the emergence of the international human protection regime; and the unique circumstances that were unfolding in and around Libya in early 2011.

Since the late 1990s, human protection has become a growing priority within the Security Council, through the inclusion of a 'protection of civilians' provision in mandates for peacekeeping operations. This started with Sierra Leone in 1997. It gained momentum in the mid-2000s, around the time that the World Summit endorsed R2P. The protection of civilians is now part of the mandate for nearly every peacekeeping operation. By 2011, the norm of human protection had become one of the key priorities for the Security Council. Indeed, since 2007, virtually all crises that involved issues around the protection of civilians made it onto the agenda of the Security Council.[9] The protection of civilians is typically included in the mandates of all new peacekeeping missions, albeit with the consent and cooperation of the host state. This can create dilemmas in how to carry out this aspect of a mandate, particularly if peacekeepers have to deal with state actors who themselves are behind the targeting of civilians. These issues notwithstanding, by 2011, while the protection of civilians had become an established priority within the Security Council, the Council had not to that point ever authorized action in the absence of consent from a host government. For this reason, the norm of human protection does not, on its own, explain Resolution 1973.

Why were Security Council members prepared to authorize this unprecedented step in 2011? The unique circumstances in Libya provide further clarity here. Five factors in particular stand out. The first is that there was credible early warning that atrocity crimes were not only likely, but imminent in a context where states accepted, and recognized the relevance of, the central norms and principles of the international human protection regime. Gaddafi's brutal treatment of dissidents went far beyond the 2011 uprising – his forty-one years of rule were characterized by the violent treatment of anyone perceived to threaten his power. As a Human Rights Watch statement pointed out, 'since he assumed power in 1969, Gaddafi has repeatedly used arbitrary arrests, torture, enforced disappearances and political killings to maintain control'.[10] In February and March 2011, there were reports that Gaddafi's forces were using similar tactics, such as ordering his military to open fire on crowds of protesters.[11] By March, around 100,000 Libyan civilians had sought refuge in neighbouring Egypt, with numbers expected to increase substantially in the event of Benghazi falling.[12] But what cemented the likelihood of atrocities clearly and starkly in the minds of international diplomats was Gaddafi's own rhetoric. As we noted earlier, speaking of his intentions in Benghazi, he threatened to 'track them down, search for them alley by alley, road by road',[13] encouraging those who supported him to target the 'cockroaches'.[14] Such language evoked memories of Rwanda in 1994, and added to the sense of urgency to do something to avert a catastrophe. Some scholars have been critical of the response that followed Resolution 1973, pointing out that the threats were issued specifically at rebels, not the general populace.[15] But this interpretation relies on a deeply flawed assumption about the willingness and intention of the regime to distinguish armed rebel fighters from their civilian supporters and mere bystanders in rebel controlled areas. In fact, a cursory glance at the Gaddafi regime's history of using violence against opponents, their supporters, and tribes belies this claim. Such a selective approach to violence would have involved Gaddafi's armed forces acting in a way they had never done before. An assumption like this is hardly a sure basis on which to decide whether or not to leave a large civilian population to its fate. Short of waiting for the death count to increase, the evidence that a massacre was about to unfold in Benghazi could not have been clearer.

Indeed, so clear was the threat that in the Security Council itself no state – not even Russia or China – disputed the view that a massacre was likely if Benghazi fell. It was this concern for the fate of the civilian population in Libya that helped persuade Moscow and Beijing – either one of which could have blocked the resolution – to abstain and allow its passage rather than veto. We know this because this is precisely how Russia itself explained its decision not to veto the draft resolution. Its Permanent Representative told the Security Council,

> I underscore yet again that we are consistent and firm advocates of the protection of the civilian population. Guided by this basic principle as well as by the common humanitarian values that we share with both the sponsors and other Council members, Russia did not prevent the adoption of this resolution.[16]

In its own words, Russia chose not to veto Resolution 1973, despite its reservations, because of its 'firm commitment' to principles of human protection. China, meanwhile, explained that it allowed passage of the resolution because it enjoyed the support of the LAS and the AU, and because of the 'special circumstances surrounding the situation in Libya' – in other words, the gravity of the threat to the civilian population.[17] To understand why states adopt certain positions, it is important to pay attention to what they themselves actually say. In this case it was striking that both Russia and China recognized their doubts about the proposed measures but judged that the threat to the civilian population in Libya was so great that in light of their commitment to human protection they would not allow their doubts to block collective action.

A second reason was the lack of other effective alternatives to remedy the obvious threat. An extensive range of non-violent measures – as laid out in Resolution 1970 – were tried, with none proving able to hold sway with the Gaddafi regime. Such measures included sanctions, travel bans, and extensive diplomacy from the UN, a number of regional organizations, and from individual countries. Nothing was successful in securing even a brief cease-fire. This is not to say that the use of violence was something that Council members were comfortable with – indeed, the choices were very stark indeed. The options were to wait for Libya to hold back on force (despite the signs suggesting its intent was the opposite) or to consider the use of force to stop the Libyan regime from committing more violence. But with the information at hand, and the lack of other options, authorizing force was becoming the only remaining choice at hand for the Council to carry out its protection responsibilities.

Even the ambivalence about the use of force expressed by Security Council members who abstained reflects the position that other options simply were not working, or could not be relied upon. Brazil, Russia, and China all expressed serious reservations about the more coercive aspects of the draft resolution. Brazil expressed doubts that the enforcement of a no-fly zone would achieve the objective of ending violence and protecting civilians.[18] Russia argued that the best way forward was to push for a ceasefire in the hope of leading to a longer term stabilization.[19] China stressed that while it thought the Security Council should engage in certain actions to help stabilize the situation in Libya, and to put an end to violence against civilians, it reiterated its opposition to 'the use of force in international relations'.[20] Yet despite these reservations, no member of the Council (and crucially no permanent member) chose to vote against the resolution. Instead, they opted to express these doubts through abstentions. The clear and growing threat of atrocities in Benghazi, combined with no credible alternative courses of action, made it almost impossible for states to vote against Resolution 1973, especially given their expressed commitments to the protection of populations.

A third reason behind the decision to intervene in Libya was the short window of time available to design a practical and timely response. Prior to the eruption of violence itself, Libya did not appear on any conflict watch list, for the simple reason that armed conflict in the country was not predicted or anticipated. Crisis Watch, for example, did not identify Libya at risk of conflict in its February 2011 report, even after the Arab Spring had started there. The Gaddafi regime had been in power for forty-one years, in which time there had been no effective challenge to its rule – it had maintained a strong hold on power, frequently abusing human rights along the way, but without apparently displaying signs of weakening. That no one had predicted the growing instability and escalating violence in Libya is not surprising. The Political Instability Task Force has found that the most stable regimes are indeed autocracies, not unlike Libya under Gaddafi. Such regimes can and indeed do continue for decades. However, when their power is threatened, the destabilization that can ensue is particularly brutal. The brutal response to Arab Spring protests triggered an opposition movement that included former elements of Gaddafi's own regime, and mobilized a rebel group that retaliated against government-backed forces, triggering a rapid escalation of fighting. The rebels made fast gains, then lost them again, leaving their stronghold of Benghazi vulnerable to Gaddafi's forces. The rapidity of these developments, as well as Gaddafi's inflammatory comments about his intentions following an anticipated victory for his forces in Benghazi, contributed to tightening the time frame within which international actors had to work in order to facilitate a reprieve of violence. Resolution 1970 represented a timely response to the early stages of this destabilization – it cobbled together a variety of non-violent yet assertive measures to address these unfolding circumstances. Diplomacy, sanctions, and punitive measures were all adopted in an attempt to bring conflict parties to mediation. Had events escalated more slowly, the Security Council would have had more time to gradually bring in increasingly coercive measures. Yet by March 17 – the date that members voted on Resolution 1973 (only three weeks after 1970) – Gaddafi's forces appeared to be on the verge of retaking Benghazi, and hence carrying out a massacre. This short time frame meant that there was only limited time to try out non-violent measures.

Fourth, the role of regional organizations in advocating for a no-fly zone was decisive. The Gaddafi regime had long been unpopular among Arab and other Islamic states in the region. The LAS, the Organization of Islamic Countries, and the Gulf Cooperation Council all called publicly for a no-fly zone, a move that likely swayed both Russia and China from exercising the veto over Resolution 1973. This added to the growing international support for those protesting in the Arab Spring across North Africa. By contrast, the AU refrained from the same call, advocating more mediation, and expressing concern about the consequences of such action precipitating regime change.[21] The AU's own constitution censures governments who come to power through unconstitutional regime change, and those that do are excluded from working as part of the Union. If China and Russia had given greater priority to the stance taken by the AU, they might have chosen to veto Resolution 1973. However, as events unfolded, the advocacy of the LAS, the OIC, and the GCC had a strong impact on the decision-making of Council members.

A fifth reason was Libya's lack of friends, both in the region and beyond. This meant that no country was prepared to block the Security Council's authorization of a no-fly zone. Even though the AU formally opposed the no-fly zone, many individual countries within the continent had no regrets about Gaddafi's rule coming to an end. Indeed, Gaddafi himself had a long history of getting involved in the domestic affairs of other countries, having backed armed groups in places such as Sierra Leone, Liberia, Sudan, and Mali. Sudan actively supported the rebels in Libya, sending armed assistance to repel Gaddafi's forces in the town of Kufra.[22] Among Arab states, Gaddafi had gone out of his way to foment tension and sever friendships. One illustration of this was Gaddafi's outburst at an Arab League Summit in Qatar in 2009, where, after publicly humiliating Saudi Arabia's King Abdullah, he went on to declare himself 'the dean of the Arab leaders, the king of kings of Africa and the leader of the faithful'.[23] This, among many other public insults, ensured that Gaddafi was alienated from other states in the Middle East. Further afield, Gaddafi had not fostered ties with either China or Russia. While Syria's ties with Russia has to some extent protected the Assad regime from a more robust Security Council response to atrocities there, Libya had no such connection to fall back on. Indeed, the Kremlin had long been wary of Gaddafi due to his support for terrorist organizations, including some with links to those in Chechnya and Dagestan.

The decision of the Security Council to authorize the use of force against a sovereign state was the product of two simultaneous sets of factors – a growing commitment to the protection of civilians and the unique circumstances in Libya, which suggested that rapidly escalating violence was headed towards atrocities. Non-violent measures to halt this escalation were attempted, but to no avail, leaving states with the view that they had little alternative but to consider a military intervention. The fact that Libya had isolated itself from other countries in the region, as well as from the broader international community, left it with no one in the Security Council to advocate on its behalf.

Why Resolution 1973 is significant

There are a number of reasons why Resolution 1973 is significant. In this section, we explain three of the most important.

First, and most notably for the purposes of this book, Resolution 1973 represents the first time that the Security Council has authorized the use of force for human protection purposes without the consent of the *de jure* sovereign state concerned. There have been times when the Council has come close to this point in the past, but never before had it gone this far. In Resolution 794 (December 1992) adopted in response to the crisis in Somalia, the Security Council authorized the Unified Task Force (UNITAF) to 'use all necessary means' to enable the provision of humanitarian aid.[24] But in that case, the Security Council judged that the Somali state had collapsed, that is, sovereignty did not apply in this case because the country had no *de jure* sovereign government. Thus, the Council formally recognized the 'unique character of the present situation in Somalia' – a nod to the fact that there was no Somali government. The resolution also noted that in the absence of a government, 'Somalis' had themselves called for international action. The Council was not, therefore, prioritizing human rights over sovereign rights in this case, since there was no rights-bearing sovereign to speak of. Towards the end of the Rwandan genocide in 1994, the Council issued Resolution 929, which authorized the establishment of a multinational force to help secure areas 'for humanitarian purposes'. This enabled the deployment of the French Operation *Turquoise*, a mission opposed by the rebel Rwandan Patriotic Front, whose forces were on the brink of defeating the government and ending the genocide.[25] Yet this case too does not qualify as an intervention without the state's consent, since the Rwandan transitional government – recognized at the time the resolution was passed as the government of Rwanda and hence the bearer of its sovereignty – consented to the intervention. In the same year, the Council authorized the use of 'all necessary means' to 'facilitate' the removal of the military regime in Haiti. However, Resolution 940 (1994) was passed with the full consent of the elected government that had been deposed from power, and indeed authorized with the explicit purpose 'to assist the legitimate Government of Haiti in the maintenance of public order'.[26] The Council continued to recognize this as the legitimate government of Haiti, and appended to Resolution 940 was a letter by President Aristide requesting external intervention.

There are other more recent resolutions where the Security Council has authorized the use of all necessary means in order to protect civilians, but all were carried out with the consent of the recognized governments in those countries. Such examples include the authorization of an intervention brigade in eastern Democratic Republic of Congo (DRC), which was mandated to work with the government of the DRC to identify threats to civilians, as well as to devise strategies to ensure their protection.[27] Even in Côte d'Ivoire, where Resolution 1975 (2011) authorized the use of 'all necessary means' to protect civilians, this was issued on the understanding that it was supported by the person that the Council recognized as the head of state. In that case, violence had erupted out of a disputed election between Alassane Ouattara and incumbent president Laurent Gbagbo. International observers reported that Ouattara had prevailed, but Gbagbo disputed this and refused to stand down and vacate the office of the presidency. The Council declared that it believed Ouattara to be the legitimate president and it was his consent that was relied upon for Resolution 1975. Thus, while the Security Council is certainly becoming increasingly proactive in its commitment to human protection, to date, Resolution 1973 remains the first and only time that it has authorized the use of force for protection purposes without the consent of a recognized government.

Another reason for why Resolution 1973 was so significant is in its illustration of the Council's willingness to try a range of strategies that did not initially involve the use of force. The authorization of the use of force did not occur in the absence of attempts to de-escalate the violence in Libya through the use of non-violent measures. Indeed, Resolution 1970, passed three weeks earlier, had recommended a number of steps that fell short of the use of force. These included punitive measures – including the referral of Libya to the Prosecutor of the International Criminal Court; an arms embargo; a travel ban on sixteen key members of the Libyan regime; and an asset freeze on property and possessions held by Gaddafi's family. In addition, the Secretary-General, as well as the Special Envoy for Libya, engaged in intense diplomacy in an attempt to persuade Gaddafi to restrain from committing violence against civilians. In this way, Resolution 1973 can be understood as part of a spectrum of measures – it reflects the idea that in terms of R2P, military intervention must only be considered in the event that other preventive measures do not work. Thus, the use of force, in this case was not the first option to be considered, but the last.[28]

Third, the resolution represents a clear test of the principle of the R2P, particularly in terms of how far the Security Council would go in its commitment to the principle. Indeed, the decisions that key member states made to bring about Resolution 1973 provide evidence that the principle is having an impact on the way states behave. As Luke Glanville points out, the decision of five abstaining countries – including Russia and China – not to block the resolution, and the Obama administration's decision to push for a stronger draft despite Libya holding no strategic interest for the USA, reflects the growing influence that the principle of R2P has. Indeed, all the abstaining countries raised concerns about the process, but not the need to protect civilians in Libya, and in doing so voted not to block military action. In the case of the USA, initial advice from Obama's defence advisers recommended that the country not involve itself in a situation that did not imperil the country's key security interests.[29] When Obama was eventually persuaded to push for a more proactive solution in Libya, justified his position by stressing that not intervening was acceptable because 'that's not who we are'.[30] As we pointed out earlier, he then went on to push for a resolution that authorized 'all necessary means' to protect civilians there.[31] The decisions by member states not to oppose military action and the decision by the Obama administration to push for more effective measures in terms of civilian protection – in the absence of national interest – reflect the extent to which the international community is prepared to go to implement strategies that provide protection for vulnerable populations.

Libya since Resolution 1973

That the authorization and implementation of Resolution 1973 were controversial should not come as a surprise. As Ramesh Thakur stresses, 'The use of force – no matter how benevolent, enlightened, or impartial in intent – has dramatic consequences.'[32] In the case of Libya, controversy arose almost immediately, and continues to this day. There has been dispute over just what 'any necessary means' actually entailed, and what its limits were. There have been accusations that NATO and its partners engaged in profound overreach. In particular, there was criticism about the fact that the NATO-led strikes led to regime change in Libya, when in fact they were mandated only to protect civilians from imminent harm – a question we will return to in more detail in Chapter 5.[33]

These critiques have been sharpened by the fact that the situation in Libya has deteriorated in the years following the intervention.[34] Though total war and butchery on the scale of Syria were avoided, seven years on from the intervention there remained no effective government, the provision of public services had not been re-established, and the violation of basic human rights remained widespread. This has provoked debate over whether Resolution 1973 and its implementation did more harm than good. More broadly, some commentators have argued that Libya's post-war problems mark a failure of human protection – one compounded by the simultaneous *lack* of decisive action over Syria. Yet despite this controversy, the evidence suggests – as we will demonstrate in the remainder of this chapter – that international society has remained committed to human protection. The key lesson from Libya is not that international society should step back from human protection but that armed intervention for humanitarian purposes must always be accompanied with broader, non-military, efforts to build sustainable human protection in the longer term.

South Africa was critical of the intervention almost from the start. South African president Jacob Zuma almost immediately went on the offensive. At a Security Council meeting on 10 May, during the NATO offensive, the South African delegate stressed that international actors should always respect the sovereignty of the country under concern, and that the mandate of civilian protection should not be stretched to incorporate other agendas, such as regime change.[35] This is despite South Africa's voting in favour of 1973, a move which came *after* advice provided to Zuma by his foreign ministry that the words 'all necessary measures' could be broadly construed, and could be used to justify regime change.[36] But as the strikes on Libya continued, Zuma's criticisms became more strident. In June, he declared in parliament that NATO was 'abusing' the resolution to bring about regime change and 'political assassinations'.[37] Other states, such as Nicaragua and Venezuela, levelled similar criticisms, accusing the Security Council of manipulating the principle of the protection of civilians for the interests of a neo-imperialist regime change, accusing some members of violating the UN Charter in the process.[38]

Other 'BRICS' countries were also critical. China was adamantly against the idea of regime change, and insisted that it should not be conflated with the protection of civilians.[39] Russia levelled similar criticism, condemning the NATO offensive three days after the resolution had passed, with Putin comparing it to a 'medieval call to a crusade', although Prime Minister Medvedev later contradicted the president, calling his words 'unacceptable'.[40] Within the Security Council itself, Russia's criticism was more circumspect, pointing out in broad terms that the goal of civilian protection should not be resolved alongside other 'unrelated issues'.[41] Brazil's opposition to the offensive grew following its decision to abstain from the vote. It also stressed that the protection of civilians was a distinct imperative from international threats to peace and security, suggesting that confusing the two would create the impression that one was being used as a 'smokescreen' for violations of sovereignty.[42]

Yet amid these criticisms, most states framed their concerns with clear support for the protection of civilians, and with the reassurance that they were all in favour of action being taken for this purpose.[43] While disagreements certainly arose, particularly in terms of the extent of the NATO-led military action, no states challenged the original authorization to use force, as set out in Resolution 1973. Criticisms of the use of force centred mostly on the way that force was carried out. In other words, the criticism targeted issues of process and interpretation.

One of the strongest critics – Brazil – raised a number of procedural issues, which addressed the problem of what they alleged was an abuse of the Security Council's practices in relation to humanitarian intervention. They proposed a measure that they claimed would create checks and balances on these practices, through an initiative called 'responsibility while protecting' (RWP). The Brazilian president, Dilma Rousseff, first proposed it at the General Assembly plenary in 2011, and it was further developed in early 2012 through an informal dialogue co-hosted by the Brazilian Mission to the UN. The initiative was warmly received and incorporated in the Secretary-General's R2P report for 2012.[44] Included in RWP was a proposal for establishing criteria when considering the use of force; a call for judicious analysis to inform decisions about the use of force; and the creation of an accountability mechanism to provide oversight on Council-mandated work. Yet ambiguities around the application of RWP remain. It is not clear what kind of criteria Brazil had in mind, beyond general principles such as last resort, proportionality, and right authority. Judicious analysis of situations could lead to delays in decision-making that make a timely response to cases involving impending or unfolding atrocity crimes impossible. And finally, the proposal of accountability mechanisms would require sweeping changes to Security Council procedures that go the heart of the way the Security Council is designed to operate, according to the authority accorded to it by the UN Charter. Such accountability could also deter states from assisting in enforcing Security Council mandates, which could potentially weaken the institution. These are important issues, which we return to in Chapter 6.

In the seven years that have passed since the implementation of Resolution 1973, there have been two key allegations about the intervention. First, some British and US intelligence officers have raised questions about the robustness of the intelligence upon which the decision to intervene was based. According to some US intelligence officers, the decision to use force was based 'more on speculative arguments of what might happen to civilians than on facts reported on the ground'.[45] Likewise, a UK parliamentary report into the 2011 intervention raised doubts about whether it had sufficiently reliable evidence about what precisely was unfolding in Libya. The report concluded that there was limited evidence to assert that Gaddafi was planning to massacre civilians in Benghazi.[46] However, the decision to intervene was made on the basis of the intelligence available to states at the time and there is no suggestion of dissembling or of manipulation of the available intelligence. That civilians in Benghazi were under imminent threat and in need of protection was not only the view of the UK, France, and the USA, it was also the opinion of other members of the Security Council, including Russia and China. Thus, the decision to authorize force (and to abstain from the veto) was based on widespread agreement among the Security Council membership that a timely response was needed to prevent a massacre. Moreover, this was also the conclusion that the LAS came to at the time.

Second, some commentators and scholars argued that the NATO-led action in Libya did more harm than good. Following the ousting of Gaddafi, an uneasy coalition took control, but never managed to govern. The social and political situation in Libya today is highly unstable. Many blame the intervention for the current fate of the country. In terms of human protection, some scholars have argued that, contrary to strengthening the international community's commitment to protecting populations vulnerable to atrocity crimes, the NATO-led operation contributed to the principle's weakening, through an erosion of consensus.[47]

The crucial moments came in the immediate aftermath of intervention when NATO and the UN decided not to insist upon the deployment of a multidimensional peace operation to restore order and build peace in Libya. During the conflict itself, the UN Secretariat had established a cell led by experienced peacebuilder Ian Martin to plan for the peace. Martin advised the deployment of a modestly sized UN peacekeeping mission to support a wider international peacebuilding effort that would help rebuild the country's shattered institutions, help establish the rule of law, maintain stability, and mediate and oversee a long-term political solution. Unfortunately, Martin's plans were leaked to the press before they could be presented formally to the UN Security Council and Libya's warring parties. Libya's National Transitional Council (NTC) flatly rejected the proposition of UN peacekeepers deploying to Libya and the idea won little support elsewhere in international society. States critical of the NATO-led intervention saw the proposed deployment as a further infringement on Libya's sovereignty and extension of Western authority. The USA, the UK, and France, meanwhile, overstretched by other commitments and by financial austerity, were only too happy to step back and not assume responsibility for establishing the peace – a move that the Obama administration at least later came to regret. It is easy to look back with hindsight and point to international society's failure to support peacebuilding in Libya as a critical moment, but blame for the failure must be spread widely. Outside the UN secretariat, few states – including NATO members and those most critical of the intervention – were prepared to support, staff, or resource a major peace operation in Libya and the Libyan authorities themselves opposed such a move. This should remind us of the critical importance of not treating armed intervention in isolation of the wider range of measures necessary to support human protection and prevent the recurrence of violence.

As international society retreated, Libya's political turmoil continued well beyond the overthrow of the Gaddafi regime in August 2011. By early 2012, violence between the various militia had escalated beyond control, with competing rivalries between tribal and territorial groups spurring ongoing violence, which by mid-2016 had resulted in the displacement of 400,000 people and the deaths of at least 5,000.[48] While national elections held in July that year were largely peaceful, the government soon fragmented, and amid an escalation of inter-militia violence that returned the country to the brink of civil war in 2014 and 2015, two rival parliaments emerged at different ends of the country.[49] The power vacuum and unfolding violence allowed Islamist militia groups like Islamic State to take control of some territory, particularly in the east of the country, close to many of the country's oil and gas installations. This growing instability and violence has had a profound effect on Libya's economy and its ability to maintain public services like electricity and clean water. While oil production returned to 85 per cent of pre-2011 levels following the overthrow of Gaddafi, by early 2014 oil production had almost ground to a halt, Current levels are roughly a quarter of production levels in early 2011. This has had a profound impact on national infrastructure and service provision. Fighting between militias, for example, has led to the hindering of electricity supply to major cities including Tripoli and Benghazi, with regular power outages lasting as long as ten hours a stretch.

Attempts by the UN to broker a political settlement received a boost in 2015, with two of the major rival factions signing an agreement on 17 December, which led to the establishment of a government of national accord (GNA).[50] However, the GNA experienced setbacks when key rival parliamentary group, House of Representatives (based in Tobruk) refused to consent to the cabinet line-up. Libya thus remains divided, with two governments continuing to operate at different ends of the country. Nevertheless, there has been recent cooperation in weakening Islamic State's hold on Sirte in May 2016, a move which came about when several rival militias coordinated their efforts. However, the security situation in Libya remains highly unstable.

These difficult circumstances have provoked some commentators to label the NATO-led intervention in Libya a failure, with some claiming that it marks a nail in the coffin of R2P. Alan Kuperman, for example, argues that the intervention turned Libya into a failed state, facilitating an environment that has spawned more human rights violations than had occurred under Gaddafi. Kuperman points out that since the interventions both Libya and nearby Mali have become 'havens' for terrorists, profiting from the proliferation of weapons in the region, both from Gaddafi's fallen regime and from countries that have provided material support to certain Islamist groups.[51] David

Chandler claims that the Libya intervention marks the death of R2P in terms of providing legitimacy for the use of force, as it was characterized by 'preventive military action' initiated 'without the promise of the assumption of "Western" responsibility for the outcomes'.[52] For Chandler, preventive military action, without the responsibility to rebuild, or 'reconstruct', marks a new kind of intervention, distinct from the commitments that Western states assumed in Kosovo and Bosnia in the 1990s. Other commentators claim that overreach in Libya has limited the future invocation of R2P to justify future military interventions.[53]

While there is no question that the current situation in Libya is highly unstable and far more precarious than it was prior to the Arab Spring, the case that the NATO-led intervention caused more harm than good is less than compelling. It relies, largely, on an image of Libya prior to the onset of the Arab Spring civil war in early 2011. The point of reference for such a claim should not, however, be Libya pre-Arab Spring. Things had already taken a turn for the worse when a civil war erupted during the early months of 2011. There was no turning back from this, nor was there any doubt about the unambiguous threats that Gaddafi had levelled against the city of Benghazi, which raised alarm throughout North Africa and the Middle East. Given that civil war had already begun, with the imminent threat of widespread atrocities by March 2011, it is difficult to envisage a scenario in which, without intervention, Libya might have suddenly turned to greater peacefulness and no such scenario is identified. Some critics talk of the need for more negotiations, but without explaining how or why, absent of military intervention, Gaddafi – who had rejected all such entreaties – would suddenly change course. Instead, without intervention, the country's civil war would likely have persisted to this day. Although the conflict might not have reached the depths of horror witnessed in Syria, there is every possibility that left unabated it may well have done: a massacre in Benghazi forcing the rebels to dig in, pushing their further radicalization, and drawing in neighbouring states. Even without Syria as a possible template, everything we know about protracted civil wars and mass atrocities tells us that many more than 5,000 civilians would have been killed between then and now had there been no intervention. Thus, as imperfect as the NATO-led intervention was, and in particular its post-intervention engagement, there is every reason to think that Libya is better off because of it than it otherwise would have been, and very little reason to think that the country's civilians would have been better served by non-intervention. Syria shows the costs of that path only too well.

The controversies over Libya have not dimmed international consensus on human protection, even if it has sharpened some of the debates. Even a cursory study of Security Council resolutions since 2011 provides clear evidence that commitment to human protection, including R2P, has strengthened considerably – what was a highly contentious principle prior to 2011 has now become commonplace. Since the Libyan crisis, R2P has been invoked by the Security Council more frequently, and with greater ease.

In terms of frequency, Resolutions 1970 and 1973 mark a distinct turning point in the Security Council's willingness to invoke R2P in a variety of resolutions, both thematic and case-specific. The numbers themselves tell a compelling story. In the period following the 2005 World Summit – where member states endorsed R2P – and prior to 2011, R2P was invoked in four resolutions. Between 2011 and June 2017, R2P was invoked fifty-eight times.[54] This very distinct increase in frequency started with the two resolutions on Libya – 1970 and 1973. Apart from Libya, R2P was referred to in resolution on country-specific issues related to Côte d'Ivoire, South Sudan, Central African Republic, Syria, Mali, Yemen, and Somalia, and on thematic issues in such areas as peacekeeping, conflict prevention, genocide, and small arms and light weapons.[55] This broad trend suggests that the international community is more committed to R2P *after* Resolution 1973 and the ensuing controversies surrounding its implementation. Contrary to claims that international consent was lost, the evidence suggests the exact opposite.

It is not just the increase in frequency of the invocation of R2P that is telling here. As Jess Gifkins points out, the use of R2P within resolutions is now occurring with far greater ease than prior to 2011. For instance, two of the resolutions in 2006 – 1674 and 1706 – each required six months of negotiations between members of the Security Council. One of the most controversial elements of both of these resolutions was R2P.[56] After 2011, it is a very different story. Often resolutions have been negotiated in less than two weeks, both for specific country cases and for broader thematic issues. Moreover, the vast majority of these resolutions passed unanimously.[57] The greater frequency and ease of drafting resolutions that invoke R2P indicate that in normative terms, the international community is taking human protection far more seriously, and with greater consensus.[58]

This is not to say that there is an absence of contention over how to protect populations from atrocity crimes. As Glanville points out, there is a great deal of 'indeterminacy' about how R2P should be carried out in specific cases. This stems from the fact that R2P is a 'positive' norm, that is, it is a norm that requires actors to *do* something rather than simply refrain from doing something.[59] How such action should be carried out will vary according to context, political will, and what actors have the capacity, opportunity, and legitimacy to implement action. In this sense, contention over the interpretation and implementation of Resolution 1973 is not an indication of a weakening of R2P, but a reflection of the norm gaining strength. Indeed, in the Security Council debates prior to and following 17 March, none of the concerns raised about the use of force challenged basic propositions about responsibility to protect civilians in Libya.

Conclusion

For the first time in its history, in 2011 the UN Security Council authorized the use of force to protect people from their own government – Libya. Before then, the Council had limited its support for armed humanitarian intervention to situations where the host government *requested or consented* to intervention (as in Haiti, Rwanda, East Timor, and Bosnia) or where the state itself had collapsed, making the whole issue moot (as in Somalia). Before 2011, where national authorities remained opposed to intervention, as in the case of Kosovo and northern Iraq in 1991, the Security Council had stopped short of authorizing it. Although the decision to intervene in Libya was the result of a range of circumstances not likely to be repeated often, this was a crucially important development because it signalled that the Security Council would not be inhibited, *as a matter of principle*, from intervening in the domestic affairs of states to protect their populations from atrocity crimes. That is not to say that such interventions will become common – they will not, for reasons we expound in the chapters to come – but it does mean that debates about whether or not to intervene will be based on prudential calculations rather than on principle. By authorizing intervention in Libya, the Security Council has established the precedent that collective action by international society to protect populations, even from their own government, can be lawful and legitimate.

Although the intervention succeeded in preventing a widely anticipated massacre in Benghazi, in limiting Gaddafi's capacity to commit
atrocities, and in significantly shortening Libya's civil war – and thus
reducing the loss of life from that which could have been expected –
what happened afterwards serves as an important reminder that military intervention cannot be treated in isolation of the other elements
of human protection. Instead, armed intervention must be understood
as only one – relatively rare – element of human protection, one
which must be supported by other, non-violent, elements. Ultimately,
the purpose of armed intervention is to end immediate killing and
create the conditions in which civilian, political, and humanitarian
capacities can be brought to the fore to support states and societies in
establishing their own buttresses against atrocity crimes.

Notes

1. United Nations Press Release, 'UN Secretary-General Special Adviser
    on the Prevention of Genocide, Francis Deng, and Special Adviser on
    the Responsibility to Protect, Edward Luck, on the Situation in Libya',
    22 February 2011, Available at: http://www.un.org/en/preventgeno-
    cide/adviser/pdf/OSAPG,%20Special%20Advisers%20Statement%20
    on%20Libya,%2022%20February%202011.pdf; UN News Centre,
    'UN Rights Council Recommends Suspending Libya, Orders Inquiry
    into Abuses', 25 February 2011, Available at: http://www.un.org/apps/
    news/story.asp?NewsID=37626#.V5H9jzcX5Y8
2. Council of the League of Arab States, Res. No.7360, 12 March 2011,
    paras. 1 and 2.
3. Josh Rogin, 'How Obama turned on a dime toward war', 18 March
    2011, Available at: http://thecable.foreignpolicy.com/posts/2011/03/18/
    how_obama_turned_on_a_dime_toward_war
4. Jo Becker and Scott Shane, 'Hillary Clinton, "Smart Power" and a
    Dictator's Fall', 27 February 2016, Available at: http://www.nytimes.
    com/2016/02/28/us/politics/hillary-clinton-libya.html?_r=0
5. See S/PV.6498, 17 March 2011.
6. Becker and Shane, 'Hillary Clinton'.
7. For a critical insider's account of the pre-vote diplomacy see Hardeep
    Singh Puri, *Perilous Interventions: The Security Council and the Poli-
    tics of Chaos* (New York: Harper Collins, 2016).
8. Those who voted in favour: Bosnia and Herzegovina, Colombia,
    France, Gabon, Lebanon, Portugal, Nigeria, South Africa, the UK, and

the USA. Those who abstained: Brazil, China, Germany, India, and Russia. There were no negative votes.

9. The only exception is Sri Lanka.
10. Human Rights Watch, 'Libya: Benghazi Civilians Face Grave Risk', 17 March 2011, Available at: https://www.hrw.org/news/2011/03/17/libya-benghazi-civilians-face-grave-risk
11. Human Rights Watch, 'Libya'.
12. David Boscoe, 'Was There Going to Be a Benghazi Massacre?', *Foreign Policy,* 7 April 2011, Available at: http://foreignpolicy.com/2011/04/07/was-there-going-to-be-a-benghazi-massacre/
13. Michael Tomasky, 'Gaddafi's Speech', *The Guardian,* 17 March 2011, Available at: https://www.theguardian.com/commentisfree/michaeltomasky/2011/mar/17/usforeignpolicy-unitednations-libya-it-will-start-fast
14. BBC News, 'Libya Protests: Defiant Gaddafi Refuses to Quit', 22 February 2011, Available at: http://www.bbc.co.uk/news/world-middle-east-12544624
15. See, for example, Alan J. Kuperman, '5 Things the US Should Consider in Libya', *USA Today,* 22 March 2011, Available at: http://usatoday30.usatoday.com/news/opinion/forum/2011-03-22-column22_ST_N.htm
16. S/PV.6498, 17 March 2011, p. 8.
17. S/PV.6498, p. 10.
18. S/PV.6498, p. 10.
19. S/PV.6498, p. 10.
20. S/PV.6498, p. 10.
21. See de Waal, 'African Roles'.
22. de Waal, 'African Roles', p. 377.
23. Abdul Hamid Ahmad, 'Libyan, Saudi Leaders Walk out of Arab Summit after a Spat', *Gulf News,* 30 March 2009, Available at: http://gulfnews.com/news/gulf/qatar/libyan-saudi-leaders-walk-out-of-arab-summit-after-a-spat-1.60102
24. UN SC Resolution 794 (1992).
25. UN SC Resolution 929 (1994).
26. UN SC Resolution 940 (1994).
27. UN SC Resolution 2098 (2013).
28. See Ruben Reike, 'Libya and the Prevention of Atrocity Crimes', in Serena K. Sharma and Jennifer Welsh (eds), *The Responsibility to Prevent* (Oxford: Oxford University Press, 2015).
29. Luke Glanville, 'Does R2P Matter? Interpreting the Impact of a Norm', *Cooperation and Conflict,* 51, no. 2 (2016), p. 192.
30. Glanville, 'Does R2P Matter?', p. 192.
31. Glanville, 'Does R2P Matter?', pp. 192–193.

32. Ramesh Thakur, 'R2P after Libya and Syria: Engaging Emerging Powers', *The Washington Quarterly,* 36, no. 2, (2013), p. 61.
33. The principal concern of Hardeep Singh Puri, *Perilous Interventions.*
34. See, for example, Rajan Menon, *The Conceit of Humanitarian Intervention* (Oxford: Oxford University Press, 2016), p. 14.
35. S/PV.6531, 10 May 2011.
36. de Waal, 'African Roles', p. 368.
37. Mail and Guardian, 'Zuma Lashes NATO for 'Abusing' UN Resolutions on Libya', 14 June 2011. Available at: http://mg.co.za/ article/2011-06-14-zuma-lashes-nato-for-abusing-un-resolutions-on-libya
38. S/PV.6531, 10 May 2011.
39. S/PV.6531.
40. Andrew Jacobs, 'China Urges Quick End to Airstrikes in Libya', 22 March 2011, Available at: http://www.nytimes.com/2011/03/23/world/asia/23beiijing.html?_r=0
41. S/PV.6531, 10 May 2011.
42. S/PV.6531.
43. This is evident in all the published notes of Security Council meetings on the topic of Libya throughout 2011. See, for example, S/PV.6528, 4 May 2011; S/PV.6531, 10 May 2011; S/PV.6531 (Resumption 1), 10 May 2011; SP/PV.6566, 27 June 2011; SP/PV.6647, 2 November 2011.
44. United Nations, *Responsibility to Protect: Timely and Decisive Response – Report of the Secretary-General,* UN Doc. A/66/844-S/2012/578, July 25, para. 50.
45. Kelly Riddell and Jeffrey Scott Shapiro, 'Hillary Clinton's "WMD" Moment: US Intelligence Saw False Narrative in Libya', *The Washington Times,* 29 January, 2015, Available at: http://www.washingtontimes.com/news/2015/jan/29/hillary-clinton-libya-war-genocide-narrative-rejec/
46. United Kingdom Parliament, *Libya: Examination of Intervention and Collapse and the UK's Future Foreign Policy Options,* 9 September 2016, Available at: https://www.publications.parliament.uk/pa/cm201617/cmselect/cmfaff/119/11905.htm
47. See, for example, Gareth Evans (2012), 'The Responsibility to Protect after Libya and Syria', Available at: http://www.gevans.org/speeches/speech476.html; Ramesh Thakur, 'R2P after Libya and Syria: Engaging Emerging Powers', *The Washington Quarterly,* 36, no. 2 (2013), pp. 61–76: 72; Graham Cronogue, 'Responsibility to Protect: Syria, the Law, Politics and Future of Humanitarian Intervention Post-Libya', *International Humanitarian Legal Studies,* 3, no. 1 (2012), pp. 124–159: 151.

48. Human Rights Watch, 'Libya: Events of 2015', *World Report 2016*, Available at: https://www.hrw.org/world-report/2016/country-chapters/libya#76b621; Chris Stephen, 'Five Years After Gaddafi, Libya Torn by Civil War and Battles with ISIS', *The Guardian,* Tuesday 16 February, Available at: https://www.theguardian.com/world/2016/feb/16/libya-gaddafi-arab-spring-civil-war-islamic-state

49. Scott Shane and Jo Becker, 'A New Libya, with 'Very Little Time Left'', *New York Times,* 27 February 2016, Available at: http://www.nyti.ms/212ZDkW

50. International Crisis Group, 'Testimony by Claudia Gazzini, Senior Analyst, International Crisis Group, for Hearing of the Senate Committee on Foreign Affairs on 'Libya: The Path Forward'', 3 March 2016, Available at: http://www.crisisgroup.org/en/publication-type/speeches/2016/gazzini-us-senate-hearing-3mar16.aspx

51. Alan Kuperman, 'Obama' Libya Debacle: How a Well-Meaning Intervention Ended in Failure', *Foreign Affairs,* March/April 2015.

52. David Chandler, 'The R2P is Dead, Long Live the R2P: The Successful Separation of Military Intervention from the Responsibility to Protect', *International Peacekeeping,* 22, no. 1 (2015), p. 2.

53. See, for example, Justin Morris, 'Libya and Syria: R2P and the Spectre of the Swinging Pendulum', *International Affairs,* 89, no. 5 (2013).

54. The Global Centre for the Responsibility to Protect keeps a running tally, comprehensively documenting references to R2P in Security Council resolutions, see Available at: http://www.globalr2p.org/resources/335.

55. Jess Gifkins, 'R2P in the UN Security Council: Darfur, Libya and Beyond', *Cooperation and Conflict,* 51, no. 2 (2016), pp. 154–155.

56. Gifkins, 'R2P in the UN Security Council', p. 157.

57. Gifkins, 'R2P in the UN Security Council', p. 159.

58. See Alex J. Bellamy, *The Responsibility to Protect: A Defense* (Oxford: Oxford University Press, 2015).

59. Glanville, 'Does R2P Matter?', p. 191.

5

The Problem of Regime Change

The use of attack helicopters by the UN mission in Côte d'Ivoire (UNOCI), operating alongside French forces, to oust Laurent Gbagbo from power in April 2011 and NATO's decision to interpret Security Council Resolution 1973 – passed a few weeks earlier, in such a way as to permit the use of air power and other forms of assistance to aid the National Transitional Council of Libya in overthrowing the Gaddafi regime – provoked a strong and negative response from some quarters in international society.[1] Several states argued that, as a matter of principle, the protection of populations from genocide and mass atrocities should never entail 'regime change'. Long-standing critics of humanitarian intervention, Nicaragua and Venezuela, used particularly blunt language to criticize what they saw as the UN's complicity in neo-imperialist interventionism dressed up in humanitarian garb. Nicaragua complained: 'Once again we have witnessed the shameful manipulation of the slogan "protection of civilians" for dishonorable political purposes, seeking unequivocally and blatantly to impose regime change, attacking the sovereignty of a State Member of the United Nations [Libya] and violating the Organization's Charter.'[2] Venezuela added: 'It is regrettable that certain countries are seeking regime change in Libya, in violation of the Charter of the United Nations.'[3]

More worryingly than these stark criticisms from two of the half a dozen or so unreconstructed opponents of international human protection was the fact that three members of the emerging BRICS (Brazil, Russia, India, China, South Africa) group – all of whom had moved over the past few years towards an accommodation with the new principle – also spoke out strongly against the actions in Côte d'Ivoire and Libya. China, a permanent member of the Security Council argued that: 'There must be no attempt at regime change or involvement in civil war by any party under the guise of protecting civilians.'[4] Brazil concurred:

> The protection of civilians is a humanitarian imperative. It is a distinct concept that must not be confused or conflated with threats to international peace and security, as described in the Charter, or with the responsibility to protect. We must avoid excessively broad interpretations of the protection of civilians, which could … create the perception that it is being used as a smokescreen for intervention or regime change.[5]

And South Africa noted that:

> international actors and external organizations … should nonetheless comply with the provisions of the United Nations Charter, fully respect the will, sovereignty and territorial integrity of the country concerned, and refrain from advancing political agendas that go beyond the protection of civilian mandates, including regime change.[6]

This argument about the inadmissibility of regime change in pursuit of the protection of people from genocide and mass atrocities has been held partly responsible for the UN Security Council's failure to reach consensus on a timely and decisive response to the crisis in Syria.[7]

Insistence that the protection of populations from atrocity crimes must never entail regime change poses the thorny question of what international society should do when states massacre large sections of their own population. How, except by regime change, might Cambodia have been saved from the Khmer Rouge? Uganda from Idi Amin? Or the Tutsis from the government-backed *Interahamwe* genocidaires Rwanda? This chapter examines the relationship between human protection and regime change and argues that although protection activities must never be used to achieve regime change, regime change is sometimes necessary for the protection of populations terrorized by their own government. Much hinges, we argue, on this causal chain. As such, the chapter proposes five tests that may help guard against the abuse of protection arguments for self-interested purposes while permitting regime in those rare and exceptional cases when it is necessary to protect populations from mass violence.

First, though, we need to define what is meant by 'regime change' and clarify its normative content, as this is a politically charged and highly contested term. As used here, regime change refers to the changing of a government by unconstitutional means. This may involve complete change – as when the government of a whole country is changed (e.g. Libya 2011) or partial change – as when a government remains in office but loses authority over a particular region, which may or may not subsequently achieve formal independence (e.g. Indonesia/East Timor, 1999–2000). As such, it is important to resist *a priori* assumptions about the normative quality of particular regime changes. Some, such as the sometimes violent changing of colonial regimes and the ending of regimes founded on racial discrimination, have been welcomed and legitimized by international society; others, such as the ousting of the genocidal Khmer Rouge regime exposed gaps between legality, legitimacy, and morality; a third category, including the unconstitutional removal of the Arbenz and Allende governments in Guatemala and Chile, respectively, were widely condemned and failed most tests of legitimacy. Given this history, unless one adopts a rigid absolutist morality which holds that governments are entitled to do whatever they like to their own population – we cannot plausibly condemn regime change *a priori*. Instead, judgements about the normative quality of changes to regimes must be based on the circumstances at hand.

There are two other definitional points that need clarifying. The term 'regime change' does not identify the agents or processes of change. In relation to the agents of change, these may be foreign states, domestic armed groups, popular uprisings, elements within a governing elite, or some combination of these. As we argued earlier, and will show in detail in the following section, regime change as a response to government-perpetrated atrocities is caused most often by domestic actors. Foreign-induced regime change in such circumstances is relatively rare. In relation to the process of regime change, armed conflict – predominantly civil war – is often a key driver. Other 'change' processes include negotiated settlements (which may involve the exiling of members of the ruling elite), the ousting of a leader by civilian members of the ruling elite, military coups, the natural death of the leader, and popular uprisings/protests.

The chapter proceeds in three parts. First, we clarify the empirical dimensions of the debate. Second, we examine in more detail the grounds for insisting that human protection must never entail regime change and argue that while these are compelling reasons for wariness about the use of force for protection purposes found in accounts of sovereignty that rest on self-determination, they do not constitute a convincing *prima facie* case against regime change in all circumstances. Third, we propose a series of checks designed to ensure that regime change may be used in extreme situations as a pathway to protection while guarding against the abuse of protection as a pathway to regime change.

Historical contours

The question of the relationship between human protection and regime change is in part an empirical one. Debates are infused with assumptions about the possibility or impossibility of achieving international society's goals of protecting populations from atrocities with or without regime change, and a deeply held belief in some quarters that protection rhetoric has been used to legitimize military interventions motivated by selfish political considerations. Because these empirical assumptions are often used to validate moral arguments, this section offers a brief examination of the history.

In the vast majority of cases, episodes in which a state perpetrates genocide or other atrocities against sections of its own population tend to end either because the perpetrators themselves decide to stop the killing – usually because they are satisfied that they have accomplished their goals – or because the government is removed from power – usually by domestic opponents. There is little reason to think that a determined state perpetrator can be persuaded to change course by diplomacy or other non-forcible measures. Atrocities are typically not an option of first resort. More often than not, governments choose not to resort to deliberately killing civilians even when they stand to gain and have the means to do so.[8] Massacring civilians is usually entered into reluctantly and only after alternative strategies have been contemplated and found wanting. Massacres are inhibited by a combination of fears about the potential for retribution against one's own population, an interest in maintaining rules governing conflict in order to limit damage to the underlying social order, the potential for third-party intervention or punishment, and ideologies or moral codes that prohibit such killing.[9] As a result, governments perpetrate atrocities usually only when they believe the stakes to be very high and in the perceived absence of alternative remedies. In such situations, they often anticipate that their actions will draw international opprobrium and attract other costs but calculate that these are worth paying to achieve their goal.[10] International responses that fall short of physical coercion are unlikely to have much effect on this calculus in the short-term, though dramatic forms of economic coercion may and regular sanctions may have some longer-term impacts.

The dilemma of protecting populations from their own murderous governments without promoting regime change cannot, therefore, be avoided by wishing up alternative, non-forcible responses likely to persuade determined perpetrators to stand down their arms. The best that can be hoped for along these lines is to strengthen the international society capacity to prevent mass atrocities in the first place or to respond in a timely and decisive manner at a very early stage in the crisis. Obviously, the best way of protecting populations from their own governments is by reducing the frequency with which governments turn their guns upon their own people. When prevention fails, however, the historical record seems to suggest that international society has limited options and that either victory for the perpetrators or regime change – usually at the hands of armed local resistance – is often unavoidable.

Despite this history, since the NATO-led intervention in Libya a significant number of states have begun to argue that the protection of populations from genocide and mass atrocities must *never* entail regime change. Because consensus is such an important facet of international legitimacy, we cannot afford to be cavalier in dismissing these arguments.[11] The next section considers their foundations in more detail.

Sovereignty, self-determination, and human rights

The chief principled objection to regime change being a product of action aimed at protecting populations from atrocities is that it is a violation of state sovereignty. There are at least two critical dimensions here. The first, and more often acknowledged, is the value of sovereignty as a principle of international order. This is more easily dispensed with because it relates more to humanitarian intervention in general than to the specific relationship between intervention and regime change. This objection is based on a logic that is now well known: in a world characterized by a plurality of radically different communities, international society is made possible by rules that permit communities to pursue their own conceptions of the good without infringing on others' right to do likewise.[12] Sitting at the heart of this system of rules of coexistence is the principle of sovereign equality, the prohibition on the use of force in international affairs (Article 2(4) of the UN Charter), and the principle of non-interference in the domestic affairs of states (Article 2(7) of the UN Charter). The interests of international peace and the potential for international cooperation are best served by maintaining these rules; their erosion would increase international insecurity and hinder cooperation.[13]

This line of thinking is a well-known aspect of the debate about humanitarian intervention. It is consistent with a pluralist conception of world politics as a society of independent units (states) bound together by constitutive and regulatory rules which guide their mutual relations but do not place demands on their internal characteristics; a rule-utilitarian view which holds that the greatest good is served by the preservation of international order;[14] legal positivist arguments about the necessity of protecting sovereign equality, without which powerful states would receive 'an almost unlimited right to overthrow [other] governments';[15] and basic communitarian assumptions about the irreconcilable diversity of the values and goals of different communities. Robert Jackson might have been speaking for all when he bluntly remarked that 'in my view, the stability of international society, especially the unity of the great powers, is more important, indeed far more important, than minority rights and humanitarian protections ... if we have to choose between these two sets of values'.[16]

Nonetheless, this argument speaks more to general problems of humanitarian intervention than to the relationship between human protection and regime change per se. As agreed by heads of state and government in 2005, the Responsibility to Protect (R2P) – the most relevant dimension of the International Human Protection regime for the present discussion – requires that the use of force or other forms of coercion to protect populations from genocide and mass atrocities be authorized by the UN Security Council (para. 139). It is partly for this reason that the UN Secretary-General, Ban Ki-moon, repeatedly argued that the principle does not alter, or seek to alter, existing international law but that it is embedded within the law.[17] Thus, any use of force conducted under the auspices of R2P or human protection more broadly would need to be consistent with existing legal rules. To that end, it is worth remembering that the use of force in both Côte d'Ivoire and Libya was expressly authorized by the UN Security Council. In short, this first line of critique is not compelling because R2P does not purport to change the rules of coexistence found in the UN Charter. Instead, R2P pursues its goals by working within this normative framework. That explains why heads of state and government were prepared to endorse the principle, why it has commanded the support of the UN General Assembly and Security Council, but also why it remains hostage to the vicissitudes of world politics.

The challenge posed by Côte d'Ivoire and Libya was therefore not constitutional in nature. Critique of regime change in both cases related not to the intervener's authority to act but to the widely held perception that they exceeded their mandate – that the interveners turned a mandate to use force to protect civilians from mass atrocities into a licence to change a regime. This brings us to the problem of abuse. The poster child for this issue is the historical fact that Adolf Hitler insisted that the 1939 invasion of Czechoslovakia was inspired by a desire to protect Czechoslovak citizens whose 'life and liberty' were threatened by their own government.[18] Traditionally, the general ban on the use of force found in the UN Charter has been held up as the primary barrier against such abuse.[19] However, critics maintain that R2P allows interveners to pursue self-interested regime change agendas while outwardly complying with the rules. As one of R2P's key champions Gareth Evans put it, when reflecting on the aftermath of Libya, the BRICS are concerned that if they give 'an inch' on the adoption of enforcement measures for protection purposes, the West and the UN itself might 'take a mile'.[20] The response to this problem has been to insist, *prima facie*, that forcible action to protect humans never result in regime change.

The historical record does not match the fear of abuse. As we observed earlier, foreign-armed intervention in response to genocide mass atrocities remains extremely rare. Armed intervention authorized by the Security Council for human protection is still more rare – the 2011 intervention in Libya being the first of its kind.[21] Nor have there been many obvious cases of 'abuse' since 1945. The most commonly discussed cases are the 1983 US intervention in Grenada, the

1994 French intervention in Rwanda, and the 2003 US-led invasion of Iraq. But the intervention in Grenada was justified more in terms of defending democracy than humanitarian considerations; although the French intervention in Rwanda was not primarily motivated by humanitarian concerns, the intervention did have a positive humanitarian effect in the short-term; and the US-led intervention in Iraq was primarily justified by reference to the problem of weapons of mass destruction (indeed, this was the whole basis of the war's legal justification).[22] The problem, then, would seem to boil down to the political question of ensuring that those who act on the authorization of Security Council mandates remain accountable to the Council itself.

The seemingly deeper objection to regime change derives from the principle of self-determination. A long strain of political and moral philosophy and action holds that political communities enjoy a 'common life' and should be free to determine their own system of governance. This right is grounded in each individual's basic human right to select his or her own mode of living.[23] This account holds that there is a 'fit' between the nation and the state, and that it should be assumed that the latter enable the former to develop and protect its own values and ideas about how its members ought to live.[24] According to Michael Walzer,

> justice is relative to social meanings: there are an infinite number of possible lives, shaped by an infinite number of possible cultures, religions, political arrangements, geographic conditions and so on. A given society is just if its substantive life is lived in a certain way – that is, in a way faithful to the shared understandings of its members.[25]

Sovereignty protects this right to self-determination because it entails a presumption against external interference in people's domestic affairs. At its heart, it holds that people might choose to live and be governed in many different ways and that outsiders have no right to impose their particular way of life on others. Ultimately, it is for peoples themselves to select their form of government by whatever means, including violence.

This view has several prominent adherents. Immanuel Kant, a theorist closely associated with a progressive vision of human potential, argued that states ought to scrupulously obey sovereignty's rule of non-interference in each other's domestic affairs. One of the core principles of his *Perpetual Peace* was that 'no state shall violently interfere with the constitution and administration of another'. This, he argued, was a basic principle of international order derived from the individual duty to respect one another's autonomy. Another liberal thinker, John Stuart Mill, insisted that foreign governments should play no part in the overthrowing of tyrannical regimes, as this should be the responsibility of peoples themselves. Mill explained:

> When the contest is only with native rulers, and with such native strength as those rulers can enlist in their defence, the answer I should give to the question of the legitimacy of intervention is, as a general rule, No. The reason is, that there can seldom be anything approaching to assurance that intervention, even if successful, would be for the good of the people themselves. The only test possessing any real value, of a people's having become fit for popular institutions, is that they, or a sufficient portion of them to prevail in the contest, are willing to brave labour and danger for their liberation. I know all that may be said, I know it may be urged that the virtues of freemen cannot be learnt in the school of slavery, and that if a people are not fit for freedom, to have any chance of becoming so they must first be free. And this would be conclusive, if the intervention recommended would really give them freedom. But the evil is, that if they have not sufficient love of liberty to be able to wrest it from merely domestic oppressors, the liberty which is bestowed on them by other hands than their own, will have nothing real, nothing permanent. No people ever was and remained free, but because it was determined to be so ... [26]

In other words, domestic political change can only be wrought by the people themselves. Where there is insufficient domestic support for the overthrow of a tyrannical regime, foreign intervention is unlikely to succeed and has the effect only of imposing an alien form of government.

The argument that this national right to self-determination translates to states and creates a powerful moral basis for the rule of non-interference has been widely voiced in international society since 1945. It was aired by several 'small' or 'new' states during negotiations about the UN Charter.[27] Chief among the concerns of Latin American states was that the new world organization should contain rules protecting the sovereign right of a state to determine its own form of government. In 1960, the General Assembly issued its Declaration on the Granting of Independence to Colonial Countries and Peoples. Adopted by eighty-nine votes to none, with nine abstentions, the declaration proclaimed that 'all peoples have the right to self-determination; by virtue of that right they freely determine their political status and freely pursue their economic, social and cultural development.' The UN's subsequent resolutions on self-determination all used this wording and in 1975 the International Court of Justice (ICJ) recognized the statement as the 'basis for the process of decolonisation'.[28] The insistence that all peoples have a right to self-determination including a right to 'freely determine their political status' was also incorporated into the General Assembly's International Covenants on Human Rights in 1966.

For many postcolonial leaders and theorists there was a direct relationship between a people's right to freely determine a state's political status and the non-interference rule. After all, there could be no effective right of self-determination if powerful states felt entitled to interfere in the affairs of the weak. As such, the General Assembly's 1970 Declaration on Principles of International Law Concerning Friendly Relations stated categorically that:

> No state or group of states has the right to intervene, directly or indirectly, for any reason whatever, in the internal or external affairs of any other state. Consequently, armed intervention and all other forms of interference or attempted threats against the personality of the state or against its political, economic and cultural elements, are in violation of international law.

In this account of sovereignty there is an implicit direct link between an individual's human right to determine his or her own way of life and form of government free of foreign and colonial interference and the rule of non-interference. Simply put, peoples have a right to determine their own destiny. Opening the door to foreign interference in the name of humanitarian principles would only pave the way to colonial or hegemonic domination. This colonizing logic was perhaps best exemplified in the work of the neo-scholastic friar Francisco de Vitoria. Writing in the sixteenth century, Vitoria had argued against the colonial acquisition of lands in the Americas on the grounds that native peoples had legitimate political institutions which exerted legitimate authority over their lands. However, he also accepted that the Spanish had a right to travel and trade in the New World and could use force to protect their rights and, more importantly, had a right to use force to overthrow despotic (cannibalistic) kings. It was this latter right – humanitarian intervention of sorts – that was seized upon as justification for the colonization of the Americas and destruction of native peoples.[29]

Commitment to this view of sovereignty as resting on the principle of self-determination remains widespread and steadfast in contemporary international society. This thinking clearly underpinned the global movement against colonialism and helped animate the often bitter and violent struggles waged to end foreign domination.[30] As we mentioned earlier, it is a position endorsed by a majority of states in the General Assembly (especially a majority of members in the G77 and Non-Aligned Movement), by many international lawyers, and by a large academic literature.

This conception of sovereignty as derived from self-determination predicated on human rights should not be confused with the 'absolutist' view that sovereigns are entitled to act however they please, a view championed by nineteenth-century German scholars such as Hegel, Fichte, Ihering, Treitschke, and Heller and closely associated with nationalism. For the German absolutists, sovereignty implied not just the absence of a superior authority but also *plenitudo potestatis* – competence to the full reach of its material power. Ihering maintained that sovereigns were limited only by their own will, while Treitschke argued that it was legitimate for a state to do anything at all to satisfy its interests and that these interests took priority over contractual obligations.[31] As a nineteenth-century French jurist Fauchille put it, 'to say a person is sovereign, not merely means to say that it does not recognize any authority above its own, but that it may issue orders at its own discretion, that it may do freely and without limitation all that it considers fit to do'.[32] The two sets of ideas (sovereignty as self-determination and absolutism) part company because the former welcomes the view that states are obliged to conduct their international relations with due respect for international legal rules (chiefly the rule of non-interference) and cannot dismiss human rights concerns per se because it is itself predicated on a human rights claim – the right to autonomy and self-determination.

The self-determinationist account can provide grounds for some limited support for foreign interference when regimes obviously deny self-determination to their peoples. It is perhaps not surprising, therefore, that it was at the behest of the UN General Assembly that the Security Council imposed a raft of mandatory enforcement measures on the governments of South Rhodesia and South Africa, including authorizing the use of force by the UK against the former. In both cases, the existence of racist minority governments exposed an obvious disconnect between the regime and the people. For similar reasons it is sometimes suggested that advocates of the self-determinationist position would not oppose armed intervention in situations where a government committed atrocities against sections of its own population. Certainly, advocates of this position tend to not dispute the legal and moral right of the Security Council to authorize collective intervention in such situations. That might explain why states such as South Africa, Nigeria, and Togo supported Resolution 1973 authorizing the use of force in Libya, while India, China, and Russia decided to not block the resolution, in a context where atrocities were imminently threatened and in which the regime in question had clearly lost the support of a large section of the people, including its own Permanent Representative to the UN, who defected early on. However, as we outlined in Chapter 4, there were a series of exceptional circumstances in the Libya case that made Resolution 1973 possible.[33] In practice, while they may admit a theoretical right to intervene against murderous states, political leaders have tended to be wary of supporting the use of force in particular cases, especially in the absence of other extenuating considerations. (The decision of Malaysia, a strident proponent of this account of sovereignty, to vote with NATO on a draft resolution critical of the Kosovo intervention in 1999 is a case in point – in that situation, Malaysia's sense of Islamic solidarity with Kosovar Albanians overrode its commitment to non-interference.)[34] As a result, the 2011 intervention in Libya remains the only instance of armed intervention against a state guilty of committing genocide and other mass atrocities against its own population to be authorized by the UN Security Council. When that sole intervention resulted in the overthrowal of the Gaddafi regime, the response of a significant portion of international society was to insist that protection should never entail regime change and demand assurances and – if necessary – institutional mechanisms, to ensure that there be no repeat.

The view that sovereignty rests on the principle of self-determination, itself widely considered an inviolable human right, lies at the core of international concern about the potential relationship between human protection and regime change. The fear is that once ground is given to enable the legitimate removal of regimes in the name of human protection, the hard-won independence of peoples in the postcolonial world and their culturally specific ways of life will become conditional upon the judgements of a small number of powerful states.[35] The historical record suggests that although in theory they might accept foreign intervention in cases where states abuse their own populations on a massive scale – on the grounds that such states could not plausibly claim to be representative of the popular will – in practice adherents to the self-determinationist account of sovereignty are predisposed towards protecting sovereigns. There is, in other words, a strong presumption in favour of the assumption that states reflect the popular will of their people that is seldom shaken by the commission of genocide and mass atrocities by those same states against the populations they are assumed to be representative of. Even when that faith is seriously shaken, there is wariness about the prospect of regime change and deep suspicion about the motives of those charged with executing protection mandates, often to a degree in excess of concerns about the targeted populations themselves. This poses a particular challenge to the implementation of human protection because, as we mentioned at the outset, its rise to prominence was based on an alignment between the principle and existing international laws and norms. Partly as a result, from the very outset the language of human protection has been suffused with the idea that it is an 'ally to sovereignty', a means of helping states realize their full sovereign potential through the discharge of responsibilities that are as inherent to sovereignty as the rule of non-interference.[36]

There are, of course, a number of problems with these views. Most significantly, the assumption that states facilitate the autonomy and self-determination of their populations – upon which the whole argument is predicated – is often proved to be false. Over the course of the past two centuries, people have been far more likely to be massacred by their own governments than by either non-state actors or foreign governments.[37] An additional problem, which stems in part from this empirical observation, is that it does not at all follow that self-determination should necessarily give rise either to a determined commitment to non-interference or to wariness towards international human protection activism. We may instead go back to first principles and focus on the autonomy of individuals as the only irreducible ontological being. From this stance, the right of self-determination makes sense only if one accepts the view that individuals have rights to autonomy and participation in government. If that proposition is denied, then it becomes very difficult to mount a moral case in defence of self-determination as a right enjoyed by nations or states.

Once this relationship between individual and collective rights is recognized, it is a short leap to the view that sovereignty should be understood as an instrumental value and not as an end in itself. That is because sovereignty ultimately resides in the people who confer authority upon the state to act in their name. As such, state sovereignty derives its moral value from the state's capacity to protect the autonomy of its citizens and facilitate their participation in government. From here, it is an equally short leap to the view that when states fail in their duty to protect the 'basic rights' of their citizens – those thought necessary for their autonomy and participation in government, the 'right to life' being chief among them – they lose their moral standing and forfeit sovereign rights.[38] There are a variety of ways of arriving at this conclusion. Simon Caney draws on Kant's concept of the rational individual to insist that all individuals have certain pre-political rights.[39] Others use St Augustine's insistence that force be used to defend public order to argue that intervention to end injustice was 'among the rights and duties of states until and unless supplanted by superior government'.[40] Alternatively, historical accounts show that in both theory and practice, sovereign rights have always been associated with responsibilities of one form or another.[41] Whichever path one takes, the basic proposition is that state sovereignty is rooted in the popular sovereignty of the people, which is in turn grounded in individual human rights. Sovereignty is conferred upon the state by the people and can be revoked by the people when the sovereign fails to protect their core rights. The point was perhaps made most eloquently by Thomas Jefferson in America's Declaration of Independence (1776).

Although this thinking lends itself more obviously to support for domestic rebellion against despotic regimes than to foreign humanitarian intervention, it shows that commitment to the principle of self-determination can just as easily provide moral support for regime change as it can non-interference. These theoretical points notwithstanding, however, it is the vision of self-determination as being tightly wedded to non-interference that tends to prevail in world politics. The challenge for the next, and final, section is to examine whether there is room for accommodation between these two accounts of self-determination and, through that, between human protection and the antipathy of a large part of international society towards regime change.

Towards responsible protection

This section presents a way of thinking about the relationship between human protection and regime change that accommodates the two key points raised in the previous sections: first, that the most common way of stopping governments that choose to massacre sections of their own population before their objectives are met is through regime change; and, second, that a large section of international community is concerned that the forcible changing of regimes could undermine the principle of self-determination and rules of international coexistence. We take our account of human protection further still in the following chapter, where we explore questions of accountability.

A useful place to start is with the common ground identified thus far. The most significant is the shared belief that – whether for the purposes of maintaining order or protecting people – international society is entitled to take collective action, including through the use of force, to promote common goals and that the UN Security Council is empowered with the authority to mandate such action. What concerned critics about the NATO-led intervention in Libya was not the question of whether the alliance had authority to act or whether the Security Council was entitled to issue such a mandate, but whether NATO was authorized to remove the regime. The various moral approaches to the question of sovereignty and self-determination surveyed in the previous section seem to accept the view that, in theory at least if not always in practice, there are situations in which collective action, including the use of force, could be legitimate to achieve common purposes. Where the approaches differed was in their presumptions in relation to regime change whether in favour of the sovereign state or the sovereignty of the people, and their degree of wariness about the motives and intentions of foreign interveners. What is clear, however, is that there is little basis in the arguments reviewed thus far for insisting, *prima facie*, that regime change must never be used as a means of protecting populations. We have also, however, found little reason to support the argument at the other extreme – that regime change by foreign intervention needs no special authorization. What we are left with is the argument we mooted in the introduction – that in some circumstances regime change may be necessary for human protection purposes, but that human protection must never be used as a vehicle for advancing regime change. This poses the question of how to disentangle the two in practice?

An appropriate starting point is the question of international authority. We want to argue that the UN Security Council can legitimately authorize forcible regime change, or measures that effect regime change. The self-determinationist position, which is related to communitarianism, holds that conceptions of the good are constituted within political communities but also that political communities may agree rules of coexistence to govern relations between them. The cornerstone of these rules in contemporary international society is the UN Charter, which confers upon the Security Council primary responsibility for international peace and security and authority to employ any means it deems to be necessary for this purpose. The Charter's drafters intentionally left it for the Council alone to determine what constituted a threat to international peace and security and placed no restrictions on the measures it might call upon in the service of peace.[42] The Council's authority therefore derives from the voluntary granting of authority by member states themselves. Two of the UN Charter's less often quoted articles make precisely this point. Article 24 (1) stresses the conferral of authority from states to the Security Council:

> In order to ensure prompt and effective action by the United Nations, its Members confer on the Security Council primary responsibility for the maintenance of international peace and security, and agree that in carrying out its duties under this responsibility the Security Council acts on their behalf.

In Article 25, states bind themselves to the Council's decisions through their unconditional commitment to 'accept and carry out the decisions of the Security Council in accordance with the present Charter'. Through accession to the Charter, therefore, states confer authority on the Security Council and recognize that it acts in the common good. As such, when the Council authorizes the use of force and/or regime change for protection purposes, it does so on the basis of the authority conferred upon it by states and acts to protect the common good and in support of commonly held values. Irrespective of which account of sovereignty is held, therefore, there is little disputing the notion that the Security Council is entitled by the authority vested in it by sovereign states to employ whatever measure it deems necessary, including regime change, in the interests of international peace and security. This rules out the case for the *prima facie* banning of regime change for human protection purposes, as well as the notion that states enjoy a right unilaterally to change unfriendly regimes.

This brings us to the more difficult argument about the presumption in favour of the state. We noted earlier that while self-determinationists might agree in theory to the possibility of UN-authorized regime change in situations where the state commits genocide or mass atrocities against sections of its population, they have been reluctant to do so in practice. Especially egregious in this regard was international society's near unanimity of condemnation of Vietnam for its ousting of the genocidal Pol Pot regime in Cambodia, whose short reign of terror accounted for a quarter of that country's population in a three-and-a-half-year period.[43]

We suggested earlier that the presumption in favour of the state is prefaced on a deeply held – if not always well-founded – suspicion about the motives or intentions of would-be interveners. That is, international society is often prepared to grant state perpetrators the benefit of the doubt because many of its members fear that some powerful states would exploit any relaxation of the principle of non-interference for their own self-interested purposes, resulting in the weakening of rules considered essential to sovereign equality. This takes us back to a long-standing debate about the importance of humanitarian motives in shaping the legitimacy of armed intervention.[44] By focusing on motives, this created an impossibly high barrier to intervention because in practice states always act out of mixed motives, especially in decisions about whether or not to go to war. Only the imprudent statesperson would commit forces to 'wars of choice' for a singular reason and without compelling national interests. As a result, scholars focused on motives found that there had been no genuinely humanitarian interventions as all had some degree of self-interest. This type of analysis supports the sceptics' view that states use humanitarian justifications to excuse the self-interested use of force. The problem with this line of argument, however, is that it misconstrues the Christian Just War tradition's attention to the moral significance of 'intentions' as synonymous with the more modern attraction to 'motives'. There are, though, important differences between motives and intentions.

Motives are the reasons why an actor chooses to behave the way she does, and intentions relate to what she intends to achieve. Motives are talked about in the plural because they are seldom, if ever, singular. For Just War thinking and many derivative ethics of war, therefore, it is the actor's *intentions* that are of critical importance. According to Just War thinking, individuals must wage war for the common good, not for self-aggrandizement or out of hatred for the enemy. This principle, often ignored or downplayed in more recent accounts of the ethics of war, is absolutely critical to the Just War tradition's basic defence of killing in war.[45] As is well known, the tradition starts from the proposition that killing in itself is wrong but sometimes necessary for the preservation of order or to right a greater wrong. When soldiers fight, they must do so with the intention of serving the common good.

How might we judge whether those proposing to use force for the purpose of protecting populations from genocide and mass atrocities are acting in good faith and with humanitarian intent? Understanding another's intent is a notoriously difficult business, but somewhat less difficult than understanding their motives because there is a stronger connection between inward intentions and outward actions. Here, we propose five checks. When all five are satisfied, we think it would be very difficult indeed to believe that an intervention was about anything other than saving populations from atrocities. As such, the checks provide a way of guarding against 'abuse' and the weakening of self-determination and non-interference principles while allowing international society the flexibility it sometimes needs to stop the perpetrators of genocide and mass atrocities in their tracks.

First, any intervention must have a mandate from the Security Council. As well as being necessary from the point of view of international authority, the insistence on a Security Council mandate adds additional political checks. Although the Council is an imperfect institution, especially from the perspective of dialogic ethics, it nonetheless imposes a strong and useful procedural check by demanding that it is not sufficient for a state simply to convince itself, or its like-minded friends, of the justice of its cause when intervening. Insisting on Security Council approval demands that would-be interveners persuade their peers – including the permanent five members – to accept the case for action.

Second, states that champion intervention should demonstrate their humanitarian intent by acknowledging – through their words and deeds – a duty to prevent genocide and mass atrocities and respond in the most effective ways possible. This requirement is potentially controversial, as states typically are not well disposed to accepting that they owe positive duties towards strangers. When it comes to the question of acting to protect foreigners from harm, states – and many political theorists – tend to be more comfortable with the language of negative rights than positive duties. However, when international society recognizes – as it has – 'failures' in relation to genocides in Rwanda and Srebrenica, it acknowledges that inaction was wrong and thereby implies a duty to act in such cases. Properly understood, rights always entail corresponding duties. Rights without duties are hollow, and since it is broadly understood that there is at least a thin layer of universal rights (including, presumably, the right to not be massacred) it follows that there must be some universal duties. Because it would be unrealistic to expect every individual to take action to realize the fundamental rights of every other individual, duties are mediated by political institutions.[46] This is not to say that there is a duty to intervene militarily whenever genocide and mass atrocities are perpetrated, but that actors should do whatever they can to protect endangered populations at a reasonable cost and without inflaming the situation further. Recognizing a right but not a duty to protect opens the door to the abuse that is so feared by those who cling to the presumption in favour of the state, because it allows states to act on their own self-interest without burdening themselves with duties. States that accept a duty to protect will not only advocate intervention when it suits other interests, but they will also dedicate resources to preventing mass atrocity crimes in the first place and to protecting civilians even when it is not politically convenient for them to do so.

The third test relates to the use of humanitarian justifications and their relationship to the known facts of the case. The simplest test of an actor's intention is to compare what they say they are doing with what is known about the case. Do actors justify their behaviour in humanitarian terms and is there a pressing humanitarian situation to respond to? For example, most advocates of human protection quickly dismissed attempts to argue that the 2003 invasion of Iraq was a legitimate humanitarian intervention on two main grounds. First, the USA did not primarily justify its actions in these terms and nor did its pre-2003 policy of maintaining harsh general sanctions on Iraq evince much concern for the civilian population in that country. Second, at the time of the intervention, there was no immediate humanitarian crisis caused by genocide and mass atrocities precipitated by the government. Most governments and analysts applied similar logic to Russia's attempt to justify its 2008 invasion of Georgia on humanitarian grounds, finding that there was no evidence to support claims that the Georgian government was perpetrating mass atrocities.

Fourth, the calibration of means and ends. Would-be interveners should select strategies that allow them to prevail without undermining humanitarian outcomes. This requires more than simply abiding by the laws of war. First, above and beyond the requirements of law, intervening militaries should pay attention to the principle of 'due care' in the selection of targets and weapons. When the purported purpose of an intervention is to save civilian lives, failure to exhibit due care casts serious doubts on the humanitarian intentions of the interveners and therefore on the legitimacy of the operation. Second, within the boundaries of what they have been mandated to do by the Security Council, interveners should choose strategies calculated to achieve the best humanitarian outcome in the shortest amount of time and with the least danger to civilians. This requirement raises difficult questions about the relative value of force protection and civilian protection. On this question, Michael Walzer offered the compelling argument that soldiers should be prepared to accept additional risks if doing so reduced the risks faced by civilians.[47] There are, however, limits to how much additional risk can be accepted by military personnel. As a rule of thumb, we might say that soldiers should be prepared to accept additional risk so long as it does not jeopardize their chances of prevailing. After all, when states intervene to end genocide and mass atrocities, the purpose is best served by rapid victory. However, few things are likely to damage the humanitarian credentials of a military operation more than the perception that it is increasing the overall risk to civilians.

Fifth, states that intervene in the affairs of others ought to recognize a duty to help the country rebuild afterwards, with a focus on re-establishing its self-determination. This is somewhat related to the idea of *jus post bellum* – the notion that the ethics of war include a commitment to building peace afterwards – but is particularly important in this setting as further surety of a state's intention to fulfil humanitarian goals. One concern might be that a demonstrative commitment to peacebuilding could give rise to a new form of imperialism through the imposition of certain institutions or modes of governance. With this in mind, perhaps the best broad vision of what is required ethically is Michael Barnett's notion of 'republican peacebuilding' – peacebuilding focused on supporting a people's capacity to govern themselves.[48] Institutional checks on this potential problem might include a requirement that peacebuilding activities be channelled through the UN's Security Council or, better still, the UN Peacebuilding Commission, which focuses on building partnerships with the state concerned.

Interventions aimed at halting genocide and mass atrocities that satisfy these five conditions – Security Council authorization; recognition of humanitarian duties; an obvious connection between justifications and known facts; the calibration of ends and means; and evident commitment to long-term peacebuilding – are pursued primarily with humanitarian intent. In such circumstances the causal flow between protection and regime change moves in the right direction such that regime change is a contribution to the pursuit of protection from genocide and mass atrocities. It would be difficult indeed to think of a situation in which these five tests were satisfied but where the causal chain flowed in the opposite direction (protection used as a vehicle for regime change). What is more, the tests present substantial hurdles that will be difficult to jump in practice. Not only should this provide reassurance to those still wary of the potentially negative impact of protection-induced regime change on the principle of self-determination, it will also ensure that the instances of protection-induced regime change remain, as they have to date, rare.

Conclusion

This chapter has examined the fraught relationship between human protection and regime change and especially the argument that international action aimed at protecting populations from genocide and mass atrocities must never entail regime change. We argued that while states were right to be wary of the capacity for humanitarian justifications to be used in support of self-interested military action, the proposed *prima facie* prohibition was misplaced for two principal reasons: first, historical experience clearly demonstrates the necessity of regime change in ending episodes of genocide and mass atrocities perpetrated by states against sections of their own population; second, accounts of sovereignty as being derived from self-determination that underpin the main arguments in favour of the prohibition do not lend strong support to the idea of a *prima facie* ban. From this, we suggested that opposition to regime change as an occasional pathway to protection outcomes was primarily based on a presumption in favour of the state, which admitted a theoretical right of collective action against state perpetrators of genocide and mass atrocities but which remained deeply wary of the practice of collective action. Underlying this wariness is a concern that powerful states might abuse the theoretical right by reversing the logic of the relationship between human protection and regime change such that the former becomes a vehicle for the latter. Recognizing those concerns, we proposed five tests that ought to be fulfilled when force is employed against a state for humanitarian purposes: (1) Security Council authorization; (2) recognition of humanitarian duties; (3) an obvious connection between justifications and known facts; (4) the calibration of ends and means; and (5) evident commitment to long-term peacebuilding. These tests create significant obstacles for would-be interveners and significantly reduce the potential for abuse to the point where it becomes difficult to conceive scenarios in which the conditions might be fulfilled by an abusive intervener. Their satisfaction would provide proof that regime change induced by external action arose from genuine humanitarian intentions and was necessary to protect populations from genocide and mass atrocities. As a result, although externally induced regime change will remain a rare and exceptional pathway to the protection of populations from genocide and mass atrocities, it is a pathway that may nevertheless be occasionally considered without fear of abuse or concern about the erosion of sovereignty and self-determination.

Notes

1. For an overview see Alex J. Bellamy and Paul D. Williams, 'The New Politics of Protection: Côte d'Ivoire, Libya and the Responsibility to Protect', *International Affairs*, 87, no. 4 (2011), pp. 825–850.
2. These four quotes from S/PV.6531, 10 May 2011.
3. S/PV.6531 (resumption 1), 10 May 2011.
4. S/PV.6531, 10 May 2011.
5. S/PV.6531, 10 May 2011.
6. S/PV.6531, 10 May 2011.
7. See, for example, Jess Gitkins, 'Syria and the Responsibility to Protect', *Global Responsibility to Protect*, 4, no. 4, 2012.

8. The tendency to use atrocities as a last resort is widely recognized in the literature. See Alexander Downes, *Targeting Civilians in War* (Ithaca, NY: Cornell University Press, 2008); Benjamin A. Valentino, *Final Solutions: Mass Killing and Genocide in the Twentieth Century* (Ithaca, NY: Cornell University Press, 2004); Stathis N. Kalyvas, *The Logic of Violence in Civil War* (Cambridge: Cambridge University Press, 2006); and Daniel Chirot and Clark McCauley, *Why Not Kill Them All? The Logic and Prevention of Political Mass Murder* (Princeton, NJ: Princeton University Press, 2006).

9. Fears of intervention and retribution are identified by Downes, *Targeting Civilians* and Valentino, *Final Solutions*. It was most evident as an inhibitor in the early days of the Second World War. See Jeffrey W. Legro, *Cooperation Under Fire: The Conduct of the Air War in the Second World War* (New York: St. Martin's Press, 1992). The others are identified by Chirot and McCauley, *Why Not Kill Them All?*, pp. 95–96.

10. Alex J. Bellamy, 'Getting Away with Mass Murder', *Journal of Genocide Research*, 14, no. 1, (2012), pp. 29–53.

11. On the role of consensus in international legitimacy see Ian Clark, *Legitimacy in International Society* (Oxford: Oxford University Press, 2005).

12. Andrew Linklater, *The Transformation of Political Community* (Cambridge: Polity, 1998), p. 59. This is the familiar 'pluralist' or 'rationalist' account of international society; for useful discussions see Barry Buzan, *From International to World Society? English School Theory and the Social Structure of Globalisation* (Cambridge: Cambridge University Press, 2004); and Andrew Linklater and Hidemi Suganami, *The English School of International Relations: A Contemporary Reassessment* (Cambridge: Cambridge University Press, 2006).

13. For example, Robert Jackson, *The Global Covenant: Human Conduct in a World of States* (Oxford: Oxford University Press, 2000).

14. Louis Henkin, *How Nations Behave: Law and Foreign Policy*, 2nd edition (New York: Columbia University Press, 1979), p. 145.

15. Oscar Schachter, 'The Legality of Pro-Democratic Invasion', *American Journal of International Law*, 78, 1984, p. 649.

16. Jackson, *Global Covenant*, p. 291.

17. Ban Ki-moon, *Report of the Secretary-General on Implementing the Responsibility to Protect*, A/63/677, 12 January 2009.

18. Ian Brownlie, *International Law and the Use of Force by States* (Oxford: Clarendon Press, 1974), pp. 217–221.

19. Simon Chesterman, *Just War or Just Peace? Humanitarian Intervention and International Law* (Oxford: Oxford University Press, 2001), p. 231.

20. Gareth Evans, 'Responding to Mass Atrocity Crimes: The Responsibility to Protect After Libya', Lecture to the Royal Institute of International Affairs, London, 6 October 2011.

21. See Bellamy and Williams, 'The New Politics of Protection'.
22. On Grenada see Karin von Hippel, *Democracy by Force: US Military Intervention in the Post-Cold War World* (Cambridge: Cambridge University Press, 2000), pp. 27–53; on Rwanda see Nicholas J. Wheeler, *Saving Strangers: Humanitarian Intervention in International Society* (Oxford: Oxford University Press, 2000); and on Iraq see Alex J. Bellamy, 'International Law and the War with Iraq', *Melbourne Journal of International Law*, 4, no. 2 (2003).
23. Michael Walzer, *Just and Unjust Wars: A Philosophical Argument with Historical Illustrations* (New York: Basic Books, 1977), p. 57.
24. Walzer, *Just and Unjust Wars*, p. 87. See also Michael Walzer, *Thick and Thin: Moral Argument at Home and Abroad* (New Haven, CT: Yale University Press, 1994).
25. Michael Walzer, *Spheres of Justice: A Defence of Pluralism and Equality* (Oxford: Basil Blackwood, 1983), pp. 312–313.
26. John Stuart Mill, 'A Few Words on Non-Intervention' [1859], in John Stuart Mill, *Essays on Politics and Culture* (ed. by Gertrude Himmelfarb) (Gloucester: Peter Smith, 1973), pp. 368–384.
27. Chesterman, *Just War or Just Peace*, p. 49.
28. Malcolm N. Shaw, *International Law*, 5th edition (Cambridge: Cambridge University Press, 2003), p. 227.
29. For a discussion see Antony Anghie, *Imperialism, Sovereignty and the Making of International Law* (Cambridge: Cambridge University Press, 2005).
30. Gareth Evans recognized that sovereignty hard-won through decolonization is not lightly given away: Gareth Evans, 'Foreward' in Ramesh Thakur, *The United Nations, Peace and Security: From Collective Security to the Responsibility to Protect* (Cambridge: Cambridge University Press, 2006), p. xiv.
31. Heinrich von Treitschke, *Politik* (Leipzig: Insel, 1899), vol. 2, p. 100.
32. Paul Fauchille, *Traité de Droit International Public* (Paris: Libraire Arthur Rousseau, 1921), p. 428.
33. Recounted in Alex J. Bellamy, 'Libya – The Norm and the Exception', *Ethics and International Affairs*, 25, no. 3 (2011), pp. 263–269.
34. Prompting Thomas G. Weiss to lament that the 'problem' in relation to humanitarian intervention was not that there was too much of it, but that there was much too little. See Thomas G. Weiss, *Humanitarian Intervention*, 2nd edition (Cambridge: Polity, 2012).
35. For an account of R2P as relating to the extension of international authority over sovereign states see Anne Orford, *International Authority and the Responsibility to Protect* (Cambridge: Cambridge University Press, 2011).
36. For example, Francis M. Deng, Sadikiel Kimaro, Terrence Lyons, Donald Rothchild, and I. William Zartman, *Sovereignty as Responsibility*.

Conflict Management in Africa (Washington, DC: The Brookings Institution, 1996). Ramesh Thakur has repeatedly argued that R2P is not an 'intervener's charter', but an attempt to restrain unilateral intervention while guiding genuine collective measures. See Ramesh Thakur, *The Responsibility to Protect: Norms, Laws and the Use of Force in International Politics* (London: Routledge, 2011).

37. A history recounted in part in Alex J. Bellamy, *Massacres and Morality: Mass Atrocities in an Age of Civilian Immunity* (Oxford: Oxford University Press, 2012).

38. Fernando Téson, 'The Liberal Case for Humanitarian Intervention', in J. L. Holzgrefe and Robert O. Keohane (eds), *Humanitarian Intervention: Ethical, Legal and Political Dilemmas* (Cambridge: Cambridge University Press, 2003), p. 93. On the idea of 'basic rights' see Henry Shue, *Basic Rights: Subsistence, Affluence and US Foreign Policy*, 2nd edition (Princeton, NJ: Princeton University Press, 1996).

39. Simon Caney, 'Human Rights and the Rights of States: Terry Nardin on Non-Intervention', *International Political Science Review*, 18, no. 1, 1997, p. 34. For a more developed exposition see Simon Caney, *Justice Beyond Borders: A Global Political Theory* (Oxford: Oxford University Press, 2005).

40. Paul Ramsey, *The Just War: Force and Political Responsibility* (Lanham, MD: Rowman and Littlefield, 2002), pp. 20 and 35–36.

41. Luke Glanville, 'The Antecedents of "Sovereignty as Responsibility"', *European Journal of International Relations*, 17, no. 2 (2011), pp. 233–255.

42. On this see the excellent discussion in Edward C. Luck, *UN Security Council: Practice and Promise* (London: Routledge, 2006), pp. 9–15.

43. Wheeler, *Saving Strangers*, pp. 90–91 and Chesterman, *Just War or Just Peace?*, p. 80.

44. Wil Verwey, 'Humanitarian Intervention in the 1990s and Beyond: An International Law Perspective', in J. N. Pierterse (ed.), *World Orders in the Making: Humanitarian Intervention and Beyond* (London: Macmillan, 1998).

45. For example, Chris Brown, *Sovereignty, Rights and Justice: International Political Theory Today* (Cambridge: Polity, 2002), pp. 108–109; and Darrel Moellendorf, *Cosmopolitan Justice* (Boulder, CO: Westview, 2002), esp. pp. 120–158.

46. Henry Shue, 'Mediating Duties', *Ethics*, 98, no. 4 (1988), p. 698.

47. Walzer, *Just and Unjust Wars*, p. 156.

48. Michael N. Barnett, 'Building a Republican Peace: Stabilizing States After War', *International Security*, 30, no. 4 (2006), pp. 87–112.

6

The Problem of Accountability

Over the previous few chapters we have demonstrated that since the turn of the century, the UN Security Council has gradually become more proactive in relation to the protection of civilians from genocide and mass atrocities. This coincides with the emergence of an international human protection regime, including the adoption of the Responsibility to Protect (R2P). From hesitant beginnings in Sierra Leone and the Democratic Republic of Congo (DRC), the Council has gradually moved human protection to the centre of UN peacekeeping, with a majority of its ongoing missions having protection mandates.[1] These mandates were established under Chapter VII of the UN Charter and permit the use of 'all necessary measures' to protect civilians.

This trend towards human protection as a core purpose of the Security Council and a more robust approach to protection accelerated markedly in early 2011. Since that time, the Council has authorized the use of force to protect populations in Libya and Côte d'Ivoire, which in both cases resulted in a change of government; mandated a UN mission (MINUSMA)[2] to assist the government of Mali to protect the population from Tuareg/Islamist militia alongside a French deployment that has applied extensive coercive force; established an international intervention brigade in the DRC mandated to use force to protect civilians against M23 and other militia but also ostensibly intended as an armed deterrent to Rwandan interference in the country's east; and authorized a UN mission (MINUSCA) to use all means necessary (i.e. force if needed) to protect civilians in the Central African Republic (CAR).[3] The Council also responded quickly to the deterioration of the situation in South Sudan in late 2013 by authorizing an unprecedented redeployment of peacekeeping forces to reinforce the beleaguered UNMISS[4] mission there.

These mandates and missions have not been without controversy. Critics complained that UN forces in Côte d'Ivoire and the NATO-led mission over Libya exceeded their mandates to protect civilians and that the Council did not hold properly accountable the UN officials and states that assumed responsibility for discharging the Council's mandates. Among UN officials and peacekeeping experts, concerns are re-emerging about the Council's growing willingness to mandate UN peacekeepers to conduct robust missions involving the use of force to protect populations in semi-hostile environments – a task for which the UN is ill-prepared. At the same time, the capacity of two permanent members of the Council to block decisive collective action on Syria – in the face of a clear majority of Council members who support such action and sharp criticism from the General Assembly, where large majorities have voiced concern about the Council's inability to take meaningful steps – has prompted a resurgence of interest in the idea of voluntary restraint in the use of the veto.

Two trends seem to be at play here. First, the deepening international consensus on R2P and the protection of civilians in armed conflict is creating new expectations about the Council's role in responding to genocide and mass atrocity crimes. Sentiments expressed in the General Assembly demonstrate a very clear – if still emerging – expectation that the Council has a responsibility to take reasonable measures to protect populations from atrocity crimes. Second, as the Council becomes more proactive, and especially as it turns to more robust measures to protect civilians from genocide and atrocity crimes, demands for accountability are becoming more significant. By accountability we mean the extent to which states follow mandates established by the Security Council; the answerability of states acting on these mandates, to the Security Council; and the procedures in place to deal with situations where states were deemed to breach mandates. These two, seemingly divergent, trends are connected inasmuch as that further deepening of consensus on the use of force or other coercive means for protection purposes – a seemingly necessary response to underlying normative shifts in international society – will require steps to address the question of accountability. With that in mind, this chapter examines the evolution of these two trends in the context of the Syrian crisis and recent discussion about the concept of 'responsibility while protecting' (RWP), proposed by Brazil to remedy problems it saw with the implementation of Resolution 1973 on Libya.[5]

Divided counsels on Syria

It is commonly argued that concerns arising from the implementation of Council Resolution 1973 on Libya prevented international society from adopting a robust response to the crisis in Syria.[6] The Council's inability to find consensus on Syria reflects a combination of concerns specific to that case and issues relating to the use of force for protection purposes more broadly. It resulted in the vetoing of three draft Security Council resolutions by China and Russia. The wider crisis in Syria has been well documented elsewhere and so need not detain us here. This section briefly examines the background to the three vetoed draft resolutions concerning Syria and their content.

The first draft resolution on Syria came to a vote on 4 October 2011.[7] It recalled the Syrian government's 'primary responsibility to protect' its population from war crimes and crimes against humanity,[8] and condemned the systematic violation of human rights and targeting of civilians by the regime. It demanded that the Syrian government take steps to remedy the problem, including by immediately ceasing violations of human rights, ending the use of force against civilians, alleviating the humanitarian situation, and allowing safe return for the displaced. It also called for an inclusive 'Syrian-led' political process.[9] The most controversial elements of the draft resolution were paragraphs 9 and 11 which, respectively, called for member states to exercise vigilance and restraint in relation to the types of assistance they provided to the Syrian government and expressed the Council's intention to review compliance with the measures within thirty days and adopt further measures under Article 41 of the UN Charter (i.e. sanctions) if necessary. Nine states voted in favour (including African Union members Gabon and Nigeria), four abstained (Brazil, India, Lebanon, and South Africa), and two permanent members voted against (China and Russia).[10] Having achieved the required nine votes, it was the two permanent member vetoes that blocked the draft's adoption.

The second draft resolution was presented for a vote on 4 February 2012,[11] in the context of the suspension of the League of Arab States' (Arab League's) monitoring mission owing to the deteriorating situation in Syria and mounting violence there. Its principal purpose was to support the Arab League Plan of Action to which Damascus had agreed on 2 November 2011. Under the plan, armed and military personnel were to be withdrawn from the streets, Arab League monitors deployed, and both foreign reporters and Arab monitors granted unfettered access. The parties to the conflict also agreed to begin a political process. However, the monitoring mission was suspended when it became clear that none of these terms were being honoured.

There were clear signs that this second draft resolution sought to accommodate some of the concerns expressed by more cautious Council members. Most notably, the draft condemned 'all violence' regardless of its source, in addition to condemning human rights violations by the Syrian regime.[12] It demanded compliance with the Arab League action plan, called for an inclusive Syrian-led political process, and called upon the Syrian government to cooperate with the Arab League. In a further sign that the new draft was trying to accommodate concerns about the earlier text, it contained no explicit reference to potential Article 41 measures, though it did stipulate that the Council would review compliance within twenty-one days and consider 'further measures' if necessary.[13] This draft secured thirteen positive votes, including those of two of the most strident critics of the NATO-led intervention in Libya: India and South Africa. Other notable supporters of the resolution were Pakistan, Togo, and Azerbaijan. However, two permanent members, China and Russia, again cast negative votes, blocking its adoption.[14]

The Council's failure to reach consensus prompted renewed diplomatic efforts. On 23 February 2012, Kofi Annan was appointed as the first joint UN–Arab League Envoy, charged with assisting the Syrian parties to reach a negotiated settlement. The result was a six-point plan, which the Syrian government agreed on 27 March to implement. The six points were: (1) work with the envoy in an inclusive Syrian-led political process; (2) stop the fighting and achieve urgently an effective UN-supervised cessation of armed violence in all its forms by all; (3) ensure timely provision of humanitarian assistance to all areas affected by the fighting; (4) intensify the pace and scale of release of arbitrarily detained persons; (5) ensure freedom of movement throughout the country for journalists and a non-discriminatory visa policy for them; and (6) respect freedom of association and the right to demonstrate peacefully as legally guaranteed.[15]

The Council then adopted two resolutions by consensus, Resolutions 2042 (2012) and 2043 (2012),[16] which voiced support for the plan and mandated the deployment of an observer mission, the UN Supervision Mission (UNSMIS), to report on compliance. When the Syrian government dragged its feet, a ceasefire intended to come into effect on 10 April in fact commenced on 14 April.

It was immediately apparent, however, that neither side was complying with the agreement. Syrian government forces refused to cease firing and withdraw unless the rebels did so first, and the Syrian armed opposition made precisely the same argument and even launched offensives at some points along the front line. On 1 May, the UN's Under Secretary-General for Peacekeeping, Herve Ladsous, reported that both sides had violated the ceasefire.[17] Attempts to persuade the parties to implement the agreement limped on, but on 25 May regime-backed militia killed over 100 civilians in Houla, prompting an outpouring of international condemnation.[18] The Council issued a press statement condemning the attack and assigning responsibility to the Syrian government. The Free Syrian Army reacted by stepping up its offensive and the regime responded in early June by vowing to crush 'anti-regime elements', effectively terminating the ceasefire and with it the Annan plan.

Within this context of a rapidly deteriorating situation and generalized non-compliance with the Annan plan, a third draft resolution was tabled in July to indicate the Council's resolve and introduce the possibility of enforcement measures against the government in the event of its continued disregard of the Council's past demands.[19] The key elements of this draft were a general demand that the parties immediately implement all aspects of the six-point plan, a demand that all parties – including the opposition – cease all armed violence, and the extension of UNSMIS's mandate by forty-five days. Most controversially, draft paragraph 4 'decided' that the Syrian government should verifiably implement its commitments to cease troop movements towards population centres, cease use of heavy weapons in these centres, and pull back military concentrations in and around such centres. The draft resolution gave the government ten days to comply and requested that the Secretary-General report to the Council on compliance. It also warned that in the event of non-compliance, the Council would adopt measures under Article 41 of the Charter. The draft text secured eleven affirmative votes, including those of India, Morocco, and Togo. Pakistan and South Africa abstained, while China and Russia again voted against the resolution.[20]

In summary, the story of the Council's failure to respond effectively during the early stages of the crisis in Syria revolves around these vetoed resolutions. However, this is not simply a story of the Council refusing to take up its protection responsibilities or a more general backtracking on the part of international society. This is clear for two reasons. First, interwoven into the story told above were moments of consensus: two states adopted resolutions supporting a peace plan self-consciously aimed at addressing the 'legitimate grievances' of the Syrian people[21] and a press statement condemning the massacre of civilians in Houla.

Second, and perhaps more interestingly, there is another story to tell: the General Assembly's response to the crisis in Syria and, in particular, its response to the Council's actions. An additional sign that the Council's inability to reach a consensus on timely and decisive action in Syria is not a product of a wider political backlash against human protection and the use of robust measures to achieves its goals is that the General Assembly resoundingly endorsed many of the measures proposed for Syria that were blocked in the Council. On 16 February 2012, two weeks after the second vetoed draft resolution, the General Assembly voted by 137 to 12 (with 17 abstentions) to adopt a resolution which contained much of the text from the rejected Council draft. The General Assembly resolution 'strongly condemned' the 'widespread and systematic violations of human rights and fundamental freedoms by the Syrian authorities', called on all armed groups to put an immediate end to violence and reprisals, supported the Arab League's peace initiative, and called on the Secretary-General to lend his support.[22] Among the states voting against the resolution were Russia, China, North Korea, Iran, Syria itself, Zimbabwe, and Venezuela. Interestingly, for our purposes, among those states that supported the resolution were some of the most strident critics of the NATO-led intervention in Libya, including Brazil, India, South Africa, and Pakistan.

A few months later, on 3 August 2012 – a day after Kofi Annan announced his decision to resign as the joint envoy for Syria, citing the parties' unwillingness to abide by their commitments and the Council's inability to impose consequences on the parties for non-compliance – the General Assembly adopted a second resolution on the situation in Syria, again by a huge majority of 132 votes to 12.[23] This resolution, principally drafted by Qatar and Saudi Arabia, proved somewhat more controversial than the first because it heaped all its criticism on the Syrian authorities and did not condemn atrocities committed by opposition groups, a problem identified especially by India. Significantly, the resolution 'deplored' the failure of the Council to adopt measures on Syria,[24] sending a clear signal that the Council's position did not reflect that of the wider UN membership. The controversy over the lack of even-handedness created more abstentions (31), including those of India and Pakistan, than in the first vote, but no more negative votes. Despite these concerns, however, Brazil and South Africa voted in favour of the resolution.

For our purposes, there are two key points that stem from this discussion. First, there are indeed heightened sensitivities about the use of coercion against member states as a tool of human protection but these do not necessarily represent a backtracking on commitments to human protection or a wholesale rejection of coercion as a potential instrument of protection in some cases. Second, Council members want to ensure the proper calibration and accountability of measures adopted by the Council and are concerned that some might interpret loosely worded mandates in an expansive fashion to justify policies of regime change sometimes only tangentially linked to human protection. There are therefore good grounds for thinking, as Gareth Evans does,[25] that without efforts to address these accountability concerns, it will be difficult to move towards a deeper consensus on timely and decisive responses to atrocity crimes – especially when the principal perpetrator is the state itself.

Responsibility while protecting

One useful way of thinking about the lessons that need to be learnt about the design and oversight of mandates to use force in order to protect populations in the wake of the controversy over Libya can be found in some aspects of the concept of RWP championed by Brazil. The concept was proposed first by Brazilian President Dilma Rousseff at the September 2011 plenary of the General Assembly. The Brazilian Permanent Mission to the UN circulated a note outlining the concept in more detail towards the end of 2011,[26] and co-hosted an informal dialogue in February 2012. Although there was some initial scepticism among some Western states, who saw the concept as an attempt to derail implementation of R2P, the initiative was widely welcomed, including by the Secretary-General, for providing fresh ideas to stimulate discussion about how to implement those most controversial aspects of human protection that relate to coercion and the use of force.

In relation to the issues of accountability mentioned earlier, there are three particularly important elements of this concept: decision-making criteria for the use of force; the provision of judicious analysis to guide decision-making; and the establishment of an accountability mechanism to oversee the Council's work.

Decision-making criteria

The concept of RWP revived long-standing proposals for the development of criteria to guide Council decision-making about the use of force. A proposal for such criteria was a centrepiece of the 2001 report of the International Commission on Intervention and State Sovereignty (ICISS), which coined the phrase 'responsibility to protect',[27] but the idea – and some of the criteria – had been aired two years earlier by British Prime Minister Tony Blair as part of his 'doctrine of the international community'.[28] These two sets of advocates articulated the need for criteria on very different bases.

First, from the perspective of the Brazilian government, Gareth Evans,[29] and others, criteria to guide decision-making guard against the abuse, misuse, or over-extension of Council mandates by ensuring that the Council adopts resolutions for the correct reasons and that there is a shared understanding among Council members of what has been agreed to. Second, from the perspective of Blair,[30] and to some extent ICISS,[31] criteria help establish a legitimate basis – founded on agreed principles – upon which to advance the case for armed intervention for human protection purposes. By this logic, once there is agreement on the principle of the need for action in the face of mass killing and on the relevant prudential checks, it becomes more difficult to justify the blocking of collective action when those conditions are met.

Although decision-making criteria have been widely taken as the centrepiece of RWP, including by Brazil itself in 2012,[32] the concept note which set out the concept in 2011 did not in fact spell out a list of criteria. Rather, it limited itself to proposing some common principles, some of which – such as 'prevention is always the best policy'[33] – were clearly not intended as decision-making criteria. Nonetheless, it is possible to discern some such criteria in the Brazilian concept note. Table 6.1 compares these with the criteria proposed by Blair and ICISS.

Table 6.1   Proposals for decision-making criteria (1999–2011)

Blair 1999	ICISS 2001	Brazil 2011
Just cause (are we sure of our case?)	Just cause (large scale loss of life/ethnic cleansing)	—
Last resort (have we exhausted peaceful means?)	Last resort (non-military measures must have been explored)	Last resort (exhaust all peaceful means)
Prudence (are there sensible military options?)	Reasonable prospects (good chance of success)	—
Long-term commitment (are we committed for the long term?)	—	—
National interests	—	—
—	Right intention (purpose must be humanitarian)	—
—	Proportional means (scale of military action should be minimum needed)	Use of force must produce as little violence as possible/must be proportionate/judicious
—	Right authority (Security Council, General Assembly, regional organization)	Right authority (Security Council or in exceptional circumstances General Assembly)
—	Operational principles (clear objectives, coordination, proportionate rules of engagement, etc.)	—
—	—	Use of force strictly limited to that which is authorized

Despite suggestions that RWP is an echo of the ICISS notion of R2P, direct overlap is limited to the 'last resort' and 'proportionality' criteria, arguably two of the most problematic when applied in a *jus ad bellum* context. On the question of 'right authority', both were notably more permissive than what the General Assembly agreed in 2005 and the Secretary-General advanced thereafter; they differed in the important respect that the ICISS countenanced the possibility that armed intervention might be legitimate even if not authorized by the Council or General Assembly. What is more, Brazil's president, Dilma Rousseff, sharply contradicted her own government's concept note when, at the opening of the 67th General Assembly in September 2012, she insisted that 'the use of force without authorization by the Council is illegal, yet it is beginning to be regarded in some quarters as an acceptable option. This is by no means the case.'[34] This was a remarkable statement given that only eleven months earlier Brazil had written to the Secretary-General that the General Assembly too, could, 'in exceptional circumstances', authorize the use of force. But it further distinguished RWP from ICISS.

Before assessing the capacity of decision-making criteria to improve accountability, it is important to stress that they enjoy relatively little political support and that what support they do have evaporates very quickly when discussion turns to what specific criteria should be used and what baselines for assessment should be employed. Key opponents of criteria have included three (US, China, Russia) of the five permanent members of the Council (P5), India, several Asian states, and even some progressive Europeans, though their reasons for scepticism were quite different.[35]

Whatever their intuitive appeal, there are few grounds for thinking that criteria would help to address concerns about accountability. First, in terms of crystallizing understanding of the circumstances in which force might be needed – and legitimate (the ostensible purpose of the ICISS's 'just cause' thresholds) – it seems reasonable to suggest that the R2P principle already achieves this goal by defining the atrocity crimes that give rise to the special responsibilities it enumerates. This perhaps explains why Brazil did not include 'just cause' thresholds among its criteria. The 2005 World Summit Outcome Document identified the crimes that governments had a responsibility to protect populations from and the circumstances in which that responsibility ought to be taken up by the international community, acting through the Council. In the Outcome Document, member states agreed that they have a responsibility to protect their populations from genocide, war crimes, ethnic cleansing, and crimes against humanity, and that the Council should stand ready to take up this responsibility, on a case-by-case basis, in situations where a government is 'manifestly failing' to protect its own population.[36] There is broad agreement that the Council should be engaged in such circumstances. For example, the Chinese government's 2005 position paper on UN reform agreed that 'massive humanitarian' crises were 'the legitimate concern of the international community'.[37]

Of course, agreement on the relevant crimes does not guarantee agreement on whether the thresholds have been breached and the most appropriate response in actual cases. This problem was raised throughout the ICISS consultation process and has been aired many times since.[38] It has also been evident in practice: in relation to Darfur, governments more or less agreed on the gravity of the threat but disagreed about the most appropriate course of action and the responsibility of the Sudanese government;[39] on Syria, the P5 disagreed about whether one side (the government) was primarily responsible or whether blame – and hence punitive action – should be shared more evenly among the armed actors.

What is more, even if voluntary recognition of criteria – and shared understandings of them – could be negotiated, there is little reason for confidence that criteria would serve the goals of accountability. In the hands of skilled diplomats, criteria would likely merely become the language used to justify predetermined positions. Indeed, in classroom exercises undergraduate students have proven capable of plausibly arguing the case for and against intervention in Kosovo and Syria by reference to criteria. Thus, in a case such as Syria, it is hard to the point of fanciful to suppose that the protagonists in the Council would employ the criteria for any other purpose than to justify their own positions. The problem is exacerbated by the fact that some criteria – precisely those on which ICISS and Brazil agreed – such as 'last resort' are vague in the extreme and open to subjective interpretation, and others, especially 'proportionality', are impossible to calculate with any degree of precision prior to the use of force (and difficult and subjective even afterwards when all the data is in). This has long been understood in the tradition of thought from which they arose: the Christian Just War tradition.

Therefore, neither criterion provides meaningful external benchmarks except, perhaps, in the most extreme of cases, such as Rwanda, and even then actual lived history shows that there remain grounds for arguing that there are viable alternatives to the use of force. Given this, it is difficult to see how criteria would have helped to avoid the controversies stemming from the implementation of Resolution 1973. The only obvious way in which criteria might have had this effect would have been by providing additional arguments and legitimacy to those governments that were uncomfortable with the resolution. Perhaps Russia and China could have used criteria to argue that the 'last resort' had not been found or that NATO's proposed action was disproportionate. In such a scenario, criteria would not have produced 'responsible protection'; it would have led to the people of Benghazi and elsewhere receiving no protection at all.

There is a counter-argument here that by setting clear thresholds for action, criteria may actually make it more difficult for states to oppose decisive action in clear cases of genocide and mass atrocities. There is not much evidence, however, to suggest that the thresholds could limit the use of the veto. In relation to the crisis in Darfur, it was suggested that Russia and China might have been 'compelled' into abstaining on a resolution authorizing intervention had such a proposal been backed by arguments grounded in shared criteria.[40] Actual voting behaviour regarding Darfur, as well as the more recent performance of Russia and China in relation to Syria, suggests that this may be wishful thinking, however. China's performance in the Council regarding the situation in Darfur suggests that it would have been more than willing to use its veto: China threatened to veto measures far less intrusive than non-consensual military intervention, such as comprehensive targeted sanctions and no-fly zones. Likewise, in relation to the situation in Syria, both Russia and China have defied large majorities in the Council and General Assembly and even voted against measures to encourage compliance with their own earlier demands (when they vetoed a resolution threatening sanctions for non-compliance with the Annan plan). Criteria could hardly be expected to alter geopolitical calculations in these cases. It is much more likely that they would simply add an extra layer of argument in defence of predetermined positions.

Moreover, when considered more systematically, the whole issue of criteria seems disconnected from the main point of concern that many member states have: the question of accountability. On that score, criteria would only rule out the blatantly obvious abuses – of which we can think of no clear examples in the Council's history; after all the Council refused US entreaties regarding Iraq without the need for criteria – and ruled in the most obvious of genocides. Again, Rwanda stands out as an example, but at the time even this was disputed; debate raged about whether the killing was part of the civil war or whether it was genocidal. Although we are all wise with hindsight, at the time even several NGOs on the ground in Rwanda were reluctant to categorize what they were seeing as genocide until several weeks into the killing. Given the immense amount of political capital that would be required to secure agreement on criteria and the limited potential gains in terms of accountability, this element of responsible protection seems less than propitious.

Judicious analysis

A second key element of Brazil's concept note on RWP was its call for judicious analysis in advance of decisions to use force. The note argued that the 'use of force must ... be preceded by a comprehensive and judicious analysis of the possible consequences of military action on a case-by-case basis'.[41] This is entirely sensible. Decision-making is clearly improved if it is based on a solid understanding of the situation at hand and likely consequences of different potential courses of action. Moreover, anything that can help the Council reach a shared understanding of the situation can assist in building a united approach to the problem. However, the UN Secretary-General's first Special Adviser on R2P, Edward Luck, detected in RWP the potential for further delaying action in response to atrocity crimes, with this demand for 'judicious' analysis chief among the factors that could be used to promote delay.[42] While information and assessment are necessary components of decision-making, building a 'judicious' assessment can take months, if not years. Further delay would be caused by the proliferation of competing assessments from different member states and other interested parties. The time required to conduct 'judicious' analysis and pit it against alternative assessments gives those states that would be opposed to decisive action a route by which to delay action indefinitely while claiming to be acting in a manner consistent with R2P. An additional problem is that states may simply refer to their own analysis, thereby entrenching and formalizing existing divisions.

There are three ways around these potential pitfalls. First, and most obviously, the requirement for analysis to be 'judicious' should be rethought. International events, especially those characterized by armed conflict and mass atrocities, are simply too fast-paced and fluid to permit truly 'judicious' analysis. The response of any government to a pressing international crisis is seldom properly described as 'judicious' and so it makes little sense to impose on the Security Council a standard of analysis which no government would expect of itself.

Second, to ensure that the burden of analysis is not entirely directed at forestalling international action, analysis should also include assessment of the possible consequences of *not* taking military action and the likely consequences of a range of other potential measures.

Third, to avoid the proliferation of analyses each claiming to be authoritative the Council should look to the UN Secretariat to provide it with the assessments it needs. As the UN system's repository of expertise on the prevention of genocide and mass atrocities, the UN's Office on Genocide Prevention and R2P would be the most promising candidate to provide this sort of advice to the Council on request and through the Special Advisers. The Office would be able to draw upon its regional experts to provide analysis of the consequences of various courses of action but its analytical capacity would need to be augmented. With greater expertise regarding their own regions, relevant regional arrangements could also feed their analysis of a situation and likely consequences of different courses of action into this process.

Accountability mechanism

The Brazilian concept note calls for 'enhanced Security Council procedures' to 'monitor and assess the manner in which resolutions are interpreted and implemented to ensure responsibility while protecting',[43] and for the Council to ensure 'the accountability of those to whom authority is granted to resort to force'.[44] These are important considerations if the Council is to continue to play an active role in the protection of populations from atrocity crimes. Council resolutions generally do contain reporting requirements, as indeed Resolution 1973 did, but there is concern that these requirements are not sufficiently complied with. For example, there was little transparency in the way in which NATO reported its activities in Libya to the Secretary-General during its Libyan campaign. Moreover, when the Libyan regime made entreaties about a negotiated ceasefire, NATO rejected those entreaties out of hand, without first discussing the issue with the Council.[45] This raised concerns among some Council members that, in effect, NATO had assumed control over the intervention, denying the Council the primacy on the issue that it is entitled to by virtue of the Charter.[46]

Brazil's calls for strengthened procedures to allow the Council to hold to account states that act on its mandate flow directly from the Libya experience. However, although there is clear merit in the argument for stronger accountability, there are problems with Brazil's initial proposal for special mechanisms to govern R2P enforcement operations. First, the UN Charter gives to the Council wide flexibility in terms of the actions it can take in pursuit of its primary responsibility for international peace and security and deliberately makes the Council self-regulating. This has allowed the Council to be innovative when it has needed to be and has helped the Council find consensus when that has proven difficult. New permanent mechanisms to regulate the Council would require a change to the Charter, which could have unintended negative consequences. Second, the Council's responsibility covers international peace and security and not just R2P cases. It would make no practical sense to have one set of rules for some Chapter VII resolutions on the use of force and another set for others – not least because 'R2P' cases could be easily re-labelled. Third, the UN has had bad experience in the past with excessive political interference in military matters. The experience of the UN Protection Force (UNPROFOR) in Bosnia is testament to what can happen when the Council tries to micromanage military operations. Fourth, excessive political requirements might inhibit states from implementing Council mandates by pushing them to the view that they cannot translate a resolution into a viable military strategy that they can sell to their publics. This would reduce implementation of Council mandates, weakening the Council's credibility and legitimacy, and inhibiting protection.

These problems should not mean that nothing be done to improve accountability. Clearly, the Council itself needs to engage in dialogue – informally at first – about how to improve this accountability loop. Instead of a new layer of procedural rules, the Council should make use of the powers it already has by writing specific accountability measures into its resolutions. The Council has already developed a strong repertoire of accountability measures that might be appropriated. One way forward may be to foster informal dialogue on the various accountability measures that the Council already has at its disposal and to inform non-permanent members in particular about what these measures are and when they might be employed.

Five such measures might be included. The first is to include *sunset clauses* in Council resolutions. This would make authorizations to use force time-limited, forcing states acting on mandates to return to the Council for a renewal. This is standard practice for UN peace-keeping operations and helps build an accountability loop. Current practice with peacekeeping operations is for a duration of six months or one year for each case. This requires that each operation remains on the agenda of the Council, with the need for a further vote in order to decide whether or not to renew or to end it. In cases regarding the use of force, an initial resolution could require a shorter time frame in order to assess the progress of each case – one or two months – which would compel states carrying out the mandate to justify progress, while at the same time enabling Council members to consider questions around mandate fulfilment.

Related to this is the second suggestion – to include *specific and frequent reporting requirements*. The Council can, and does, require reports from those acting on its mandates. In the case of Libya, Resolution 1973 required that implementing states report their activities to the Secretary-General.[47] In future, the Council might also require that the Secretary-General brief it on these reports or demand that implementing states report directly to the Council. It would be reasonable to make considerations about renewal of mandates on the basis of such reports. This would compel more transparency from states committed to carrying out mandates, and would also require them to justify specific actions carried out to fulfil such mandates. It would also be an opportunity for both the Council and states committed to action to reflect on the unfolding circumstances of any given operation, taking into account questions around proportionality and unintended consequences.

The third suggestion is for the Council to include *specific limitations* to rule out certain courses of action. For example, Resolution 1973 forbade the deployment of ground troops as an occupying force in Libya. The inclusion of such limitations could be a means to assure sceptical governments that boundaries will be placed around the use of force. Providing clearer guidelines around the precise limits of military action would inevitably make clearer the question of whether or not mandate overreach actually occurs.

The fourth suggestion is *direct action*: the Council might directly mandate or require diplomatic activity, the dispatch of envoys, or acceptance of negotiated agreements – that is, should it wish to ensure that diplomacy be continued, the Council could simply mandate it. It could, for example, nominate its own envoy and determine that states acting under its mandates must facilitate the work of that envoy.

And the fifth suggestion is to mandate *information gathering*: to supplement or replace reporting from implementing states, the Council might mandate its own fact-finding missions to gather information about the implementation of its mandates. Fact-finding missions are already deployed for a range of reasons, including for the purposes of investigating widespread human rights violations and identifying possible cases of mass atrocity perpetration or the risk of future perpetration. Similarly, it could authorize fact-finding missions to supplement information proved by states carrying out mandates, ensuring that such information is fair and balanced, and takes into account a broad range of actors relevant to any particular situation.

Pursuing this route to greater accountability would reduce the likelihood of unintended negative consequences, would allow the tailoring of accountability measures to individual circumstances, and would make use of the Council's existing authority under the UN Charter.

Conclusion

The Council's response to the crisis in Syria ought to be viewed in the wider context of its evolving practice on human protection and its general history and politics. As Edward Luck explained, the Council's efforts are constrained and shaped by two conditions: there are some problems that do not have feasible near-term solutions; and the Council is 'not above the vagaries of international politics. Indeed it is all about politics: local, national, regional and global.'[48] As a result, from case to case the Council is inconsistent and unpredictable and it is not always possible to draw clear connections between its handling of different situations. Such inconsistencies – inevitable given the nature of the Council and of international order – should not blind us, however, to the deeper, longer-term transformations in the Council's practice, chief among which is the rise to prominence of human protection, in part facilitated by R2P. As the Council has become more assertive in the field of human protection – an assertiveness increasingly demanded by the international community more broadly, as evidenced by the General Assembly's position on the Council's response to the crisis in Syria – so too have demands arisen for greater accountability. This is to be expected, as the more active the Council becomes, the more UN member states will want to ensure that it acts for the common good.

In that regard, the concept of 'responsibility while protecting' marks a useful contribution to thinking about how best to balance the Council's protection responsibilities with increasing demands for accountability. Drawing on this concept, we argue that the best approaches to strengthening the Council's accountability in relation to use of force for protection purposes would be to strengthen the flow of information and analysis from the UN Secretariat to the Council and to improve the Council's own working practices to enhance oversight of its mandates and accountability.

Notes

1. Siobhan Wills, *Protection of Civilians* (Oxford: Oxford University Press, 2011).
2. UN Multidimensional Integrated Stabilization Mission in Mali.
3. UN Security Council Resolution 2149 (10 April 2014).
4. UN Mission in the Republic of South Sudan.
5. 'Responsibility While Protecting: Elements for the Development and Promotion of a Concept' in UN Doc. A/66/551-S/2011/701 (11 November 2011) *Letter dated 9 November 2011 from the Permanent Representative of Brazil to the United Nations addressed to the Secretary-General*, Annex.
6. For example, Ramesh Thakur, 'R2P after Libya and Syria: Engaging Emerging Powers', *The Washington Quarterly*, 36, no. 2 (2013), p. 62.
7. UN Doc. S/2011/612 (4 October 2011).
8. S/2011/612, p. 1 (preamble).
9. S/2011/612, para. 5.
10. UN Doc. S/PV.6627 (4 October 2011), p. 2.
11. UN Doc. S/2012/77 (4 February 2012).
12. S/2012/77, para. 3.
13. S/2012/77, para. 15.
14. UN Doc. S/PV.6711 (4 February 2012), p. 2.
15. See UN Security Council Resolution 2042 (2012), Annex: Six-Point Proposal of the Joint Special Envoy of the United Nations and the League of Arab States.
16. UN Security Council Resolution 2042 (14 April 2012) and Security Council Resolution 2043 (21 April 2012).
17. 'Herve Ladsous, Under-Secretary-General for Peacekeeping Operations, Press Conference, 1 May 2012. Near verbatim transcript.' United

Nations Public Affairs Section (1 May 2012). Available at: http://www. un.org/en/peacekeeping/articles/usg_ladsous_press_conf01052012.pdf, accessed 5 May 2014.

18. For example, 'Annan condemns "appalling crime" on Syria visit as Damascus denies Houla killings', *Al Arabiya News* (28 May 2012), Available at http://english.alarabiya.net/articles/2012/05/28/217134. html, accessed 5 May 2014.

19. UN Doc. S/2012/538 (19 July 2012).

20. S/PV.6810 (19 July 2012), p. 2.

21. See point 1 of Annan's Six-Point plan: SC Res. 2042 (2012), Annex.

22. UN General Assembly Resolution 66/253 (21 February 2012).

23. GA Res. 66/253 B (7 August 2012).

24. GA Res. 66/253 B, para 11.

25. Gareth Evans, 'Responding to Atrocities: The New Geopolitics of Intervention' in, *SIPRI Yearbook 2012: Armaments, Disarmament and International Security* (Oxford: Oxford University Press for the Stockholm International Peace Research Institute, 2012), pp. 15–38.

26. 'Responsibility While Protecting: Elements for the Development and Promotion of a Concept' in UN Doc. A/66/551-S/2011/701 (11 November 2011) *Letter dated 9 November 2011 from the Permanent Representative of Brazil to the United Nations addressed to the Secretary-General*, Annex.

27. International Commission on Intervention and State Sovereignty (ICISS), *The Responsibility to Protect: Report of the International Commission on Intervention and State Sovereignty* (Ottawa: International Development Research Centre, 2001).

28. Tony Blair, 'Doctrine of the International Community', Chicago, 24 April 1999, Available at: www.britishpoliticalspeech.org/speech-archive.htm?speech=279

29. Evans, 'R2P after Libya and Syria'.

30. Blair, 'Doctrine of the International Community'.

31. ICISS, *The Responsibility to Protect.*

32. See the statement of Her Excellency Ambassador Maria Luiza Ribeiro Viotti, Permanent Representative of Brazil to the United Nations, delivered during the General Assembly's annual dialogue on the responsibility to protect, 5 September 2012, Available at: responsibilitytoprotect.org/Brazil(1).pdf.

33. 'Responsibility While Protecting' in UN Doc. A/66/551-S/2011/701 (11 November 2011).

34. Statement by Her Excellency Dilma Rousseff, President of the Federative Republic of Brazil, at the Opening of the General Debate at the 67th Session of the United Nations General Assembly, New York,

25 September 2012, Available at: http://gadebate.un.org/sites/default/files/gastatements/67/BR_en.pdf

35. Jennifer M. Welsh, 'Conclusion: Humanitarian Intervention after 11 September' in Jennifer M. Welsh (ed.), *Humanitarian Intervention and International Relations* (Oxford: Oxford University Press, 2004), p. 180.

36. GA Res. 60/1 (24 October 2005), para. 139.

37. *Position Paper of the People's Republic of China on the United Nations Reforms*, 8 June 2005, Available at: http://www.china.org.cn/english/government/131308.htm

38. See Thomas G. Weiss and Don Hubert, *The Responsibility to Protect: Supplementary Volume to the Report of the International Commission on Intervention and State Sovereignty* (Ottawa: IDRC, 2001), pp. 351–352.

39. Alex J. Bellamy, 'Responsibility to Protect or Trojan Horse? The Crisis in Darfur and Humanitarian Intervention after Iraq', *Ethics and International Affairs*, 19, no. 2 (2005), pp. 31–54.

40. Nicholas J. Wheeler and Justin Morris, 'Justifying the Iraq War as a Humanitarian Intervention: The Cure is Worse than the Disease' in Ramesh Thakur and Waheguru Pal Singh Sidhu (eds), *The Iraq Crisis and World Order* (Tokyo: UN University Press, 2006), pp. 444–463: p. 460.

41. 'Responsibility While Protecting' in UN Doc. A/66/551-S/2011/701 (11 November 2011), para. 7.

42. Opening statement by Edward C. Luck, Special Adviser to the UN Secretary-General on the Responsibility to Protect at the 'Informal Discussion on the Responsibility While Protecting Initiative' Organized by the Permanent Mission of Brazil, New York, 21 February 2012, Available at: http://www.globalr2p.org/media/files/edluckrwp.pdf, accessed 4 May 2014.

43. Opening statement by Edward C. Luck, para. 11(h).

44. Opening statement by Edward C. Luck, para 11(i).

45. 'Libya: Rebels and Nato dismiss Gaddafi ceasefire offer', *BBC News* (30 April 2011), Available at: http://www.bbc.co.uk/news/world-africa-13249923, accessed 4 May 2014.

46. Discussed in Alex J. Bellamy and Paul D. Williams, 'The New Politics of Protection: Cote d'Ivoire, Libya and the Responsibility to Protect', *International Affairs*, 87, no. 4 (2011), esp. p. 847.

47. UN Security Council Resolution 1973 (17 March 2011), paras. 4 (relating to protection of civilians) and 8 (relating to no-fly zone).

48. Edward C. Luck, *The Security Council* (London: Routledge, 2006), pp. 7–8.

7
Consistency and Complications

Should international society aim for consistency of action in situations where it does authorize humanitarian intervention? It is unlikely that consistency of response to such extreme cases where atrocities are perpetrated and peaceful means are inadequate will ever be possible. Nor is it the case that consistency – understood as using the same measures in different cases – is necessarily desirable. Every case is different, and involves different sets of local, national, and geopolitical actors. As such, some degree of selectivity and inconsistency is not only inevitable, it is necessary.[1] In the rare cases where humanitarian intervention becomes a feasible option for confronting impending or unfolding atrocities, its precise character will always be different. The calculus of context-driven demands, political will, and geopolitical dynamics never precisely align across cases, rendering impossible the prospect of consistency. Even if international society were able to guarantee a constant level of political will in all cases, an unlikely proposition given the commitment of states to their decision-making sovereignty, the contextually specific nature of environments where atrocities are committed provokes unique challenges that require carefully tailored responses from a variety of different actors.

If there is one aspect of humanitarian intervention that does yield consistency, it is in the fact that all cases where the use of force is used without the consent of the state concerned will generate significant complications that are often felt for years. However well crafted, it is inevitable that foreign intervention will have profound implications for states and communities in ways that go beyond the original intent of the action. Indeed, many of the long-term implications are unforeseen at the point of intervention, products of the 'fog of war' described by Clausewitz. Thus, while foreign interventions can save lives in the immediate term, they can also provoke longer-term instability. This potential needs to be understood and managed.

The purpose of this chapter is twofold: to explore the problem of consistency; and to identify the often unforeseen complications that arise from cases of humanitarian intervention. Humanitarian intervention should not be viewed in isolation to a range of measures that can and are adopted in response to cases of impending and unfolding atrocities, most of which are non-coercive in character. We argue that while humanitarian interventions have sometimes been instrumental in halting atrocities, it is impossible to avoid the sometimes negative implications that deploying the use of force brings about. By contrast, other measures, institutions, and practices contained within the human protection regime, those that are more preventive in character, rarely provoke such complications – though they are not without their own potential risks.[2] Rather than pushing for better and more consistent humanitarian intervention, we argue that a more pragmatic objective is to broaden the capacity for prevention by strengthening the international human protection regime in an effort to reduce the occasions where international society is compelled to consider the need for humanitarian intervention.

The question of consistency

While the Chapter VII responses to the crises in both Libya and Côte d'Ivoire represented significant advances in international thought and practice with respect to human protection, they do not represent a good model for how international responses will take shape (or subsequently have taken shape) in the future. As we observed with relation to Libya in Chapter 4, the decision to intervene was enabled by a combination of factors unlikely to be often repeated. What is more, although the intervention saved lives, it bequeathed a much more mixed legacy to Libya. The fact that international responses to different crises is not consistent has been a common point of critique, with critics pointing out that the Security Council's asymmetrical structure, reliant as it is on the consensus of its permanent five members, prevents a more consistent response to crises involving imminent or unfolding atrocities. This criticism was levelled by Noam Chomsky in a 2009 speech during the UN's first informal meeting on the Responsibility to Protect (R2P). Chomsky accused international society of 'selectivity' in terms of international responses to humanitarian crises characterized by atrocities. This, he argued, leads to double standards, where some cases are ignored due to lack of interest, while others are pursued under the pretence of R2P, veiling ulterior motives.[3] It is indeed true that for as long as its permanent members wield the veto, the Security Council will continue to be inconsistent, its decisions driven by a combination of principle, prudential calculations about international peace and security, and judgements about self-interest. We should recognize that even at the level of principle and responsibility, the permanent members face competing demands – indeed, a 'dual responsibility'. As Justin Morris explains, the Security Council's primary responsibility is to international peace and security, not human protection, and there are cases where the demands of the two may not align, forcing states to make difficult choices between these important sets of values.[4]

As a result of this dual responsibility, when it comes to the use of force for human protection perhaps, inconsistency is not only inevitable, it is also necessary. Any response to atrocities will be contingent on a range of factors, including context, political will, and capacity. Circumstances in every case will demand tailored responses. At the same time, both the political will and the capacity of agents to carry out intervention will also vary, meaning that when there is consensus on the need to intervene, the type of response will necessarily reflect these contingencies. We should therefore expect mixed motives; anything else would be unrealistic and generate a stymied politics of protection in which the pursuit of the perfect ruled out the practice of the good. This does at times mean that atrocities are perpetrated without a timely and decisive response by international society, due to a lack of will or because of competing geopolitical interests. Syria provides an unwelcome example of a situation where local complexity, regional competition, and clashing geopolitical interests stymied efforts to protect civilians from atrocities.

Of course, consistency was never part of the agreement on R2P at the 2005 World Summit. Recognition of inconsistency was written into the agreement. The agreed Outcome Document stated that international society was prepared to 'take collective action, in a timely and decisive manner, through the Security Council, in accordance with the Charter, including Chapter VII, *on a case by case basis ...*'[5] In other words, paragraph 139 made it abundantly clear that its intention *was not* to establish an inflexible duty of consistency in response to cases of mass atrocities. To criticize Pillar Three responses for not being consistent is to ignore the original intent that member states expressed with regards to the principle of R2P. Of course, such a stipulation leaves the principle open to accusations of selectivity and double standards – if each case is dealt with differently, what is to prevent international actors from picking and choosing on the basis of national interest rather than concerns over human protection?

This very concern was addressed in the UN Secretary-General's 2012 report on R2P, which focused on this very question of timely and decisive responses to atrocity crimes. Published amid the controversy over the NATO-led intervention in Libya, the Secretary-General offered important insights, with the aim of limiting the possibility of selectivity and double standards. Most importantly, the Secretary-General stressed that while the R2P principle should be applied as consistently as possible, it is imperative that actors tailor their responses according to the 'circumstances on the ground', as well as the 'informed judgement' of the possible implications of such action.[6] Therefore, it would be 'counterproductive', to say the least, to apply the principle in the same way in every situation. Yet the Secretary-General also acknowledged that such variation ran the risk of generating accusations of selectivity and double standards. Although the Security Council will inevitably attract controversy both in its action (as in Libya) and in its lack of action (as in Syria), the Secretary-General pointed out that 'the overall trend has been towards greater Council engagement' when it comes to responding to cases involving human rights violations that contain a high risk of atrocities.[7] Given that human protection involves a far broader array of measures than simply humanitarian intervention, the combination of measures that international society chooses in response to particular crises will never be the same. Moreover, humanitarian intervention is necessarily the last measure to be considered – if one were to uphold a consistent response in all cases, then such interventions would not be a last resort.[8] When confronting atrocities, we should first ask not whether or not there should be armed intervention, but rather what is the most effective way of protecting the vulnerable population.

Much of the recent criticism around inconsistency and double standards came in response to the divergent responses by the Security

Council to crises in Libya and Syria in 2011. The fact that the Security Council did not authorize a no-fly zone over Syria in order to provide greater protection for civilians, who were being targeted by barrel bombs dropped from the air, led some to claim that the principle of R2P was only utilized when it was in the interests of powerful actors to do so. However, there are good prudential as well as political reasons why the responses to these cases were different. First, as we described in Chapter 4, the Security Council's authorization of Resolution 1973 followed appeals by regional actors, namely the League of Arab States (LAS), the Organisation of Islamic Conference (OIC), and the Gulf Cooperation Council (GCC), for the establishment of a no-fly zone. These appeals forced the Security Council to consider the matter, and played a part in preventing the use of veto by Russia or China. Timing was also an issue, concerning the rapid response needed to respond to Gaddafi's threats to target civilians in Benghazi.

Beyond that, a similar response would not have worked in Syria for at least three political and prudential reasons. First, a military response to the escalating violence did not have the support – either overt or tacit – of the permanent members of the Security Council, which meant that any resolution that proposed a Chapter VII response would have been vetoed by Russia and China. In the event, the decision by one side (supporters of the opposition, such as the USA, Saudi Arabia, Turkey, and Qatar) to escalate into civil war prompted a counter-intervention by the other side (Russian intervention in support of Assad). Together, these interventions served only to escalate the level of violence. Second, military action was not supported by every country in the region, as was the case with Libya. The LAS did not issue an appeal to the Security Council, as it had in Syria. It is widely believed that appeals by the LAS and other regional organizations were instrumental in the decisions of both Russia and China opting to not use their veto power with Resolution 1973. The third reason is that Syria had key allies in the region who were openly hostile to the idea of a no-fly zone or another form of Chapter VII intervention and were prepared to provide military support to the Assad regime. Principal among these allies are Russia and Iran, both of whom have provided direct military aid to the Syrian regime. As such, the unfolding crisis in Syria did not yield any clear-cut opportunities to use properly authorized humanitarian intervention as a tool to protect populations. In this context, the resort to force by one side would have produced only an equal and counter-balancing escalation of force by the other, to the further detriment of the civilian population. This does not mean that international society has done nothing about Syria, or that it has failed to agree on anything. Indeed, international actors have attempted to implement a range of measures, both to broker ceasefires and agreements and to provide limited humanitarian protection for civilians in Syria. Tragically, this has not been sufficient to halt atrocities.

Comparing the cases of Syria and Libya, therefore, shows us that not only is 'consistency' impossible – unless we opt for the minimum common denominator, consistency of inaction – but it is also undesirable since the options used in one case would have likely only exacerbated problems in the other. A consistent response does not guarantee a consistent outcome. Indeed, the same international response to such a range of unique crises would guarantee extreme inconsistency in the outcomes, given the contextually specific nature of each situation. And, above all else, human protection is concerned with outcomes.

None of this should be read as an argument that international responses to impending or unfolding atrocities are adequate – indeed, in many cases, they are not. Apart from the civil war in Syria the ongoing atrocities in Somalia, the escalating violence against civilians in South Sudan, and the widespread and systematic human rights violations in North Korea are examples of cases where international responses to unfolding atrocities have been grossly inadequate. As has been pointed out, often inconsistency in such responses arises out of both geopolitical dynamics and a lack of political will. Although the emergence of a human protection regime has seen a growing commitment to halting and preventing atrocities – and underlying shifts in practice (responses to atrocities are more likely and more comprehensive than they once were) – there may always be cases where international responses will either be inadequate or fail to sway the determination of elites to carry out such violence. The question is how does international society reduce the frequency of this and increase the chances of offering protection in some form to vulnerable populations? The answer, we think, lies in strengthening the international human protection regime.

Moreover, the use of force for the purposes of human protection inevitably produces adverse consequences that would not arise with less extreme action. It is to this that we now turn.

Consequences of humanitarian intervention

While the use of force can sometimes save lives imperilled by atrocities, the act of resorting to such an extreme and invasive measure for the purposes of protection inevitably has consequences. In the following section, we discuss two cases of humanitarian intervention – Somalia in 1992–5 and Kosovo in 1999. While both interventions were effective in protecting populations that were under immediate threat of ethnic cleansing (in Kosovo) and human-induced famine (in Somalia), in both instances, the use of force provoked further complications that still affect these countries today.

Somalia

Somalia's descent into state failure and civil war was triggered by the collapse of the Siad Barre regime in early 1991. In the decade leading up to the collapse, Barre's attempts to implement liberal market reforms as part of an International Monetary Fund-imposed structural adjustment programme led to economic chaos.[9] This was compounded by Barre's own repressive leadership, which was characterized by widespread violence against the population. The Somali currency depreciated, foreign debt escalated, and the cash crop economy was no longer able to secure revenue needed to pay for important food staples.[10] Throughout the 1980s, civil war escalated, as armed groups from various parts of the country challenged Barre's regime, eventually toppling it in 1991. At the same time, a severe drought compounded the crisis, leading to famine and the deaths of up to 248,000 people.[11]

In the wake of renewed international concern in humanitarian crises, the UN first authorized the provision of humanitarian relief, and then mandated an enforcement mission with the goal of restoring peace and stability within the country. The UN Operation in Somalia (UNOSOM) was authorized by the Security Council in April 1992. This allowed for a relatively small peacekeeping contingent to land in Somalia to monitor a recently agreed ceasefire between two of the main warlord factions – one led by Mohamed Farrah Aideed, and the other by Ali Mahdi.[12] Yet the ceasefire did not hold, which led the Security Council to consider a more robust operation that invoked Chapter VII of the UN Charter, which mandated an expanded peacekeeping contingent to use force in order to bring about peace and stability. The new contingent was given the name the Unified Task Force in Somalia (UNITAF), which comprised a US-led contingent of 38,000 peacekeepers.[13] Their tasks included clearing the main highways of warlord-controlled checkpoints for the purpose of ensuring protection for aid convoys.[14] From March 1993, the Security Council authorized the establishment of UNOSOM II, an international mission that saw the US-led UNITAF give way to a UN-led international force, which had a similar Chapter VII mandate, with a contingent of 28,000 peacekeepers.[15]

The US-led intervention in Somalia was initiated with the purpose of providing humanitarian relief amid a growing famine in 1992. While UNITAF and UNOSOM II were charged with ensuring a secure environment for aid provision, one dimension of the operation was to secure passage for the provision of humanitarian aid throughout the country, confronting warlords who had apprehended food aid for their own gain. However, in the immediate surrounds of Mogadishu, UNITAF's commander, Robert F. Oakley, initially lent recognition to the city's two main warlords, Aideed and Mahdi, at the expense of other clan leaders, as well as the possibility of a future civilian-led administration.[16] As the US-led mission approached its transfer to UNOSOM II, UNITAF's efforts to incorporate more grassroots involvement in the political process precipitated a deterioration of relations with Aideed.[17] This led to confrontations in the streets, resulting in numerous peacekeeping casualties, including twenty-four dead Pakistani peacekeepers in July 1993, and eighteen dead US soldiers in October of the same year.[18] Subsequently, the USA removed its contingent, as did many European nations, significantly weakening the mission.[19]

The intervention in Somalia had both economic and political implications that further weakened the state and further empowered armed non-state actors. In economic terms, the actors who profited most from the three missions were criminal businessmen and warlords. Both mission personnel and other international humanitarian actors entered an environment where the formal economic system had failed, and had, in the context of civil war, been replaced by what Aisha Ahmad describes as 'tax- and regulation-free trade opportunities in both licit and illicit goods'.[20] This was a situation that favoured criminal businessmen and warlords. At the same time, this new arrangement marginalized established members of the business community, particularly in Mogadishu.[21] It was into this environment that international society injected hundreds of millions of dollars in aid.[22] There is no surprise then, that the groups who were best poised to take advantage of this were businessmen who had connections to different warlord factions.

As Ahmad has pointed out, the economic impact of intervention manifested in two negative ways. First, collusion between warlords and the new criminal business class ensured that contracts related to food aid delivery were won by these coalitions. During famine and state failure, food acted as hard currency, and whoever had it held power. Because various warlords controlled the main roads between cities, any provision of aid had to pass through their checkpoints, which meant that only businesses that could prove they could effectively transport aid through such obstacles would end up with contracts. Thus, only businesses working in partnership with warlord factions were able to demonstrate this. In turn, this helped warlords accumulate sufficient wealth 'to maintain their political power'.[23]

Even after the arrival of the peace enforcement contingents, UNI-TAF, and its successor UNOSOM II, this coalition of illicit traders and warlords continued to prosper. While UNITAF succeeded in clearing the roadblocks and checkpoints established by various warlord factions in late 1992,[24] Aideed's faction proved particularly adept at setting up fake non-governmental organizations to win lucrative contracts. This entailed businessmen creating proposals for aid provision, usually for invented displacement camps. They would then take the proposal to a Somali official working within an aid organization, which, for an agreed kickback would approve the contract.[25] Furthermore, the influx of food aid undermined the country's agricultural sector. While the drought in 1991 severely limited food production at the time, efforts to rebuild the sector were profoundly compromised by the presence of free food, driving down prices and rendering local production unviable. This prompted farmers to cease production, leading some in rural communities to blame the more recent famine in 2011 not on the natural forces, but on 'the destruction of farming'.[26]

All this inevitably had profound political implications for Somalia. Such arrangements allowed the warlord factions to continue their economic dominance and political control of Mogadishu and surrounds, and, as Ahmad argues, 'kept Somalia in a state of perpetual state failure'.[27] The consequence of empowering criminal businessmen and their affiliated warlord factions was the continued flourishing of such armed clan groups, particularly in the wake of UNOSOM II's withdrawal in 1995. New factions emerged from established factions, precipitating further conflict, all of which was financed by the food aid, whose provision was serviced by UNITAF and UNOSOM. Ultimately, this further weakened both state institutions and legitimate businesses that had been originally sidelined after the collapse of Siad Barre's government in 1989.

The intervention in Somalia between 1992 and 1995 undoubtedly exacerbated the instability that led to and followed the collapse of Barre's government. It inadvertently strengthened the hand of warlords like Aideed and Mahdi, and enriched the criminal networks of businessmen tied to them. This then added fuel to inter-clan conflicts. That is not to say that the intervention was not instrumental in mitigating the effects of the human-induced famine – estimates are that the humanitarian relief that operated after transport networks was secured saved the lives of between 10,000 and 15,000 people. Admittedly, this is a small number compared to the lives lost prior to the relief, though the worst effects of the famine had already passed by late 1992.[28] However, the economic and political impacts of the intervention contributed to the erosion of security within a country that continues to endure entrenched conflict and atrocities.[29]

Moreover, as peacekeeping casualties began to mount in 1993, the US contingent rapidly drew down. The failures of UNITAF in particular had a knock-on effect on other humanitarian emergencies, especially Rwanda.[30] The timing of the drawdown of troops is worth noting – US troops left Somalia in August 1993, around the time that plans for a peacekeeping contingent were being drawn up for Rwanda. Indeed, the size of the contingent that Force Commander Roméo Dallaire had requested for the Rwandan mission was twice that of what he eventually was given – the UN Assistance Mission for Rwanda (UNAMIR) was hamstrung from the very beginning of that mission.[31]

Kosovo

The NATO-led intervention in Kosovo was effective in putting an end to the atrocities against the Albanian population which were being committed by the Serbian government. Kosovar Albanians had been subject to nearly three decades of mounting discrimination by Belgrade. This reached its nadir in the 1990s, with the rise of Milosevic and Serb nationalism. Milosevic overturned the 1974 constitution, which had ensured a measure of autonomy for Kosovo. He overthrew elected officials in the province, whose power was then transferred to Belgrade. This preceded a programme of 'Serbianization' in the province, which involved the prohibition of Albanian as an official language; the exclusion of Albanian teachers; the imposition of a Serbian curriculum in schools; and the segregation of Albanians and Serbs in schools. Inevitably, these changes provoked protests throughout Kosovo, which were responded to through repressive state violence. Hundreds of Kosovar Albanians were arrested and tortured; others were routinely and systematically intimidated; and by 1998, thousands were targeted and killed by Serb paramilitary groups.[32] Serbian police routinely engaged in disproportionate violence against the Kosovar Albanian population, while condoning violence committed by Serb groups. One such example was in Donji Prekaz in March 1998, where Serb paramilitaries killed forty people in their attempt to apprehend one member of the Kosovo Liberation Army (KLA).[33] After many similar operations across Kosovo, in the same year, the total number of Albanian casualties from February to October reached 2,000, most of whom were civilians. In the same period, up to 300,000 civilians were forcefully displaced.[34] Overall, from 1996 to 1999, the Serbian security forces, and affiliated militia groups, were culpable of displacing almost the entire Albanian population in Serbia, as well as committing further massacres that resulted in up to 50,000 casualties between 1998 and early 1999.[35] More than three decades of discrimination against the Albanian population in Kosovo escalated to persecution and violence in the 1990s. By 1999, all indications were that this violence would continue to escalate until the entire province was ethnically cleansed of its Albanian population.

It was this ethnic cleansing that provoked an international response characterized by the use of force. By early 1999, approximately 1.5 million Kosovar Albanians had been displaced. More than seventy villages were destroyed, and there were reports of the systematic rape of women and girls by Serbian soldiers.[36] The ethnic cleansing of the Albanians had continued unabated despite warnings from the international community. Finally, in March 1999, after gridlock in the Security Council, NATO led an attack on Serbian forces in Kosovo, as well as in Belgrade, in an effort to force them to end this cleansing. NATO-led airstrikes forced the Serbian government to concede to withdrawing from Kosovo. This then allowed the displaced Albanian population to return to their homes.[37] In terms of halting the Serbian government's ethnic cleansing of the Kosovar Albanian population, the intervention was effective. It was authorized in response to the Serbian government-sponsored ethnic cleansing against the Albanian population; and it managed to stop such atrocities by forcing the Serbian police and army to leave Kosovo.

The NATO bombing began on 24 March 1999 and lasted until 10 June. It followed failed attempts to broker an agreement between the Milosevic government. The KLA's head at the time, Hashim Thaci, eventually agreed to the terms, but the Serbs remained recalcitrant. With the memory of Srebrenica still fresh in the minds of NATO leaders, the intervention proceeded without Security Council authorization, following Russia and China threatening to veto such action. From 10 June, Serbian forces began to withdraw from Kosovo, while the NATO-led Kosovo Force (KFOR) began filling the security vacuum. The Security Council authorized the establishment of the UN Interim Admission in Kosovo (UNMIK), which then became responsible for repatriating refugees, civil administration, security administration, and economic reconstruction.[38]

Yet the NATO-led intervention was not without its complications. The bombings themselves caused approximately 500 civilian deaths, according to Human Rights Watch.[39] Moreover, some of the worst massacres committed by Serbian forces occurred during the bombings, prior to their departure from Kosovo. One such massacre occurred in the village of Meja on 27 April, with up to 377 men and boys killed.[40] In addition, the intervention triggered a cycle of reverse ethnic cleansing that unfolded in the wake of the Serbian withdrawal. Most of the ethnic Serb, Roma, and Turkish population were subsequently driven out of Kosovo, leaving behind an ethnically homogeneous population of ethnic Albanians. While the intervention succeeded in stemming abuses against the Kosovar Albanians, it triggered retributive abuse against other minorities. This violence not only provoked a reverse ethnic cleansing, but it also affected parts of the Albanian community. Such violence unfolded in three stages.

The first stage involved revenge attacks on Serbs and other minorities by returning refugees and KLA fighters. Much of this violence stemmed from perceptions that the Serbs as well as other minorities had collaborated with the government in Belgrade in order to target Albanians. Much of this violence seemed to be revenge-driven, motivated both by their own trauma of displacement and by perceptions that non-Albanian groups had assisted Yugoslav security forces in their persecution of the Albanian population.[41] This retributive violence was largely committed by extremist elements that were claiming to be part of the KLA – gangsters as well as 'angry/traumatised Kosovar Albanian mobs'.[42] Their activities started after the NATO bombing campaign began in March 1999. They staged a number of highly publicized beatings and murders of ethnic Serbs, which led to the mass exodus of 170,000 Serbs, fleeing to both Serbia and Montenegro.[43] In addition to Serbs, Roma groups were also targeted extensively, with a large number of members of this community being murdered, subsequently driving out almost all of this minority group.[44] Members of the Roma community alleged that neither KFOR nor UNMIK showed any concern about this violence.[45]

The second stage involved an intensification of acts of revenge and reverse ethnic cleansing. Such acts were principally committed by certain elements from within the KLA. In the chaos that materialized after the intervention, and after the withdrawal of Serbian security forces, violence often broke out between different Kosovar Albanian groups, on the basis that some had informed on others. At the same time, some KLA members continued with its determination to drive out all remaining Serbs from Kosovo.[46]

In the third stage, violence was committed largely by rogue elements of the KLA – combatants who had refused to relinquish weapons. With the conflict drawing to a close, these groups of former combatants, often with nothing better to do, engaged in criminal activity, 'exploiting the rich pickings of urban Kosovo', mostly in Pristina. The rise in criminal violence is partly a product of the demobilization process. Out of the 10,000 registered combatants within the KLA, 5,000 were incorporated into the newly formed Kosovo Protection Corps, out of which only 3,000 were to serve as full-time members. As the International Crisis Group reported at the time, 'that leaves at least 5,000 battle-hardened men looking for something to do'.[47]

In short, the reverse ethnic cleansing, the rise of criminal gangs, and the late and poorly constructed entry of NATO-led ground forces illustrate how the Kosovo intervention was certainly not absent of complications. Although the UNMIK was effective in laying solid groundwork for institution building and the rebuilding of key infrastructure,[48] there is no indication that the nascent state's continued ethnically homogeneous population will return to its former diverse self.

The interventions in Somalia and in Kosovo were instrumental in protecting populations from famine, war, and ethnic cleansing, yet precipitated other forms of destabilization. This was especially the case in Somalia, where the actions of UNITAF and (albeit to a lesser extent) UNOSOM II empowered warlords and allowed for the flourishing of the criminal economy. In Kosovo, the intervention guaranteed the return of displaced Kosovar Albanians, but inadvertently led to the revenge targeting of ethnic Serbs and other minorities. These examples illustrate the fact that any use of force for the purposes of protection – without government consent – will provoke major consequences. While the aim of such interventions is to protect populations who are being targeted by states or other domestic actors, such interventions themselves are inevitably destabilizing, much more so than non-coercive strategies. Clearly, humanitarian interventions solve some problems, but at the expense of creating others. That is why it is imperative that we understand both the problem of atrocities and the responses to it in a more comprehensive fashion.

The case for prevention

We have argued that, although it can save lives, humanitarian intervention is not a comprehensive response to the problem of atrocities. The sources of atrocity crimes are often deeply rooted and complex and not amenable to temporary external solutions. Armed intervention creates as well as addresses problems. Those with the will to intervene may not be the same actors as those who have the capacity to do so.[49] For example, in the late stages of the Rwandan genocide in June 1994, France was the only state prepared to deploy its forces. But the legitimacy of the French commitment at that particular stage was questioned widely, particularly owing to the fact that they (among other Security Council members) voted in favour of significantly decreasing the size of UNAMIR. That they had suddenly expressed a willingness to deploy troops on short notice invited accusations of their desire to preserve its sphere of influence by supporting the creation of a 'power base' for Hutu refugees who were escaping the victorious Tutsi-led Rwandan Patriotic Front (RPF).[50] In short, the circumstances that might allow for effective humanitarian intervention, the requisite political will, as well as the existence of legitimate actors to carry out such intervention, rarely align.

Yet humanitarian intervention cannot be understood in isolation from non-coercive measures. Indeed, in situations where the risk of atrocities is escalating, the question of prevention should always be the priority, though prevention remains underdeveloped in both theory and practice, especially when compared to intervention. Throughout, we have argued that humanitarian intervention is best understood as falling at one extreme of a spectrum of measures and strategies – most of which are preventive in nature – to confront the risk of atrocities, or to respond to cases of unfolding violence. As part of this broad spectrum, humanitarian intervention cannot be seen as an option to be reliably considered if other measures fail, because as we know, the cumulative circumstances that make intervention a practical consideration rarely coalesce. Humanitarian intervention, more than other non-coercive measures, is contingent upon context, geo-political dynamics, and political will. No matter how effective such interventions have been in protecting populations from the immediate threat of mass atrocities, no such instance in recent history has been without complications. Preventive strategies, by contrast, carry fewer risks.

There are four reasons why the preventive dimension requires urgent attention. First, incorporating a range of preventive strategies alongside reactive options in response to impending and unfolding cases of mass atrocities enables a more context-specific approach. Every situation naturally demands responses that are tailored to its unique circumstances, meaning the more options available, the better chance of fashioning a response that addresses these particular dynamics. Scholarship into the causes of genocide and other forms of mass violence has highlighted just how unique each episode of mass violence is. Jack Goldstone of the Political Instability Task Force, for instance, argued that 'the precise combination of factors by which a particular state becomes "unhappy" may be regarded as specific to that regime'.[51] While commonalities across cases have been identified, each situation has its unique calculus that belies any attempts to standardize responses. This is not to say that humanitarian interventions are the same in every instance – indeed, as pointed out earlier, consistency is neither possible nor desirable. However, limiting options to the use of force risks the prospect of the international community relying on 'cookie-cutter responses'.[52] As Adam Lupel and Ernesto Verdeja point out, 'responding to massive human rights violations involves a number of different levels, actors, and tools'.[53] The use of force is one tool among many.

Second, prevention considerably increases the number of actors who may be legitimately engaged, significantly expanding the pool of global capacity committed to preventing and ending atrocity crimes. Humanitarian interventions are usually undertaken by state actors, deploying national armed forces, or coalitions of militaries. Not everyone has the capacity or the legitimacy to intervene, and often the legitimacy of actors deploying the use of force in such circumstances is questioned. For example, as mentioned above, there was great controversy about the French deployment of soldiers to Rwanda in the aftermath of the 1994 genocide, given its ties to some of the perpetrators. Yet at the time they were the only state – with the capacity to send forces – who were willing to do so. By contrast, preventive strategies are undertaken by a much broader range of actors, as we have pointed out in Chapter 3. They can be part of regional or international organizations, domestic as well as international civil society groups, diplomats, heads of state, and local community leaders. The legitimacy of such actors can come from the Security Council, as well as through regional bodies and bilateral arrangements.

While external pressure has had a limited impact in influencing domestic leaders to end atrocities (as we discussed in Chapter 1), the decision to commit atrocities in the first place is, in most cases, a last resort. The decision to perpetrate atrocities is usually taken after leaders have decided that they are unable to achieve their goal by adopting other strategies. Given that it is usually the option of last resort not the first, this suggests that there are opportunities to engage and dissuade leaders before the determination to commit such violence has materialized. Indeed, having both the desire and the capacity to commit atrocities, even in times of upheaval, is not enough, as Scott

Straus claims. According to Straus, the ability for leaders to commit atrocities can only unfold once three conditions are in place: 'elite consolidation, subnational (local) alliances, and popular compliance.'[54] In terms of elite compliance, if there is opposition among influential elites, consolidating a path to mass atrocities is difficult, if not impossible. Atrocities can only be carried out if such opposition can be resolved. Moreover, the importance of subnational alliances is crucial, because actors such as local elites, police officers, provincial militia groups, and civil society groups are instrumental in the carrying out of destructive policies by national elites. Indeed, alliance with subnational actors should not be taken as given. Studies into the ways that violence unfolds at a micro level within civil wars highlights the reality that local dynamics and broad political objectives are often loosely connected.[55] Even when these two factors are in play, there is usually some degree of 'popular compliance'. That is, mass violence involves the overcoming of any potential popular opposition to such a process. This does not mean that the broader public need directly participate in the violence – though often some do – it simply means that a substantial sector of the population 'remain passively supportive or indifferent'.[56] The complexity of this process underscores the point that such violence is not inevitable, and that the seeds of resistance come from within not from outside. More attention should be paid to the relationships between outsiders and insiders, and in particular to how external actors can support the sources of local and national resilience to atrocity crimes that are already in place.[57] Moreover, in the intricate balance of compliance and alliance that needs to be secured before such strategies of mass violence can be consolidated, opportunities for prevention can arise. While it is rare for external actors to pressure elites to end atrocities once they start, the process towards consolidating policies of mass violence yields far more opportunities for both external and domestic actors to set up roadblocks.

Third, although not without their own downsides and controversies, non-coercive preventive strategies typically produce fewer negative side effects than humanitarian intervention. The implications of intervention are often felt for years, and sometimes decades, after the use of force has been deployed. The cases of Libya, Kosovo, and Somalia all provide illustrations of the profound complications that humanitarian intervention can provoke in subsequent years, despite having met the objective of protecting populations against mass atrocities and human-induced famine. While the intervention in Libya was instrumental in preventing a massacre in Benghazi and shortening the country's civil war, the ensuing power vacuum after the removal of Gaddafi's regime left the country with rival governments, all claiming to be the legitimate power. That said, of course, we should recognize the limits of non-coercive preventive action. Diplomacy was tried with Gaddafi, and it failed. Indeed, at no stage in the crisis did the Libyan government display an intention to moderate its behaviour in the face of multiple international entreaties for it to do so. The receptiveness of national leaderships stands out, here, as a key criterion for the success of preventive leadership. Our point here, though, is not that intervention be eschewed but that energy and resources also be placed into prevention.

Finally, well-targeted prevention is cheaper than intervention. This was a claim initially made by the Carnegie Commission in its report on conflict prevention in 1997, and it remains true. According to the Carnegie Commission, the costs of prevention are a small fraction of the costs of reacting to deadly violence, not to mention the added costs of rebuilding, and the healing of traumatized populations.[58] Indeed, while the third-party intervention was instrumental in halting the 2008 post-election violence in Kenya at an early stage, this limited period of violence and displacement cost the Kenyan economy close to US$3.6 billion.[59] Compound that with the costs of a military response and the expenses climb even higher.

Conclusion

In this chapter we have argued that international responses to atrocities will be necessarily different between cases. On the one hand, the political configurations surrounding any particular case will be different – so inconsistency is simply a matter of political reality. On the other, what constitutes an effective response to one case will not necessarily translate into other cases owing to the differences between them. Beyond that, we argued that while the use of force is sometimes necessary to save populations from atrocities, it also always carries counter-productive effects. The 1992 intervention in Somalia, for example, further empowered armed clan groups and criminal businessmen, while diminishing the likelihood of a return to a civilian government. As such, some clans profited from the influx of humanitarian aid, which then provided the finances to continue their violent conflict. In Kosovo, the NATO-led intervention put an end to the Serbian government's persecution of Kosovar Albanians, but enabled reprisal violence against Serbs and other ethnic minorities, provoking further displacement. It is inevitable that deploying the use of force, even for the objective of protecting populations from mass atrocities, will have some destabilizing effects. Nevertheless, humanitarian intervention is one extreme option along a spectrum of measures aimed at protection, the overwhelming majority of which are non-coercive in character. Taking this broad spectrum into account, the goal is not necessarily to ensure greater consistency with cases of humanitarian intervention, but to ensure that fewer atrocities are perpetrated in the first place, thus lessening the need to consider the use of force at all. That, we argue, is the fundamental purpose of the international human protection regime.

Notes

1. See Chris Brown, 'Selective Humanitarianism: In Defence of Inconsistency', in Dean Chatterjee and Don Scheid (eds), *Ethics and Foreign Intervention* (Cambridge: Cambridge University Press, 2003), pp. 31–50.
2. As James Pattison ably points out, these measures also carry normative pros and cons. See James Pattison, *The Alternatives to War: From Sanctions to Nonviolence* (Oxford: Oxford University Press, 2018).
3. See Alex J. Bellamy, *The Responsibility to Protect: A Defense* (Oxford: Oxford University Press, 2015), p. 134.
4. Justin Morris, 'The Responsibility to Protect and the Great Powers: The Tensions of Dual Responsibility', *Global Responsibility to Protect,* 7, nos. 3–4 (2015), pp. 398–421.
5. United Nations General Assembly, '2005 Summit Outcome Document', A/60/L.1, 20 September 2005. Emphasis added.
6. Ban Ki-moon, *Responsibility to Protect: Timely and Decisive Response,* A/66/874-S/2012/578, 2012, p. 6.
7. A/66/874-S/2012/578.
8. See Bellamy, *Responsibility to Protect,* p. 140.
9. Aisha Ahmad, 'Agenda for Peace or Budget for War? Evaluating the Economic Impact of International Intervention in Somalia', *International Journal,* 67, no. 2 (2012), pp. 313–331. p. 320; Lidwien Kapteijns, 'Test-Firing the "New World Order" in Somalia: The US/UN

Military Humanitarian Intervention of 1992–1995', *Journal of Genocide Research*, 15, no. 4 (2013), pp. 421–442: 423.

10. Ahmad, 'Agenda for Peace or Budget for War?', p. 320.

11. Steven Hansch, Scott Lillibridge, Grace Egeland, Charles Teller, and Michael Toole, *Lives Lost, Lives Saved: Excess Mortality and the Impact of Health Interventions in the Somalia Emergency* (Washington, DC: Refugee Policy Group, 1994), p. 94.

12. United Nations Security Council Resolution 751 (1992); Kapteijns, 'Test-Firing the "New World Order"', p. 426.

13. 28,000 of which were US troops. See Kapteijns, 'Test-Firing the "New World Order"', p. 425.

14. United Nations Security Council Resolution 794 (1992).

15. United Nations, *Somalia – UNOSOM II, Facts and Figures,* Available at: http://www.un.org/en/peacekeeping/missions/past/unosom2facts.html, accessed 14 December 2016.

16. Kapteijns, 'Test-Firing the "New World Order"', p. 426.

17. Kapteijns, 'Test-Firing the "New World Order"', p. 430.

18. Kapteijns, 'Test-Firing the "New World Order"', pp. 432–433.

19. John L. Hirsch, 'Somalia', in Sebastian von Einsiedel, David M. Malone, and Bruno Stagno Ugarte (eds), *The UN Security Council in the 21st Century* (Boulder, CO: Lynne Rienner, 2016), p. 599.

20. Ahmad, 'Agenda for Peace or Budget for War?' p. 322.

21. Ahmad, 'Agenda for Peace or Budget for War?' p. 322.

22. For 1992/3 alone, total UN funding for humanitarian relief was US$203,546,049. Between April 1992 and July 1994, the USA contributed US$311,000,000 to humanitarian relief. See John G. Summer, *Hope Restored? Humanitarian Aid in Somalia* (Refugee Policy Group, 1994), Available at: http://pdf.usaid.gov/pdf_docs/PNABZ357.pdf

23. Ahmad, 'Agenda for Peace or Budget for War?' p. 324

24. This was initially done with the cooperation of Aideed and Mahdi. See Human Rights Watch, *Somalia, Beyond the Warlords: The Need for a Verdict on Human Rights Abuses,* Report Vol. 5, No 2 (1993), Available at: https://www.hrw.org/reports/1993/somalia/

25. Ahmad, 'Agenda for Peace or Budget for War?' p. 326.

26. Ahmad, 'Agenda for Peace or Budget for War?' p. 326.

27. Ahmad, 'Agenda for Peace or Budget for War?' p. 326.

28. Kapteijns, 'Test-Firing the "New World Order"', p. 426.

29. See Nicolas de Torrente and Fabrice Weissman, 'A War Without Limits: Somalia's Humanitarian Catastrophe', *Harvard International Review,* 30, no. 4 (2009), pp. 14–19: p. 14.

30. See Nicholas J. Wheeler and Justin Morris, 'Humanitarian Intervention and State Practice at the End of the Cold War', in Rick Fawn and Jeremy Lankins (eds), *International Society After the Cold War: Anarchy and Order Reconsidered* (London: Macmillan, 1996), p. 156.

31. Roméo Dallaire, *Shake Hands with the Devil: The Failure of Humanity in Rwanda* (Croydon: Arrow Books, 2004), p. 75.
32. Alex J. Bellamy, 'Human Wrongs in Kosovo: 1974–99', *The International Journal of Human Rights*, 4, no. 3–4 (2000), pp. 105–126, 119–120.
33. Bellamy, 'Human Wrongs in Kosovo', p. 120.
34. Bellamy, 'Human Wrongs in Kosovo', p. 121.
35. Bellamy, 'Human Wrongs in Kosovo', p. 120.
36. Bellamy, 'Human Wrongs in Kosovo', p. 120.
37. Human Rights Watch, *The Crisis in Kosovo* (1999), Available at: https://www.hrw.org/reports/2000/nato/Natbm200-01.htm
38. Tim Judah, *Kosovo: What Everyone Needs to Know* (Oxford: Oxford University Press, 2008), p. 94.
39. See Human Rights Watch, *Under Orders: War Crimes in Kosovo* (New York: Human Rights Watch, 2001), p. 16. The total casualties during the war amounted to 10,000. See Judah, *Kosovo*, p. 91.
40. Judah, *Kosovo*, p. 90.
41. International Crisis Group, *Violence in Kosovo: Who's Killing Whom?* (ICG Balkans Report No. 78, 1999), p. 3.
42. Bellamy, 'Human Wrongs in Kosovo', p. 121.
43. Bellamy, 'Human Wrongs in Kosovo', p. 105.
44. Judah, *Kosovo*, p. 91.
45. International Crisis Group, *Violence in Kosovo*, p. 4.
46. International Crisis Group, *Violence in Kosovo*, p. 4.
47. International Crisis Group, *Violence in Kosovo*, p. 5.
48. Judah, *Kosovo*, p. 95.
49. See, for example, James Pattison, *Humanitarian Intervention and the Responsibility to Protect: Who Should Intervene?* (Oxford: Oxford University Press, 2010), pp. 8–12.
50. Nicholas J. Wheeler, *Saving Strangers: Humanitarian Intervention in International Society* (Oxford: Oxford University Press, 2000), pp. 232–235.
51. Jack A. Goldstone, 'Toward a Fourth Generation of Revolutionary Theory', *Annual Review of Political Science*, 4 (2001), pp. 139–187: 173.
52. Adam Lupel and Ernesto Verdeja, 'Responding to Genocide', in Adam Lupel and Ernesto Verdeja (eds), *Responding to Genocide: The Politics of International Action* (Boulder, CO: Lynne Rienner, 2013), p. 9.
53. Lupel and Verdeja, 'Responding to Genocide', p. 9.
54. Scott Straus, *Making and Unmaking Nations: War, Leadership and Genocide in Modern Africa* (Ithaca, NY: Cornell University Press, 2015), p. 79.
55. See, for example, Stathis Kalyvas, *The Logic of Violence in Civil War* (Cambridge: Cambridge University Press, 2006).
56. Straus, *Making and Unmaking Nations*, p. 83.

57. See, for example, Stephen McLoughlin, 'From Reaction to Resilience in Mass Atrocity Prevention: An Analysis of the 2013 Report *The Responsibility to Protect: State Responsibility and Prevention*', *Global Governance,* 22, no. 4 (2016), pp. 473–490.
58. Carnegie Commission on Preventing Deadly Conflict, *Preventing Deadly Conflict: Final Report* (Washington, DC: Carnegie Commission, 1997), pp. xlvi, 20.
59. East West Institute, *A New Road for Preventive Action: Report from the First Global Conference on Preventive Action,* 2011, Available at: www.ewi.info/idea/new-road-preventive-action

8

Human Protection in Crisis?

Only a few years ago, a flurry of publications proclaimed that international society was finally winning 'the war on war'; that human societies were becoming ever more peaceful; that international activism in support of peace was having a decisive impact.[1] Over the preceding few decades, both the incidence and lethality of armed conflict had been in steady decline, prompting renewed speculation about the obsolescence of major war.[2] Regions once blighted by armed conflict, genocide, and mass atrocities, such as East Asia, had moved towards sustainable peace.[3] Much of this progress was underpinned by the international human protection regime, described earlier, as a complex of norms, institutions, and practices focused on the minimization of suffering as a result of atrocity crimes and the protection of vulnerable populations.[4] This regime made it more difficult – though not impossible – for actors to achieve their goals by targeting civilians and more likely that international society would impose costs for such crimes and take action to protect the intended victims.[5] It did so by deepening and broadening international society's engagement with human protection. Where it once focused on humanitarian intervention, now international society adopted a more comprehensive approach, which included a new focus on the prevention of atrocity crimes.

However, since the start of the 'Arab Spring' in early 2011, trends have moved in the opposite direction. The number of armed conflicts increased until 2015, though there has been a slight reduction again since that time. During this time, some reports suggest a six-hundred-fold increase in the annual number of civilian casualties in war. Atrocity crimes are committed regularly, and with seeming impunity, in Syria, Yemen, Iraq, South Sudan, and elsewhere. Displacement – both internal and international – has reached a level not seen since the end of the Second World War. Wherever we look, the forces that promoted human protection and the constructive management of difference over the past few decades are in retreat. Meanwhile, the forces of racism, xenophobia, nationalism, and what Martin Ceadal called 'warism' are everywhere on the march.[6] The effects can be seen not only in the outpouring of mass violence especially in the Middle East and parts of sub-Saharan African, but also in the increasing tendency of powers – both 'great' and regional – to utilize and support violence to support their narrow sectarian interests and (with some notable exceptions) the declining international support provided to important elements of the human protection regime, such as international refugee law. Today, international society confronts a global crisis of human protection that challenges the progress made over the past few decades.

This chapter examines this global crisis of human protection. It enquires into its causes and consequences and asks whether there are steps that can be taken to address it. It proceeds in three parts. The first examines the crisis confronting the international human protection regime today. The second advances an explanation for the increased violence. The third outlines steps that peoples, governments, and international organizations can take to address the crisis and evaluates their prospects. We argue that while human protection confronts a potentially existential crisis, there are grounds for thinking that it will survive into the future – but that this very much depends on the choices made by political leaders, civil society, and others. Ultimately, like William Cooper (discussed in the Introduction), we all have choices to make as to whether, or not, we help support human protection. The future capacity of the regime to prevent atrocities and protect vulnerable populations depends on the choices we all make.

The crisis of human protection

Since around 2011, indicators of armed conflict, atrocities, and global displacement have all moved in the wrong direction, prompting expressions of concern and alarm. Michael Ignatieff warned of a 'new world disorder' characterized by a rise of 'violence and hate' while Louise Arbour argued that the new trend showed that international society's approach to protection 'just doesn't work'.[7] Jennifer Welsh, meanwhile, writes eloquently of the 'return of history' to world politics as barbarism (warfare unregulated by international humanitarian law), mass migration, a renewed Cold War, and increasing inequality challenge the liberal order from within.[8] After declining some 72 per cent after the 1990s, the number of major civil wars grew from four to eleven after 2011, with the cumulative battle deaths reaching levels in 2014 and 2015 not seen since the end of the Cold War.[9] Minor civil wars have also increased, reaching a level not seen since the mid-1990s.[10] These increases can be largely ascribed to two major factors: the lethality of armed conflicts in the Middle East, in particular in Syria but also in Iraq and Yemen; and the increased violence unleashed by Islamist non-state armed groups such as Islamic State, al-Qaeda, and its affiliates, Boko Haram and al-Shabaab.[11] These groups overtly challenge established international norms and openly advocate what Hugo Slim described as 'anti-civilian norms' – ideas that contest the normative foundations of the international human protection regime.[12] Among the negative trends, the frequency and scale of atrocity crimes have increased dramatically. Since 2011, civilian populations in the Central African Republic (CAR), Democratic Republic of Congo (DRC), Myanmar, Iraq, Libya, South Sudan, Sudan, Syria, Yemen, and elsewhere have been subjected to mass violence. As a result, global trends show a sharp increase in 'one-sided' violence against civilians, beginning in 2013; and while atrocity crimes declined in 2015 from their peak a year earlier, they remained at levels not seen since 2001.[13] In Syria alone, more than a quarter of a million people have been killed and more than 10 million displaced by a civil war in which government forces and non-state armed groups have paid scant regard to their legal obligations towards civilians. Estimates suggest that in South Sudan at least 50,000 civilians have already been killed in a civil war in which civilians are targeted more than opposing forces. Between them, Syria, South Sudan, and the crisis in the CAR account for a large part of the global increase in 'one-sided violence'.

The increased incidence of atrocity crimes has contributed significantly to a global crisis of displacement. Today, there are more refugees and displaced persons than at any point since the adoption of the United Nations Convention on Refugees in 1951. In 2016, the UN High Commissioner for Refugees (UNHCR) estimated that there were some 21.3 million refugees, more than 40.8 million internally displaced people, and more than 65 million people forcibly displaced from their homes by armed conflict and atrocity crimes.[14] A majority of the world's displaced people come from countries that have recently experienced atrocity crimes, including Syria, Somalia, South Sudan, Sudan, DRC, CAR, Iraq, Yemen, and Nigeria. The flow of refugees from the Middle East caused a major refugee crisis in Western Europe that fundamentally undermined the European Union's migration policies, created significant political discord, contributed to Brexit, and was instrumental in the rise of far-right extremism (across the region) and authoritarian government (in Hungary, for example). Closer to the epicentre of the crisis, huge refugee populations in Turkey and Jordan have added to political instability there. Globally, and with a few exceptions, states have responded to this crisis not by recommitting to refugee protection but by weakening their compliance with international refugee law.

The principal cause of this global human protection crisis is the increasing number of atrocity crimes and direct violations of International Humanitarian Law. From the use of chemical weapons against civilians in Syria to the brazen atrocities committed by violent extremists in Syria and Iraq and the indiscriminate use of air power against civilian populated areas in Syria and Yemen, the deliberate targeting of civilians and violation of International Humanitarian Law have become a regular feature of many modern armed conflicts. Reported attacks on protected buildings, such as hospitals and schools, and on protected persons such as humanitarian workers have increased. In 2016, a marked humanitarian convoy in Syria was attacked, most probably by the Russian air force. In 2017, a convoy of displaced children in Syria was also hit. The besieging of civilian communities, the denial of humanitarian relief, and the use of civilians as human shields have become commonplace features of the modern battlefields in places such as Aleppo and Mosul. In Syria and Yemen, the situation of civilians besieged or otherwise unable to flee conflict zones has become so dire since 2015 that many have reportedly confronted the very real danger of starvation and often die for want of basic medical assistance.[15]

To understand precisely what is going on, we need to understand that violence is driven by different concerns in different contexts. Globally, we can identify three principal clusters.[16] The first cluster, which accounts for the majority of cases of increased death rates and displacement, is the interconnected series of conflicts in the Middle East triggered by forces unleashed by the 2003 US-led invasion of Iraq and the 2011 'Arab Spring'. The underlying causes of the armed conflicts in Syria, Iraq, Yemen, and Libya lay in crises of governance caused by the failure of authoritarian rulers to legitimize their rule or improve the lives of their populations. Confronted by internal demands for reform, governments turned their guns on their own populations. Rebellions in Syria, Iraq, and Yemen were all caused and then escalated by the systematic discrimination against and violent abuse of individuals and groups not aligned to the government. In all of these conflicts, the deliberate targeting of civilians has been justified through the articulation of violent extremist ideologies that make no distinctions between soldiers and civilians, ideologies that have gained in strength as the cycle of violence has escalated. Foreign actors have also played significant roles in stoking the violence, a particular challenge to the international human protection regime we will return to later. In the case of Syria, for example, Turkey, Iran, Hezbollah, Qatar, Saudi Arabia, and Russia directly contributed to the violence. Each of these states has directly supported armed groups responsible for atrocity crimes and none has taken action to restrain atrocities committed by their Syrian clients. What is more, in Syria and Yemen, the frequency of atrocity crimes is at least in part due to the sense of impunity granted to perpetrators by their Great Power allies: Russia in the case of the Syrian government, and the USA in terms of the Saudi-led coalition in Yemen and Iraq. These states have inhibited accountability for atrocity crimes in the Middle East.

The second cluster relates specifically to the rise of violent extremism in the Middle East, parts of sub-Saharan Africa (parts of Nigeria, Somalia, Mali), parts of Central Asia (Afghanistan, parts of Pakistan), Europe, and parts of Southeast Asia (parts of Myanmar). Responses to violent extremism have also sometimes been particularly bloody. For example, since 2011, Boko Haram has been responsible for more than 11,000 deaths, more than 6,000 of which resulted from one-sided massacres of civilians. The Nigerian government's response has been no less brutal. Some 7,000 Boko Haram suspects have died in custody during that time. Many of these conflicts have their roots in specific localities. For example, it was a combination of local political intrigues and heavy-handed policing that transformed Boko Haram from a small extremist sect into an armed militia capable of withstanding the attentions of the

Nigerian army.[17] In these contexts, political entrepreneurs exploit ethnic and religious divisions for their own ends and have developed extremist anti-civilian ideologies that reject fundamental principles of common humanity. In some situations, such as in the DRC, competition for natural resources continues to be a cause of conflict that can give rise to atrocity crimes.

The third cluster of crises are those that predate 2011 but remain unresolved. Conflicts in South Sudan, Sudan, Somalia, the DRC, Nigeria, CAR, Mali, and Myanmar may have experienced peaks of violence in the past few years but their origins predate the global escalation of violence and peaks of violence occurred prior to 2011. These are what John Mueller refers to as the 'remnants' of war.[18] Myanmar, for example, has not experienced a single year of peace since independence in 1948.[19] In these situations, colonial orders have yet to be fully replaced by legitimate state institutions capable of imposing the rule of law across their entire territory. Here, the rule of law is weak, and factions struggling for power have committed atrocity crimes and have sought to advance the interests of one part of the community at the expense of others. In the CAR, for example, sectarian politics pitted one community against another and gave rise to widespread atrocity crimes.

Beyond the increased commission of atrocity crimes, a second element of the crisis confronting the international human protection regime is the declining will of states to uphold their legal obligations and shared principles and act collectively to prevent grave violations or respond to them by protecting populations in a timely and decisive fashion. This was a core message in the UN Secretary-General's 2016 report on the Responsibility to Protect (R2P), which emphasized a growing gap between the legal obligations and political commitments accepted by states and their actual practice.[20] Three specific aspects of this problem were identified.

First, there is evidence of declining compliance with fundamental tenets of International Humanitarian, Human Rights, and Refugee Law, not just by the violent extremists and authoritarian states that perpetrate atrocity crimes but by states of good standing and even some champions of human protection. In the face of the crisis of human protection described earlier, some states have wound back their commitment to crucial norms and principles. The US administration, for example, has eased targeting restrictions aimed at protecting civilians from indiscriminate or disproportionate attacks.[21]

Several others, including Hungary and Australia, have adopted refugee policies which, the UNHCR believes, contradicts their legal obligations under the Refugee Convention and associated protocol. Burundi has withdrawn from the International Criminal Court (ICC), and South Africa and Kenya threatened to do likewise, placing this new institution under immense political pressure. Others, such as the Philippines, could follow suit largely because the Court has become an inconvenience to states that may be responsible for committing crimes against humanity.

The second problem is that increased involvement of external states in crisis situations is enabling the perpetration of atrocity crimes. There has been a significant increase in the involvement of external states in civil wars. In 1990, only 4 per cent of civil wars were 'internationalized' through the direct involvement of other states. By 2015, that figure had increased to 40 per cent and many of these, including Syria and Yemen, experienced interventions by multiple external states.[22] Some of these external actors – such as Russia in Syria and Saudi Arabia in Yemen – have used force in support of actors responsible for widespread and systematic atrocity crimes, have supported such uses of force, and have themselves directed attacks that have resulted in large-scale civilian casualties. Some of these attacks, such as the Russian bombing of a UN aid convoy in Syria in September 2016, and repeated Saudi bombings of schools and hospitals in Yemen, may in themselves constitute war crimes. These and other states have supplied the arms and ammunition used to commit atrocity crimes or have turned a blind eye to their transportation to the perpetrators of atrocities – in contravention of the Arms Trade Treaty. Qatar, for example, is one of the principal suppliers of arms and ammunition to extremist groups linked to the Muslim Brotherhood in Syria. While their crimes are not on the same scale as those perpetrated by Syrian government forces, there is little doubt that these groups have committed atrocity crimes against non-combatants in Syria. States and state leaders have also used their political influence to shield the perpetrators of atrocities. For example, in 2016, South Africa's Constitutional Court ruled that the South African government breached its legal obligations by not arresting Sudanese president Omar al-Bashir and transferring him to the ICC as required by the Rome Statute, to which South Africa is a party. Meanwhile, Russia and China have repeatedly blocked efforts to hold those responsible for atrocity crimes in Syria accountable, vetoing draft Security Council resolutions referring the situation to the ICC. This resistance to legal accountability prompted the UN General Assembly to take the unprecedented step of establishing its own mechanism to support the future criminal prosecution of those responsible for atrocity crimes in Syria.[23]

The immediate problem here is, of course, material. External supporters enable violence and prolong the killing. Research shows that in cases where external intervention fails to deliver a rapid decisive outcome, they tend to make civil wars longer and deadlier.[24] Syria provides an apt example, since the involvement of external actors such as Russia, Turkey, Iran, Hezbollah, Saudi Arabia, and Qatar has served only to extend the violence and further complicate peace efforts. The deeper problem here though is a normative one. This is because some of the leading supporters of the protagonists in these conflicts are the great powers themselves – those states that have a special responsibility to support international peace and security and the R2P principle. Where R2P calls for the exercising of responsible sovereignty, we are instead seeing the return of what Hedley Bull described, in a different context, as the 'great irresponsibles'. By pursuing their own sectarian interests at the expense of their global responsibilities, the great powers may be 'forfeiting the claims they had begun to build up ... to be regarded by others as responsible managers of international society as a whole'.[25] The gap between the responsibilities for world order and basic decency bestowed upon the permanent members of the UN Security Council in particular and their actual behaviour is in danger of becoming a chasm that could delegitimize the core principles and institutions of global governance. To return to Bull, 'great powers cannot expect to be conceded special rights if they do not perform special duties'.[26] Should the great powers continue to abandon their responsibility for managing international society in favour of the pursuit of their own sectarian interest, we might expect to find not only a more disorderly and violent world, but also a world in which other states and societies look beyond established norms and institutions for answers to the problems they face.

A third problem, which stems from the first two is that international society is too often failing to do what is necessary to prevent atrocity crimes and protect populations from them. As crises remain unresolved and new ones emerge, international society's capacity to respond effectively is reduced. Despite all of their commitments to preventing atrocities, states are still too often reluctant to act until they see the casualties mounting. Commitment to act has sometimes been lacking even when atrocities occur. For example, the risk of atrocity crimes in Syria was predicted almost at the outset of the crisis there in 2011, yet the world could not find sufficient will or consensus to prevent it. The USA, for example, responded initially by ruling out strong action in Syria before switching emphasis to demand an immediate end to the violence and that Assad 'step aside'. But at no stage have either the USA or its Western allies shown themselves willing to take the steps necessary to achieve their often stated goals.[27] In Yemen, warnings about the dangers confronting the civilian population have not been translated into much other than humanitarian aid; and even then humanitarian support for Yemen has been so inadequate that by 2017 the UN was moved to argue that Yemen was the world's gravest humanitarian emergency and that significant populations confronted the risk of famine and severe malnutrition.[28] A year earlier, the International Committee of the Red Cross (ICRC) observed that the humanitarian situation in Yemen was at a 'tipping point'.[29] Other times, early warnings of atrocity crimes have translated into preventive actions only very slowly, as in the CAR and Burundi. Early warning remains a problem in some situations, as in South Sudan, Libya, and Iraq where the outbreak of conflict and atrocities was not widely predicted in advance. Another example comes from the treatment of those fleeing atrocities. The granting of safe passage and asylum to populations threatened by atrocity crimes remains one of the most direct ways in which states can support human protection but – with only a few notable exceptions, such as Germany – national policies have moved their national politics in the opposite direction, adopting a less hospitable and more punitive approach to asylum seekers, largely inconsistent with the 1951 Convention on the Status of Refugees and the subsequent 1967 Protocol, and certainly inconsistent with the spirit and intention of human protection.

From this brief survey, it seems clear that the international human protection regime established over many decades is confronting a series of potentially existential challenges from which it might not emerge intact. This crisis stems not only from increasing violations of basic international rules forbidding atrocity crimes, but also from the simultaneous decline of international commitment to upholding these rules and protecting people from violations of them. Whether or not the human protection regime will survive intact is as yet unclear, but as with all regimes the answer depends upon the choices that states make. There are, therefore, steps that can be taken to reinforce the international human protection regime, some of which are outlined in the following section. Before that, however, we need to better understand precisely what has driven this recent upsurge in violence and the apparent downturn in internationalism.

A crisis explained

Why has the world taken this turn towards the more violent? There are, a number of theories but none of them entirely are persuasive as a global explanation. One of the most popular theories is Pankaj Mishra's, which holds that what we are seeing is merely the latest phase of a backlash against modernization and globalization.[30] Mishra maintains that Western-style modernization uprooted traditional cultures and societies but failed to replace them with new locally grounded and legitimated ideas about how we should live. That was not much of a problem for those who benefited materially from the global transformation, but it created a reservoir of resentment among those who did not benefit, those on the receiving end of the ever-widening inequalities between rich and poor. Extremist ideologues – entrepreneurs of disenchantment – exploited this resentment to their own advantage. Romantics responded to modernity with nationalism and mythology; anarchists, communists, and fascists with wildly utopian visions of a world reordered; Islamists with dreams of the caliphate and the restoration of their own – extremist – accounts of Shari'a. In Mishra's vision, today's jihadists and white extremists are simply contemporary manifestations of the same forces that brought anarchist terrorism, socialism, and fascism to the streets of Europe in the nineteenth and early twentieth centuries.

This account is illuminating, inasmuch as it points to the inevitability of violent resistance to transformational change and shows that far from being unique and novel, the extremism of today draws from the same reservoirs of human resentment that drove extremism a century ago. It also does a good job of explaining why it is that extremists and especially their leaderships tend to come, not from the very bottom of society, but from the educated middle classes, those often acculturated by the modern but who, for one reason or another, choose to rebel against it in the name of the genuinely disenfranchised. But it is a one-sided accounting of the contemporary world that pays little attention to the goods wrought by modernization not least among them sharp declines in poverty, increases both in the quality and length of life, or of how modernization has driven greater peacefulness.[31] There may have been more atrocities in 2015 than in 2010, but even this peak was well below the average in the 1990s, or the 1970s, 1960s, and 1950s for that matter. While recognizing that human protection does indeed confront a crisis, we must be careful to keep things in their proper historical perspective.

Mishra's thesis is also too general in its explanation: why has this type of violence emerged only in some places and not in others that have undergone similar transformations? Here, we suspect that the ideologues – and the ideologies they pedal play a more significant role than Mishra's account suggests.[32] So too do local conditions. The rise of Boko Haram, for example, had next to nothing to do with industrialization and modernization and everything to do with local politics and the authorities' mistreatment of opposition activists. Likewise, it was not 'modernization' that sparked the Sunni rebellion in Iraq that eventually gave rise to Islamic State. After all, many of Iraq's Sunnis had profited under Saddam's modernization schemes. Rather, it was the collapse of Saddam's regime; their loss of privilege, wealth, and security; and the sometimes brutal discrimination against them by the Shi'ite-controlled government in Baghdad that drove their resentment – all of this a direct product of the US decision to invade in 2003.

An alternative account suggests that the nature of the problem lies not in the fact of violence, but rather in our interpretation of it, that is, the elevated normative expectations created by the international human protection regime were not, as we claimed earlier, products of a universally understood conception of humanity and human rights but rather of a liberal moment in world politics made possible by Western hegemony after the Second World War and its triumph after the Cold War. As E. H. Carr explained in 1939, perhaps 'common morality' is actually nothing more than the interests and preferences of the powerful masquerading as universal moral truth.[33] What if this were true of the campaign against atrocity crimes? If Carr was right, then central components of the struggle against atrocities – human rights and humanitarian law, human rights institutions, R2P, international criminal justice – would be better understood as products of a Western liberal governed international system rather than normative standards genuinely shared by the society of states. And, if that is correct, the relative decline of the West should result in the relative decline of Western liberal values measured in terms of declining compliance and the declining will and capacity of states and institutions to ensure compliance. From this perspective, we are witnessing end times of human rights, as Stephen Hopgood eloquently expounded.[34]

But there is reason to doubt the association of West with liberalism and fundamental ideas about human protection, not least because it exaggerates the extent to which Western states actually championed these rights and also because it simultaneously neglects the ideas, struggles, and advocacy of non-Western leaders, activists, and communities. The campaign against colonialism was prefaced on the idea that *all* humans enjoyed certain fundamental rights, not least to life and liberty. Western states were among those most implacably opposed to these notions. It was African and other postcolonial states that argued – in the context of apartheid South Africa – that governments were not entitled to discriminate on the grounds of race or to treat their populations however they saw fit, arguments which at the time were often met with opposition in the West, not least the USA and the UK. More recently, one of the core elements of the international human protection regime, R2P, was devised by a commission co-chaired by an Algerian (Mohammed Sahnoun), placed on the UN's agenda by a Ghanaian (Kofi Annan), and negotiated by a General Assembly led by a diplomat from Gabon. Rwanda, South Africa, and Pakistan played pivotal roles in those negotiations. It was Guatemala that proposed the UN General Assembly's first resolution affirming the principle, over the objections of many European states. In all this, it bears remembering that John Bolton – the US Ambassador to the UN at the time – remained implacably opposed to the concept and that by the time that the UN got around to adopting R2P, the African Union had already adopted more forceful language on atrocity responses into its own constitution.

The same is true of other elements of the international human protection regime. There was little diplomatic pressure, and certainly no coercive inducement, placed on states to agree, sign, and ratify the

Rome Statute of the ICC. The USA, recall, is not a party. Treaties, resolutions, and positions have to persuade a majority of states to be adopted by the UN. It is a long time since the West had the numbers to control a consistent majority in the UN. This is precisely why Carr's diagnosis of 'moral universalism' as simply the preferences of the powerful is not an accurate description of our context today. The annals of diplomatic history are littered with failed attempts to advance human rights. Only those that command the support of a majority drawn from every part of the world can become established as norms. Most, if not all, of the barriers against genocide have commanded the support of a sustained majority of states. They are, we think, signifiers of an 'overlapping moral consensus' – to borrow a phrase from the philosopher John Rawls – against atrocity crimes, not a thinly veiled Western moral hegemony.[35]

Setting these two explanations alongside one another does highlight one critical point: that our explanation of the present must address two distinct, though interconnected, questions: why is violence increasing and why is international society less able to control and constrain it?

In relation to the first question, Mishra's account does a good job at exposing how radical social and economic transformations can give rise to violent backlashes, though as I mentioned earlier it was not always modernization that lay at the centre of the problem – local politics and foreign invasions have proven equally significant in recent rimes. Nonetheless, fragmentation, inequality, instability, and ideology provide us with a useful way of understanding violent extremism.

What is more, violent extremism is only one of the things making our world more violent. Another, perhaps larger problem, is the incomplete globalization of international society. By this, we mean the project of establishing an order of responsible sovereign states capable of maintaining order within their boundaries without having to resort to mass violence. Many of the conflicts that give rise to genocide and mass atrocities today might be characterized as wars of state formation and consolidation – wars over where the boundaries of a state should be, what ideological and constitutional form it should take, and who should control it and on what basis. Of these, many occur in countries where the states have barely – if ever – exercised legitimate control over the whole of their territory. In Sudan,

South Sudan, Somalia, DRC, CAR, Mali, and Myanmar there have been many more years of war than of peace since independence, and atrocity crimes have been long-standing features of these wars in part because of their practical utility and in part because the association of peoples and territories lay at their core. But in addition to these residual conflicts, the 'Arab Spring' gave rise to a new set of conflicts, caused in part by the failure of the Middle East's authoritarian governments to build internal legitimacy and improve the lives of their peoples and in part by external intervention. Addressing these issues requires the full panoply of the international human protection regime. Recall that we argued it is only since the start of this century that the regime has become fully established; it will take decades more for it to influence positive changes in these long-time conflict zones.

All of this is happening in an era of *declining internationalism*, a period in which 'onlookers [are too] preoccupied with their own, to them more pressing, concerns' to do what is necessary to protect shared international human protection norms.[36] This is a trend driven in part by stagnating and declining economies in the post-Global Financial Crisis world, which has prompted governments to look inwards rather than outwards. It is also a trend driven by the dashing of overly optimistic accounts of what outside intervention can achieve. Critiques of peacebuilding in the Balkans or of intervention in Libya reinforce the view that time, energy, and resources dedicated to the protection of people in other countries are, essentially, wasted. Not only do they represent the redirection of precious resources, but they are also unlikely to succeed. Here we see an alliance of sorts between leftist-minded critics of peacebuilding – who see it as neo-imperialism writ large – and rightist-minded realists who see it as contrary to the national interest. As a result, and as Jennifer Welsh explained, 'Liberal democracy itself is less stable, and less admirable, than it was at the end of the Cold War.' And that: 'It should also be less confident about its longevity.'[37]

Sentiments such as these have encouraged states to retreat from the promotion of global norms abroad, with two principal effects. First, by reducing expectations of foreign intervention, sanctions, or censure, retreating internationalism has altered the balance of costs and payoffs associated with mass atrocities in favour of the payoffs. On the costs side, the chances of prosecution, intervention, sanctions, and embargoes have declined. On the payoff sides, the chances of self-interested foreign support have sometimes increased. Second, the decline of internationalism has elevated suffering by limiting the aid granted to vulnerable populations and the survivors of mass violence. Such heightened suffering will only add to the reservoir of resentment from where the ideologues of extremism draw their support.

Can human protection survive?

Today, the international human protection regime confronts a series of challenges that together constitute an existential threat. Even the principle that there are limits to what states and other armed groups are entitled to do to their own, and other, populations is being questioned and challenged in ways not seen since the height of the Cold War.[38] In this concluding section, we offer some ways of thinking about how to address the crisis and strengthen human protection. We must be realistic, however, about the practical and political constraints that confront the sector. We must also acknowledge that advocates for change are operating within a narrower political space than they were a decade or so ago. In particular, in the future there will be increasing demands for protective action but fewer resources with which to carry it out; there will likely be limited political leadership on these issues emanating from the West owing to the likely absence of US leadership under Trump and increased division and retrenchment in the European Union; and there will likely be continued pushback by some states against some key human protection agendas. For example, sexual violence in armed conflict is likely to be more narrowly understood by some states and the ICC can expect to face continued pressure and opposition.

The first step, we think, is to strengthen accountability. Actors with protection responsibilities should be held to account in clear and transparent ways. International norms, such as those contained in the international human protection regime, shape shared understandings and limit the behaviours that can be justified and legitimized by reference to them, such that actors will be inhibited from acting in ways that cannot be plausibly justified by the imposition of social costs. However, what a norm prescribes in a certain situation is never fixed and absolute, opening space for contestation and norm avoidance. The capacity of an international regime, then, to constrain and enable courses of action consistent with it is influenced by both the clarity of the norm itself and by the range of relevant intervening variables, in particular the extent to which actors are made to account for their actions.[39] Recent debates surrounding international society's inadequate response to the crisis in Syria and controversial reaction to the 2011 crisis in Libya underscore the need to strengthen accountability for, and while, protecting. As we noted earlier, the principal challenge confronting the international human protection regime is the widening gap between normative commitments and a daily lived reality. The unity of the UN Security Council in effectively averting mass atrocities is crucial to closing that gap, but because it is divided politically, the Council is often falling short of what is expected of it. Indeed, in December 2016 the General Assembly was moved to express its 'alarm that the responsibility of the Security Council to ensure prompt and effective action has not been further discharged' with respect to the situation in the Syrian Arab Republic.[40] To remedy this, international institutions bestowed with protection responsibilities need to be held accountable to the states and societies they serve.

At the same time, however, those invested with responsibility should also exhibit responsibility while protecting. Perceptions of selectivity, double standards, and the absence of accountability breed mistrust and make it more difficult to forge international consensus.[41] Accountability for and while protecting are interrelated, since it is only if international society achieves the latter that it can be hopeful of securing the former. Over the past few years, governments have raised a number of different proposals for strengthening the transparency of the Security Council's decision-making as it responds to atrocity crimes. We discussed this issue at length in Chapter 6. These include calls for voluntary veto restraint by the Accountability, Coherence and Transparency (ACT) Group, which enjoys the support of more than one hundred member states, and a separate initiative on veto restraint led by France and Mexico. In addition to these ideas, the Security Council should also periodically review its contribution to human protection through, among other things, an annual thematic debate on atrocity prevention, in which the Council's actions are reviewed in a holistic way, practical operational matters assessed and debated, and future priorities discussed and agreed. In addition to its responsibility to act if necessary, the Security Council should also act responsibly. Learning the lessons of Libya, the Security Council should ensure that those who act on its mandates remain accountable to it. It is a basic principle of accountability that those authorized to undertake certain actions must be accountable to those that authorize them. It is when these lines of accountability are broken that trust breaks down and doubts and suspicions inhibit effective decision-making. The Council could achieve stronger accountability by imposing time limitations on protection mandates, as is common practice in peacekeeping. It might also require specific reporting by those acting on its mandates.

Second, the preventive components of human protection need a practice turn. There is strong political consensus on the merits of atrocity prevention, and since 2005 there have been rapid advances in our understanding of what atrocity prevention is, understanding the warning signs, risk factors, and triggers and the 'toolbox' of policy responses.[42] But global thought on prevention remains too abstract and generic, which consequently limits its capacity to shape behaviour. States are typically risk-averse, meaning that it is easier to persuade them to act after the fact, when costs and consequences can be calculated and causation attributed, than it is to persuade them to act prospectively.

There are a number of steps that could be adopted by international organizations, individual states, and scholars to advance thought and practice on prevention. For example, the UN Secretary-General could utilize his annual report on R2P to articulate a clear strategy for atrocity prevention to guide the organization's political and operational work, and improve its capacity for early warning and assessment so that it can advise with confidence, better configure the UN institutionally to respond to emerging crisis, and establish new ways of engaging with states at an earlier stage in a crisis. Likewise, individual governments could take steps to mainstream atrocity prevention concerns into their foreign and development policies. The Obama administration led the way on this with the establishment of the Atrocity Prevention Board, but only a handful of other states, including Australia, Costa Rica, Denmark, Ghana, Kenya, Paraguay, and Tanzania have followed suit.

There is also a need for stronger research on atrocity prevention. We need to better understand the precise preventive strategies, policies, and levers of influence that can be used, and by whom, to address specific threats and risks. This is a wide-ranging agenda on which there is ongoing work, including for example a UN study examining past experience of prevention to learn lessons of best practice and develop system-wide guidance on atrocity prevention. This sort of research is necessary in order to better clarify what it is states are expected to do, beyond not committing atrocities, and build shared understandings around those points.

Third, new political leadership is imperative. If human protection is to survive, it will need to find political leaders willing to support it and prepared to take risks to advance it. The UN's former special envoy on Syria, Lakhdar Brahimi, observed that one of the principal problems in that case was the fact that none of the significant regional or global powers prioritized the well-being of Syria's civilian population above their own sectarian interests.[43] In that context, there was relatively little that the UN could do to bring the parties closer to peace. Naturally, the UN Secretary-General Antonio Guterres will have to play a leadership role on human protection, but it is well established that the Secretary-General can do relatively little without the support of member states. Within this context, the traditional friends of human protection, states such as Australia, Germany, Denmark, Switzerland, Spain, Canada, and to an extent the UK and France need to assume more of a leadership role. However, given the priorities of the Trump administration and the internal divisions within the EU, it is unlikely that the traditional champions will be able to shoulder the burden of leadership themselves. New leadership will therefore have to come from outside the West. There are several opportunities. For example, China has a well-known aspiration to lead in UN peacekeeping and recently assumed command of the UN's mission in South Sudan. Rather than resisting Chinese pretensions to leadership through the UN, the West should embrace it and explore ways of transferring greater responsibility for international peace and security to it. Likewise, Brazil briefly assumed a leadership position on R2P, advancing the concept of Responsibility While Protecting to bridge the divide between the West and the rest over Libya. Indonesia, meanwhile, has expressed its intention to expand its commitment to UN peacekeeping, has indicated strong support for human protection goals, and has taken an increasingly active role in responding to crises in Southeast Asia. The traditional friends of human protection need to do more to encourage others to take the lead and should be prepared to transfer responsibility to others. Fourth, more attention needs to be paid to effectively implementing the protection mandates that already exist. The UN already has significant mandates that it struggles to implement in full. These include robust mandates to use 'all means necessary' to protect civilians caught in the midst of civil wars in South Sudan, CAR, Mali, Darfur, and the DRC. As well as thinking about what *more* can be done to strengthen atrocity prevention, it is imperative that steps are taken to ensure that existing protection-related mandates are discharged as well as they can be. Since 2014, the UN has undertaken system-wide reviews of its peacekeeping, peacebuilding, and gender activities which revealed a number of shortcomings and identified tangible steps for making progress. These need to be understood and practices improved, especially with regard to strengthening the protection of civilians; understanding the effects of robust peacekeeping operations and mitigating adverse effects; reducing sexual exploitation and abuse by peacekeepers; widening the pool and increasing the quality of peacekeepers; improving the operational effectiveness of peacebuilding to support consolidated peace; pushing back against restrictions to humanitarian access and attacks on humanitarian workers; and ensuring full compliance with international refugee law and the guiding principles on internal displacement.

Fifth, a renewed focus is needed on embedding human protection into the everyday at the national and local levels. The ultimate vision of the international human protection regime is of a world of responsible sovereign states that protect their own populations from atrocity crimes and other serious violations of their human rights as a matter of habit. The national and local levels have generally received little attention, yet they are crucial to the long-term prospects for human protection. In 2015, the High Level Advisory Panel on R2P in Southeast Asia, chaired by former ASEAN Secretary-General Surin Pitsuwan recommended that states should continue, and further develop, dialogue among stakeholders on building a national architecture to support the prevention of atrocity crimes. It argued that governments should take steps to develop their own national architecture to protect their peoples from genocide, war crimes, ethnic cleansing, and crimes against humanity. This should include active steps to ensure that there is no impunity for atrocity crimes committed either at home or overseas.[44] Of course, as we have argued throughout, there is no single template that can be applied in every country. In some cases, as in Tanzania, prevention architecture might be built around a national committee for genocide prevention. In the USA, an Atrocities Prevention Board was established to coordinate policy. Some countries, such as Argentina, have adopted a legislative approach while others vest their national human rights institutions with responsibilities for prevention and others take a less formal approach. Governments and societies need to determine for themselves which approach best suits their own circumstances and needs. In some cases, a national human rights commission may be part of this national architecture. Whatever approach is adopted, a focus on national measures for human protection is long overdue.

Conclusion

After decades of concerted progress in thought and practice about the prevention of atrocity crimes and protection of vulnerable populations, progress which has seen a military focus on humanitarian intervention replaced by a more comprehensive and multifaceted regime focused on human protection, there is no doubt that human protection confronts a major crisis. Part of this is simply a function of the increase in global violence. Partly the crisis is an inevitable backlash against the regime itself, for human protection is an agenda designed to make some powerful actors less comfortable. But there are also powerful global trends pushing against human protection, forces of racism, nationalism, xenophobia, and extremism. These forces have made the political context for human protection in the immediate more difficult, at precisely the time when it is needed most. But the greatest strength of the international human protection regime is that it derives from a sustained consensus about the moral imperative of limiting civilian suffering in war and ending atrocity crimes – a point of 'overlapping consensus' between the world's many different moral and legal traditions. With consensus comes legitimacy – a legitimacy that still holds today, evidenced by the fact that few, if any, argue that the turn towards a world more violent in its treatment of civilian populations is a welcome development or express satisfaction with international society's inability to better protect populations. It is that legitimacy, if it can be preserved, that creates grounds for thinking that the crisis of human protection which international society faces today can be overcome, and progress on the further development of a human protection regime sustained.

Notes

1. Joshua S. Goldstein, *Winning the War on War: The Decline of Armed Conflict Worldwide* (New York: Dutton, 2011) and Steven Pinker, *The Better Angels of Our Nature: Why Violence has Declined* (New York: Penguin, 2012).
2. John E. Mueller, *The Remnants of War* (Ithaca, NY: Cornell University Press, 2007).
3. Alex J. Bellamy, *East Asia's Other Miracle: Explaining the Decline of Mass Atrocities* (Oxford: Oxford University Press, 2017).
4. Elaborated in Alex J. Bellamy, 'The Humanization of Security: Towards an International Human Protection Regime', *European Journal of International Security*, 1, no. 1 (2016), pp. 112–133.
5. Alex J. Bellamy, *Massacres and Morality: Mass Killing in an Age of Civilian Immunity* (Oxford: Oxford University Press, 2012).
6. Martin Ceadal, *Thinking about Peace and War* (Oxford: Oxford University Press, 1987).
7. Michael Ignatieff, 'The New World Disorder', *The New York Review of Books*, 25 September 2014 Available at: http://www.nybooks.com/articles/archives/2014/sep/25/new-world-disorder/?pagination=false, accessed 15 April 2017; and Doug Saunders, 'Why Louise Arbour is Thinking Twice', *Globe and Mail*, 28 May 2015, Available at: http://www.theglobeandmail.com/globe-debate/why-louise-arbour-is-thinking-twice/article23667013/
8. Jennifer Welsh, *The Return of History: Conflict, Migration and Geopolitics in the Twenty-First Century* (Toronto: House of Anansi Press, 2017).
9. UCDP/PRIO Armed Conflict Dataset version 4-2016.
10. UCDP/PRIO Armed Conflict Dataset.
11. Sebastian von Einseidel, 'Civil War Trends and the Changing Nature of Armed Conflict', United Nations University Centre for Policy Research, Occasional Paper No. 10, March 2017, p. 2.
12. Hugo Slim, *Killing Civilians: Method, Madness and Morality in War* (London: Hurst and Co., 2008).
13. Eric Melander, Therese Pettersson, and Lotta Themner, 'Organised Violence, 1989–2015', *Journal of Peace Research*, 53, no. 5 (2016).

Also see Monty G. Marshall and Benjamin R. Cole, *Global Report 2014: Conflict, Governance and State Fragility* (Vienna, VA: Center for Systemic Peace, 2014), pp. 18–19.

14. UNHCR, *Global Trends: Forced Displacement in 2015* (Geneva: UNHCR, 2016).

15. Rick Gladstone, 'UN Warns of Starvation Peril in Rebel Side of Aleppo', *New York Times*, 10 November 2016, Available at: https://www.nytimes.com/2016/11/11/world/middleeast/aleppo-un-starvation-risk-russia.html

16. A potential fourth relates to the former Soviet Union and the continuation of conflicts arising from its collapse. This includes the conflict in Ukraine.

17. Wisdom Oghasa Iyekekpolo, 'Boko Haram: Understanding the Context', *Third World Quarterly*, 37, no. 12 (2016), pp. 2211–2228.

18. John Mueller, *The Remnants of War* (Ithaca, NY: Cornell University Press, 2004).

19. Richard Cockett, *Blood, Dreams and Gold: The Changing Face of Burma* (New Haven, CT: Yale University Press, 2015), p. xiii.

20. United Nations, *Mobilizing Collective Action: The Next Decade of the Responsibility to Protect: Report of the United Nations Secretary-General*, A/70/999-S/2016/620, 22 July 2016.

21. Charlie Savage and Eric Schmitt, 'Trump Eases Combat Rules in Somalia intended to Protect Civilians', *New York Times*, 30 March 2017, Available at: https://www.nytimes.com/2017/03/30/world/africa/trump-is-said-to-ease-combat-rules-in-somalia-designed-to-protect-civilians.html

22. UCPD/PRIO Armed Conflict Dataset version 4-2016.

23. The International, Impartial and Independent Mechanism to assist in the Investigation and Prosecution of those Responsible for the Most Serious Crimes under International Law committed in the Syrian Arab Republic since March 2011, established by General Assembly Resolution 71/248, 21 December 2016.

24. David Cunningham, 'Blocking Resolution: How External States Can Prolong Civil Wars,' *Journal of Peace Research*, 47, no. 2 (2010), pp. 115–127.

25. Hedley Bull, 'The Great Irresponsibles? The United States, the Soviet Union and World Order', *International Journal*, 35, no. 3 (1980), p. 437.

26. Bull, 'Great Irresponsibles', p. 446.

27. This is the central critique of Western policy towards Syria levelled throughout Samer M. Abboud, *Syria* (Cambridge: Polity, 2015).

28. United Nations, 'Yemen Emergency Food Security and Nutrition Assessment – 2016 Preliminary Results', 8 February 2017, Available at: http://fscluster.org/yemen/document/yemen-emergency-food-security-and-0

29. International Committee of the Red Cross (ICRC), 'Crisis in Yemen: Tipping Point for International Humanitarian Action', 20 May 2015, Available at: https://www.icrc.org/en/document/crisis-yemen-tipping-point-international-humanitarian-action

30. Pankaj Mishra, *Age of Anger: A History of the Present* (New York: Farrar, Straus and Giroux, 2017).

31. As explained by Azar Gat, *The Causes of War and the Spread of Peace: But Will War Rebound?* (Oxford: Oxford University Press, 2017).

32. Jonathan Maynard Leader, 'Rethinking the Role of Ideology in Mass Atrocities', *Terrorism and Political Violence*, 26, no. 5 (2014), pp. 821–841.

33. E. H. Carr, *The Twenty Years' Crisis 1919–1939: An Introduction to the Study of International Relations* (Basingstoke: Palgrave Macmillan, 2001 [1939]).

34. Stephen Hopgood, *The Endtimes of Human Rights* (Ithaca, NY: Cornell University Press, 2013).

35. John Rawls, *A Theory of Justice* (Cambridge, MA: Harvard University Press, 1971), p. 340.

36. Peter Hayes, *Why? Explaining the Holocaust* (New York: W. W. Norton, 2017), p. xv

37. Welsh, *Return of History*, p. 17.

38. Ruti G. Teitel, *Humanity's Law* (New York: Oxford University Press, 2011).

39. Another is the regime's capacity to shape the perceived costs and benefits associated with rule-breaking and rule-following. Given the aforementioned political constraints, this is an unlikely proposition and so is not explored here.

40. A/RES/71/130, 9 December 2016.

41. See Hardeep Singh Puri, *Perilous Interventions: The Security Council and the Politics of Chaos* (New York: Harper Collins, 2016).

42. For example, Serena K. Sharma and Jennifer M. Welsh (eds), *The Responsibility to Prevent: Overcoming the Challenges of Atrocity Prevention* (Oxford: Oxford University Press, 2015) and Sheri P. Rosenberg, Tibi Galis, and Alex Zucker (eds), *Reconstructing Atrocity Prevention* (Cambridge: Cambridge University Press, 2015).

43. Cited by Charles Glass, *Syria Burning: ISIS and the Death of the Arab Spring* (London: Verso, 2015).

44. *Mainstreaming the Responsibility to Protect in Southeast Asia: Pathway Towards a Caring ASEAN Community*, Report of the High Level Advisory Panel on the Responsibility to Protect in Southeast Asia, 9 September 2014.

Bibliography

Abboud, Samer M., *Syria* (Cambridge: Polity, 2016).

Adler, Emmanuel and Peter Haas, 'Conclusion: Epistemic Communities, World Order and the Creation of a Reflective Research Program', *International Organization*, 46, no. 1 (1992), pp. 367–390.

Adler, Emmanuel and Vincent Pouliot, 'International Practices: Introduction and Framework', in Emmanuel Adler and Vincent Pouliot (eds) *International Practices* (Cambridge: Cambridge University Press, 2011).

Ahmad, Abdul Hamid, 'Libyan, Saudi Leaders Walk out of Arab Summit after a Spat', *Gulf News*, 30 March 2009, Available at: http://gulfnews.com/news/gulf/qatar/libyan-saudi-leaders-walk-out-of-arab-summit-after-a-spat-1.60102

Ahmad, Aisha, 'Agenda for Peace or Budget for War? Evaluating the Economic Impact of International Intervention in Somalia', *International Journal*, 67, no. 2 (2012), pp. 313–331.

Akhaven, Payam, *Reducing Genocide to Law: Definition, Meaning, and the Ultimate Crime* (Cambridge: Cambridge University Press, 2015).

Al Arabiya News, 'Annan Condemns "Appalling Crime" on Syria Visit as Damascus Denies Houla Killings', *Al Arabiya News*, 28 May 2012, Available at: http://english.alarabiya.net/articles/2012/05/28/217134.html

Antony Anghie, *Imperialism, Sovereignty and the Making of International Law* (Cambridge: Cambridge University Press, 2005).

Annan, Kofi, *Interventions: A Life in War and Peace* (New York: Penguin, 2012).

Balas, Alexandru, Andrew P. Owsiak, and Paul F. Diehl, 'Demanding Peace: The Impact of Prevailing Conflict on the Shift from Peacekeeping to Peacebuilding', *Peace and Change*, 37, no. 2 (2012), pp. 195–226.

Balch-Lindsay, Dylan and Andrew Enterline, 'Killing Time: The World Politics of Civil War Duration, 1820–1992', *International Studies Quarterly*, 44, no. 4 (2000), pp. 615–542.

Ban Ki-moon, *Report of the Secretary-General on Implementing the Responsibility to Protect*, A/63/677, 12 January 2009.

Ban Ki-moon, *Responsibility to Protect: Timely and Decisive Response*, Report of the Secretary-General, A/66/874-S/2012/578, 2012.

Ban Ki-moon, *The Responsibility to Protect: State Responsibility and Prevention*, Report of the Secretary-General, A/67/9290S/2013/399, 9 July 2013.

Ban Ki-moon, *Fulfilling our Collective Responsibility: International Assistance and the Responsibility to Protect*, Report of the Secretary-General, A/68/947-S/2014/449, 11 July 2014.

Barbour, Brian and Brian Gorlick, 'Embracing the Responsibility to Protect: A Repertoire of Measures Including Asylum for Potential Victims', *International Journal of Refugee Law*, 20, no. 4 (2008), pp. 533–566.

Barnes, Catherine, 'The Functional Utility of Genocide: Towards a Framework for Understanding the Connection between Genocide and Regime Consolidation, Expansion and Maintenance', *Journal of Genocide Research*, 7, no. 3 (2005), pp. 309–330.

Barnett, Michael N., 'Building a Republican Peace: Stabilizing States After War', *International Security*, 30, no. 4 (2006), pp. 87–112.

Barrett, John Q., 'Raphael Lemkin and "Genocide" and Nuremberg, 1945–1946', in Christoph Safferling and Eckart Conze (eds), *The Genocide Convention Seventy Years After its Adoption* (The Hague: TMC Asser Press, 2010).

Bass, Gary J., *Stay the Hand of Vengeance* (Princeton, NJ: Princeton University Press, 2000).

BBC News, 'Libya Protests: Defiant Gaddafi Refuses to Quit', 22 February 2011, Available at: http://www.bbc.co.uk/news/world-middle-east-12544624

BBC News, 'Libya: Rebels and Nato Dismiss Gaddafi Ceasefire Offer', *BBC News*, 30 April 2011, Available at: http://www.bbc.co.uk/news/world-africa-13249923

Beardsley, Kyle and Holger Schmidt, 'Following the Flag or Following the Charter? Examining the Determinants of UN Involvement in International Crises 1945–2002', *International Studies Quarterly*, 56, no. 1 (2012), pp. 33–49.

Becker, Jo and Scott Shane, 'Hillary Clinton, 'Smart Power' and a Dictator's Fall', 27 February 2016, Available at: http://www.nytimes.com/2016/02/28/us/politics/hillary-clinton-libya.html?_r=0

Bellamy, Alex J., 'Human Wrongs in Kosovo: 1974–99', *The International Journal of Human Rights*, 4, nos 3–4 (2000), 105–126.

Bellamy, Alex J., *Kosovo and International Society* (London: Palgrave, 2001).

Bellamy, Alex J., 'International Law and the War with Iraq', *Melbourne Journal of International Law*, 4, no. 2 (2003).

Bellamy, Alex J., 'Responsibility to Protect or Trojan Horse? The Crisis in Darfur and Humanitarian Intervention after Iraq', *Ethics and International Affairs*, 19, no. 2 (2005), 31–54.

Bellamy, Alex J., 'Military Intervention', in D. Bloxham and D. Moses (eds), *Oxford Handbook of Genocide Studies* (Oxford: Oxford University Press, 2009).

Bellamy, Alex J., Mass *Atrocities and Armed Conflict: Links, Distinctions and Implications for the Responsibility to Protect*, Policy Analysis Brief for the Stanley Foundation, February 2011.

Bellamy, Alex J., 'Libya – The Norm and the Exception', *Ethics and International Affairs*, 25, no. 3 (2011), pp. 263–269.

Bellamy, Alex J., *Massacres and Morality: Mass Killing in an Age of Civilian Immunity* (Oxford: Oxford University Press, 2012).

Bellamy, Alex J., 'Getting Away with Mass Murder', *Journal of Genocide Research*, 14, no. 1 (2012), pp. 29–53.

Bellamy, Alex J., 'When States Go Bad: The Termination of State Perpetrated Mass Killing', *Journal of Peace Research*, 52, no. 5 (2015), pp. 565–576.

Bellamy, Alex J., 'The First Response: Peaceful Means in the Third Pillar of the Responsibility to Protect', *The Stanley Foundation*, December 2015.

Bellamy, Alex J., 'The Humanization of Security: Towards an International Human Protection Regime', *European Journal of International Security*, 1, no. 1 (2016), pp. 112–133.

Bellamy, Alex J., *East Asia's Other Miracle: Explaining the Decline of Mass Atrocities* (Oxford: Oxford University Press, 2017).

Bellamy, Alex J. and Adam Lupel, *Why We Fail: Obstacles to the Effective Prevention of Atrocity Crimes*, Policy Brief, International Peace Institute, New York, 2015.

Bellamy, Alex J. and Edward C. Luck (eds), *The Responsibility to Protect: Promise to Practice* (Cambridge: Polity, 2018).

Bellamy, Alex J. and Paul D. Williams, 'The New Politics of Protection: Côte d'Ivoire, Libya and the Responsibility to Protect', *International Affairs*, 87, no. 4 (2011), pp. 825–850.

Bellamy, Alex J. and Paul D. Williams, 'Protecting Civilians in Uncivil Wars', in Sara E. Davies and Luke Glanville (eds), *Protecting the Displaced: Deepening the Responsibility to Protect* (The Hague: Martinus Nijhoff, 2010), pp. 127–162.

Best, Geoffrey, *War and Law Since 1945* (Oxford: Clarendon Press, 1997).

Blair, Tony, 'Doctrine of the International Community', Chicago, 24 April 1999, Available at: http://www.britishpoliticalspeech.org/speech-archive.htm?speech=279

Bookstein, Amelia 'Beyond the Headlines: An Agenda for Action to Protect Civilians in Neglected Conflicts', *Humanitarian Exchange Magazine,* issue 25, December 2003.

Boscoe, David, 'Was There Going to Be a Benghazi Massacre?', *Foreign Policy,* 7 April 2011, Available at: http://foreignpolicy.com/2011/04/07/was-there-going-to-be-a-benghazi-massacre/

Boutellis, Arthur and Paul D. Williams, *Peace Operations, the African Union and the United Nations: Toward More Effective Partnership* (New York: International Peace Institute, 2013).

Brahimi, Lakhdar, *Report of the Panel on UN Peace Operations*, A/55/303 – S/2000/804, 21 August 2000, p. x.

Brown, Chris, *Sovereignty, Rights and Justice: International Political Theory Today* (Cambridge: Polity, 2002).

Brown, Chris, 'Selective Humanitarianism: In Defence of Inconsistency', in Dean Chatterjee and Don Scheid (eds), *Ethics and Foreign Intervention* (Cambridge: Cambridge University Press, 2003).

Brownlie, Ian, *International Law and the Use of Force by States* (Oxford: Clarendon Press, 1974).

Bull, Hedley, *The Anarchical Society: A Study of Order in World Politics* (London: Macmillan, 1977).

Bull, Hedley, 'The Great Irresponsibles? The United States, the Soviet Union and World Order', *International Journal*, 35, no. 3 (1980), pp. 437–447.

Buzan, Barry, *From International to World Society? English School Theory and the Social Structure of Globalisation* (Cambridge: Cambridge University Press, 2004).

Call, Charles T. and Elizabeth M. Cousens, 'Ending Wars and Building Peace: International Responses to War-Torn Societies', *International Studies Perspectives,* 9, no. 1 (2008), pp. 1–21.

Callahan, Mary P., *Making Enemies: War and State-Building in Burma* (Ithaca, NY: Cornell University Press, 2003).

Campbell, Kenneth J., *Genocide and the Global Village* (New York: Palgrave, 2001).

Bibliography

Caney, Simon, 'Human Rights and the Rights of States: Terry Nardin on Non-Intervention', *International Political Science Review,* 18, no. 1 (1997), pp. 27–37.

Caney, Simon, *Justice Beyond Borders: A Global Political Theory* (Oxford: Oxford University Press, 2005).

Carnegie Commission on Preventing Deadly Conflict, *Preventing Deadly Conflict: Final Report* (Washington, DC: Carnegie Commission, 1997).

Carr, E. H., *The Twenty Years' Crisis 1919–1939; An Introduction to the Study of International Relations* (Basingstoke: Palgrave Macmillan, 2001 [1939]).

de Carvalho, Benjamin and Ole Jacob Sending, *The Protection of Civilians in UN Peacekeeping: Concept, Implementation and Practice* (Berlin: Nomos, 2012).

Ceadal, Martin, *Thinking about Peace and War* (Oxford: Oxford University Press, 1987).

Chandler, David, 'The R2P is Dead, Long Live the R2P: The Successful Separation of Military Intervention from the Responsibility to Protect', *International Peace-keeping,* 22, no. 1 (2015).

Charvet, John and Elisa Kaczynska-Nay, *The Liberal Project and Human Rights: The Theory and Practice of a New World Order* (Cambridge: Cambridge University Press, 2008).

Chauville, Roland, 'The Universal Periodic Review's First Cycle: Successes and Failures', in Hilary Charlesworth and Emma Larking (eds), *Human Rights and Universal Periodic Review: Rituals and Ritualism* (Cambridge: Cambridge University Press, 2014).

Chesterman, Simon, *Just and Unjust Interventions: Humanitarian Intervention in International Law* (Oxford: Oxford University Press, 2001).

Chirot, Daniel and Clark McCauley, *Why Not Kill Them All? The Logic and Prevention of Mass Political Murder* (Princeton, NJ: Princeton University Press, 2006).

Clark, Ian, *Legitimacy in International Society* (Oxford: Oxford University Press, 2005).

Clarke, Walter S. and Jeffrey Herbst (eds), *Learning from Somalia: Lessons of Armed Humanitarian Intervention* (Boulder: Westview, 1997).

Cockett, Richard, *Blood, Dreams and Gold: The Changing Face of Burma* (New Haven, CT: Yale University Press, 2015).

Cohen, Roberta, 'Developing an International System for Internally Displaced Persons', *International Studies Perspectives,* 7, no. 2, (2006), pp. 87–101.

Cohen, Roberta and Francis M. Deng, *Masses in Flight: The Global Crisis of Internal Displacement* (Washington, DC: The Brookings Institution, 1998).

Cohen, Roberta and Francis Deng, 'From Sovereignty as Responsibility to R2P', in Alex J. Bellamy and Tim Dunne (eds), *The Oxford Handbook on the Responsibility to Protect* (Oxford: Oxford University Press, 2016).

Collier, Paul, *Wars, Guns & Votes: Democracy in Dangerous Places* (London: The Bodley Head, 2009).

Collier, Paul and Dominic Rohner, 'Democracy, Development and Conflict', *Journal of the European Economic Association,* 6, no. 2–3 (2008), pp. 531–540.

Collier, Paul, V. Elliott, H. Havard, A. Hoeffler, A. Reynal-Querol and N. Sambanis, *Breaking the Conflict Trap: Civil War and Development Policy* (Oxford: Oxford University Press for the World Bank, 2003).

Contessi, Nicola P., 'Multilateralism, Intervention and Norm Contestation: China's Stance on Darfur in the UN Security Council', *Security Dialogue*, 41, no. 3 (2010), pp. 323–343.

Council of the League of Arab States, Res. No.7360, 12 March 2011.

Cribb, Robert, ed., *The Indonesian Killings 1965–1966: Studies From Java and Bali* (Melbourne: Centre of Southeast Asian Studies, Monash University, 1995).

Cronin, Bruce, *Institutions for the Common Good: International Protection Regimes in International Society* (Cambridge: Cambridge University Press, 2003).

Cronogue, Graham, 'Responsibility to Protect: Syria, the Law, Politics and Future of Humanitarian Intervention Post-Libya', *International Humanitarian Legal Studies*, 3, no. 1 (2012), pp. 124–159.

David Cunningham, 'Blocking resolution: How external states can prolong civil wars', *Journal of Peace Research*, 47, no. 2 (2010), pp. 115–127.

Cushman, Thomas, 'Is Genocide Preventable? Some Theoretical Considerations', *Journal of Genocide Research*, 5, no. 4 (2003), pp. 523–542.

Dallaire, Romeo, *Shake Hands with the Devil: The Failure of Humanity in Rwanda* (New York: Cornerstone, 2011).

Daniel, Donald C. F., 'Contemporary Patterns in Peace Operations: 2000–2010', in Alex J. Bellamy and Paul D. Williams (eds), *Providing Peacekeepers: The Politics, Challenges and Future of United Nations Peacekeeping Contributions* (Oxford: Oxford University Press, 2013).

Davies, Sara E., Kimberley Nackers and Sarah Teitt, 'Women, Peace and Security as an ASEAN Priority', *Australian Journal of International Affairs*, 68, no. 3, (2014), pp. 333–355.

Davies, Sara E. and Luke Glanville (eds), *Protecting the Displaced: Deepening the Responsibility to Protect* (The Hague: Martinus Nijhoff, 2010).

Davies, Sara E. and Jacqui True, 'Reframing Conflict-Related Sexual and Gender Based Violence: Bringing Gender Analysis Back In', *Security Dialogue*, 46, no. 6 (2015), pp. 495–512.

Davies, Sara E., Sarah Teitt, Eli Stamnes, and Zim Nwokora (eds), *Responsibility to Protect and Women, Peace and Security: Aligning the Protection Agendas* (The Hague: Brill, 2013).

de Waal, Alex and Bridget Conley-Zilkic, 'Reflections on How Genocidal Killings are Brought to an End', *Social Science Research Council* (Berlin: Nomos, 2006).

Deng, Francis M., 'Divided Nations: The Paradox of National Protection', *The Annals of the American Academy of Political and Social Science*, 603 (2006), p. 218.

Deng, Francis M., Sadikiel Kimaro, Terrence Lyons, Donald Rothchild, and I. William Zartman, *Sovereignty as Responsibility: Conflict Management in Africa* (Washington, DC: The Brookings Institution, 1996).

Diehl, Paul F. and Alexandru Balas, *Peace Operations*, 2nd edition (Oxford: Polity, 2014).

Dikötter, Frank, *Mao's Great Famine: The History of China's Most Devastating Famine, 1958–1962* (London: Bloomsbury, 2010).

Dikötter, Frank, *The Tragedy of Liberation: A History of the Chinese Revolution 1945–1957* (London: Bloomsbury, 2013).

Dikötter, Frank, *The Cultural Revolution: A People's History, 1962–1976* (London: Bloomsbury, 2016).

Louise Doswald-Beck (1987), 'The Civilian in the Crossfire', *Journal of Peace Research*, 24 (3), pp. 251–262.

Downes, Alexander B., *Targeting Civilians in War* (Ithaca, NY: Cornell University Press, 2008).

Downes, Alexander B. and Jonathan Monten, 'Forced to be Free? Why Foreign Imposed Regime Change Rarely Leads to Democratization', *International Security*, 37, no. 4 (2013), pp. 90–131.

Durr, Olivier, 'Humanitarian Law of Armed Conflict: Problems of Applicability', *Journal of Peace Research*, 24, no. 3 (1987), pp. 263–273.

East West Institute, *A New Road for Preventive Action: Report from the First Global Conference on Preventive Action*, 2011, Available at: www.ewi.info/idea/new-road-preventive-action

von Einseidel, Sebastian, 'Civil War Trends and the Changing Nature of Armed Conflict', United Nations University Centre for Policy Research, Occasional Paper No. 10, March 2017.

Evans, Gareth, 'Responding to Mass Atrocity Crimes: The Responsibility to Protect After Libya', Lecture to the Royal Institute of International Affairs, London, 6 October 2011.

Evans, Gareth, 'Responding to Atrocities: The New Geopolitics of Intervention', in *SIPRI Yearbook 2012: Armaments, Disarmament and International Security* (Oxford: Oxford University Press for the Stockholm International Peace Research Institute, 2012).

Evans, Gareth, 'The Responsibility to Protect after Libya and Syria', 2012, Available at: http://www.gevans.org/speeches/speech476.html

Fauchille, Paul, *Traité de Droit International Public* (Paris: Libraire Arthur Rousseau, 1921).

Fein, Helen, *Accounting for Genocide: National Response and Jewish Victimization During the Holocaust* (New York: The Free Press, 1979).

Finnemore, Martha, *National Interests in International Security* (Ithaca, NY: Cornell University Press, 1996).

Flint, Julie and Alex de Waal, *Darfur: A New History of a Long War* (London: Zed, 2008).

Forrer, John and Conor Seyle (eds), *The Role of Business in the Responsibility to Protect* (Cambridge: Cambridge University Press, 2016).

Forsythe, David P., *The Humanitarians: The International Committee of the Red Cross* (Cambridge: Cambridge University Press, 2005).

Fortna, Virginia Page, *Does Peacekeeping Work? Shaping Belligerents' Choices After Civil War* (Princeton, NJ: Princeton University Press, 2005).

Freeman, Alwyn V., 'War Crimes by Enemy Nationals Administering Justice in Occupied Territory', *American Journal of International Law*, 41, no.3 (1947), pp. 579–610.

Gallagher, Adrian, 'What Constitutes a Manifest Failing? Ambiguous and Inconsistent Terminology and the Responsibility to Protect', *International Politics*, 28, no. 4 (2014), pp. 428–444.

Gat, Azar, *The Causes of War and the Spread of Peace: But Will War Rebound?* (Oxford: Oxford University Press, 2017).

Gifkins, Jess, 'R2P in the UN Security Council: Darfur, Libya and Beyond', *Cooperation and Conflict*, 51, no. 2 (2016), pp. 377–393.

Gilligan, Michael and Stephen John Stedman, 'Where do Peacekeepers Go?', *International Studies Review,* 5, no. 4 (2003), pp. 37–54.

Gladstone, Rick, 'UN Warns of Starvation Peril in Rebel Side of Aleppo', *New York Times,* 10 November 2016, Available at: https://www.nytimes.com/2016/11/11/world/middleeast/aleppo-un-starvation-risk-russia.html

Gilpin, Robert, *War and Change* (Cambridge: Cambridge University Press, 1981).

Glanville, Luke, 'The Antecedents of "Sovereignty as Responsibility"', *European Journal of International Relations,* 17, no. 2 (2011), pp. 233–255.

Glanville, Luke, *Sovereignty and Responsibility to Protect: A New History* (Chicago, IL: Chicago University Press, 2014).

Glanville, Luke, 'Does R2P Matter? Interpreting the Impact of a Norm', *Cooperation and Conflict,* 51, no. 2 (2016).

Glanville, Luke, 'Responsibility to Perfect: Vattel's Conception of Duties Beyond Borders', *International Studies Quarterly* (2017 forthcoming).

Glass, Charles, *Syria Burning: ISIS and the Death of the Arab Spring* (London: Verso, 2015).

Goertz, Gary, Paul F. Diehl and Alexandru Balas, *The Puzzle of Peace: The Evolution of Peace in the International System* (Oxford: Oxford University Press, 2016).

Goldstein, Joshua S., *Winning the War on War: The Decline of Armed Conflict Worldwide* (New York: Penguin, 2011).

Goldstone, Jack A., 'Toward a Fourth Generation of Revolutionary Theory', *Annual Review of Political Science* 4 (2001), pp. 139–187.

Goldstone, Richard J., *For Humanity: Reflections of a War Crimes Investigator* (New Haven, CT: Yale University Press, 2000).

Government of Brazil, 'Responsibility While Protecting: Elements for the Development and Promotion of a Concept', in UN Doc. A/66/551-S/2011/701 (11 November 2011) *Letter dated 9 November 2011 from the Permanent Representative of Brazil to the United Nations addressed to the Secretary-General,* Annex.

Gow, James, *Triumph of the Lack of Will: International Diplomacy and the Lack of Will* (London: C. Hurst and Co., 1997).

Haas, Peter, 'Do Regimes Matter? Epistemic Communities and Mediterranean Pollution Control', *International Organization,* 43, no. 3 (1989), pp 377–403.

Hafner-Burton, Emilie M., *Making Human Rights a Reality* (Princeton, NJ: Princeton University Press, 2013).

Hamilton, Rebecca, *Fighting for Darfur: Public Action and the Struggle to Stop Genocide* (London: Palgrave Macmillan, 2011).

Hansch, Steven, Scott Lillibridge, Grace Egeland, Charles Teller, and Michael Toole, *Lives Lost, Lives Saved: Excess Mortality and the Impact of Health Interventions in the Somalia Emergency* (Washington, DC: Refugee Policy Group, 1994).

Harff, Barbara, 'The Etiology of Genocides', in Isidor Wallimann and Michael N. Dobkowski (eds), *Genocide and the Modern Age: Etiology and Case Studies of Modern Death* (Syracuse, NY: Syracuse University Press, 1987).

Harff, Barbara, 'No Lessons Learned from the Holocaust? Assessing Risks of Genocide and Political Mass Murder since 1955', *American Political Science Review,* 97, no. 1 (2003), pp. 57–73.

Hartigan, Richard Shelly, *Lieber's Code and the Laws of War* (New York: Transaction, 1983).

Hayes, Peter, *Why? Explaining the Holocaust* (New York: W. W. Norton, 2017).

Henkin, Louis, *How Nations Behave: Law and Foreign Policy*, 2nd edition (New York: Columbia University Press, 1979).

High Level Advisory Panel on the Responsibility to Protect in Southeast Asia, *Mainstreaming the Responsibility to Protect in Southeast Asia: Pathway Towards a Caring ASEAN Community*, Report of the High Level Advisory Panel on the Responsibility to Protect in Southeast Asia, 9 September 2014.

Hirsch, John L., 'Somalia', in Sebastian von Einsiedel, David M. Malone and Bruno Stagno Ugarte (eds), *The UN Security Council in the 21st Century* (Boulder, CO: Lynne Rienner, 2016).

Howard, Lise Marje, *UN Peacekeeping in Civil Wars* (Cambridge: Cambridge University Press, 2007).

Holzgrefe, J. L., 'The Humanitarian Intervention Debate', in J. L. Holzgrefe and R. Keohane (eds), *Humanitarian Intervention: Ethical, Legal and Political Dilemmas* (Cambridge: Cambridge University Press, 2005).

Hopgood, Stephen, *The End Times of Human Rights* (Ithaca, NY: Cornell University Press, 2013).

Hultman, Lisa, 'UN Peace Operations and the Protection of Civilians: Cheap Talk or Norm Implementation?', *Journal of Peace Research*, 50, no. 1, (2013), pp. 59–73.

Hultman, Lisa, Jacob Kathman and Megan Shannon, 'United Nations Peacekeeping and Civilian Protection in Civil War', *American Journal of Political Science*, 57, no. 4 (2013), pp. 875–891.

Human Rights Watch, *Somalia, Beyond the Warlords: The Need for a Verdict on Human Rights Abuses*, Report, vol. 5, no 2. (1993), Available at: https://www.hrw.org/reports/1993/somalia/

Human Rights Watch, *The Crisis in Kosovo* (1999), Available at: https://www.hrw.org/reports/2000/nato/Natbm200-01.htm

Human Rights Watch, *Under Orders: War Crimes in Kosovo* (New York: Human Rights Watch, 2001).

Human Rights Watch, 'Libya: Benghazi Civilians Face Grave Risk', 17 March 2011, Available at: https://www.hrw.org/news/2011/03/17/libya-benghazi-civilians-face-grave-risk

Human Rights Watch, 'Libya: Events of 2015', *World Report 2016*, Available at: https://www.hrw.org/world-report/2016/country-chapters/libya#76b621

Human Security Report, *Human Security Report 2013: The Decline in Global Violence· Evidence, Explanation and Contestation* (Burnaby, BC: Simon Frazer University, 2013).

Hyeran, Jo and Beth A. Simmons, 'Can the International Criminal Court Deter Atrocity?', *Social Science Research Network*, 2014.

ICRC, 'Crisis in Yemen: Tipping Point for International Humanitarian Action', 20 May 2015, Available at: https://www.icrc.org/en/document/crisis-yemen-tipping-point-international-humanitarian-action

Ignatieff, Michael, 'The New World Disorder', *The New York Review of Books*, 25 September 2014, Available at: http://www.nybooks.com/articles/archives/2014/sep/25/new-world-disorder/?pagination=false

Independent Commission, *Report of the Independent Inquiry into the Actions of the United Nations During the 1994 Genocide in Rwanda*, 12 December 1999.

International Commission on Intervention and State Sovereignty, *The Responsibility to Protect* (Ottawa: International Development Research Centre, 2001).

International Crisis Group, 'Testimony by Claudia Gazzini, Senior Analyst, International Crisis Group, for Hearing of the Senate Committee on Foreign Affairs on 'Libya: The Path Forward'', 3 March 2016, Available at: http://www.crisisgroup.org/en/publication-type/speeches/2016/gazzini-us-senate-hearing-3mar16.aspx

Iyekekpolo, Wisdom Oghasa 'Boko Haram: Understanding the Context', *Third World Quarterly*, 37, no. 12 (2016), pp. 2211–2228.

Jackson, Robert, *The Global Covenant: Human Conduct in a World of States* (Oxford: Oxford University Press, 2000).

Jacobs, Andrew, 'China Urges Quick End to Airstrikes in Libya', 22 March 2011, Available at: http://www.nytimes.com/2011/03/23/world/asia/23beiijing.html?_r=0

Judah, Tim, *Kosovo: What Everyone Needs to Know* (Oxford: Oxford University Press, 2008).

Kaldor, Mary, *New and Old Wars: Organized Violence in a Global Age* (Cambridge: Polity, 1997).

Kalyvas, Stathis N., *The Logic of Violence in Civil War* (Cambridge: Cambridge University Press, 2006).

Kardam, Nuket, 'The Emerging Global Gender Equality Regime from Neoliberal and Constructivist Perspectives in International Relations', *International Feminist Journal of Politics*, 6, no. 1 (2004), pp. 85–109.

Kathman, Jacob and Reed Wood, 'Managing Threat, Cost, and Incentive to Kill: The Short- and Long- Term Effects of Intervention in Mass Killing', *Journal of Conflict Resolution*, 55, no. 5, (2011), pp. 735–760.

Keohane, Robert, *After Hegemony: Cooperation and Discord in the World Political Economy* (Princeton, NJ: Princeton University Press 1984).

Kemp, Walter A., *The OSCE in a New Context* (London: Royal Institute of International Affairs, 1996).

Kiernan, Ben, *The Pol Pot Regime: Race, Power, and Genocide in Cambodia under the Khmer Rouge, 1975–79* (New Haven, CT: Yale University Press, 1996).

Kiernan, Ben, *Blood and Soil: A World History of Genocide and Extermination from Sparta to Darfur* (New Haven, CT: Yale University Press, 2007).

Hun Joon Kim, *The Massacres at Mt. Halla: Sixty Years of Truth Seeking in South Korea* (Ithaca, NY: Cornell University Press, 2014).

Hunjoon Kim and Kathryn Sikkink, 'Explaining the Deterrence Effects for Human Rights Prosecutions in Transitional Countries', *International Studies Quarterly*, 54, no. 4 (2010), pp. 939–963.

Klose, Fabian, ed., *The Emergence of Humanitarian Intervention: Ideas and Practice from the Nineteenth Century to the Present* (Oxford: Oxford University Press, 2015).

Krain, Matthew, 'Democracy, Internal War, and State-Sponsored Mass Murder', *Human Rights Review*, 1, no.3 (2000), pp. 40–48.

Krain, Matthew, 'International Intervention and the Severity of Genocides and Politicides', *International Studies Quarterly*, 49, no. 2 (2005), pp. 363–387.

Krasner, Stephen D., 'Structural Causes and Regime Consequences: Regimes as Intervening Variables', in *International Regimes* ed. Stephen D. Krasner (Ithaca, NY: Cornell University Press 1999), pp. 1–21.

Krasner, Stephen D., *Sovereignty: Organized Hypocrisy* (Princeton, NJ: Princeton University Press, 1999).

Kressel, Neil J., *Mass Hate: The Global Rise of Genocide and Terror* (Cambridge, MA: Westview Press, 2002).

Kroslak, Daniela, *The Role of France in the Rwandan Genocide* (London: C. Hurst and Co., 2008).

Kuper, Leo, *Genocide: Its Political Use in the Twentieth Century* (New Haven, CT: Yale University Press, 1982).

Kuperman, Alan J., 'The Moral Hazard of Humanitarian Intervention: Lessons from the Balkans', *International Studies Quarterly,* 52, no. 1(2008), pp. 49–80.

Kuperman, Alan J., '5 Things the US Should Consider in Libya', *USA Today,* 22 March 2011, Available at: http://usatoday30.usatoday.com/news/opinion/forum/2011-03-22-column22_ST_N.htm

Kuperman, Alan, 'Obama' Libya Debacle: How a Well-Meaning Intervention Ended in Failure', *Foreign Affairs,* March/April 2015.

Lankov, Andrei, *The Real North Korea: Life and Politics in the Failed Stalinist Utopia* (Oxford: Oxford University Press, 2013).

Leader, John Maynard, 'Rethinking the Role of Ideology in Mass Atrocities', *Terrorism and Political Violence,* 26, no. 5 (2014), pp. 821–841.

Leatherman, Janie L., *Sexual Violence and Armed Conflict* (Oxford: Polity, 2011).

Legro, Jeffrey W., *Cooperation Under Fire: The Conduct of the Air War in the Second World War* (New York: St. Martin's Press, 1992).

Lesch, David W., *Syria: The Fall of the House of Assad* (New Haven, CT: Yale University Press, 2013).

Levy, Jack and William R. Thompson, 'The Decline of War? Multiple Trajectories and Diverging Trends', *International Studies Review*, 15, no. 3, (2013), pp. 405–411.

Linklater, Andrew, *The Transformation of Political Community* (Cambridge: Polity, 1998).

Linklater, Andrew and Hidemi Suganami, *The English School of International Relations: A Contemporary Reassessment* (Cambridge: Cambridge University Press, 2006).

Lischer, Sarah Kenyon, 'Military Intervention and the Humanitarian "Force Multiplier"', *Global Governance,* 13, no. 1 (2007), pp. 99–118.

Loescher, Gil, Alexander Betts and James Milner, *The Untied Nations High Commissioner for Refugees (UNHCR): The Politics and Practice of Refugee Protection into the Twenty-First Century* (London: Routledge, 2008).

Lu, Catherine, *Just and Unjust Interventions in World Politics: Public and Private* (New York: Palgrave, 2006).

Luck, Edward C., *UN Security Council: Practice and Promise* (London: Routledge, 2006).

Luck, Edward C., *The Responsibility to Protect at Ten: The Challenges Ahead*, Policy Analysis Brief for the Stanley Foundation, June 2015.

Luck, Edward C. and Dana Luck, 'The Individual Responsibility to Protect', in Rosenberg et al, *Reconstructing Atrocity Prevention* (Cambridge University Press, 2015).

Lupel, Adam and Ernesto Verdeja, 'Responding to Genocide', in *Responding to Genocide. The Politics of International Action,* edited by Adam Lupel and Ernesto Verdeja (Boulder, CO: Lynne Rienner, 2013).

MacFarlane, S. Neil and Yuen Foong Khon, *Human Security and the UN: A Critical History* (Bloomington, IN: Indiana University Press, 2006).

McLoughlin, Stephen, 'From Reaction to Resilience in Mass Atrocity Prevention: An Analysis of the 2013 Report *The Responsibility to Protect: State Responsibility and Prevention*', *Global Governance*, 22, no. 4 (2016), pp. 473–490.

McLoughlin, Stephen, *The Structural Prevention of Mass Atrocities: Understanding Risk and Resilience* (London: Routledge, 2014).

McLoughlin, Stephen and Deborah Mayersen, 'Reconsidering Root Causes: A New Framework for the Structural Prevention of Genocide and Mass Atrocities', in Bert Ingelaere, Stephan Parmentier, Jacques Haers and Barbara Segaert (eds), *Genocide, Risk and Resilience: An Interdisciplinary Approach* (Basingstoke: Palgrave, 2013).

Mamdani, Mahmood, *Saviors and Survivors: Darfur, Politics and the War on Terror* (New York: Bantam Doubleday Dell, 2009).

Mail and Guardian, 'Zuma Lashes NATO for 'Abusing', UN Resolutions on Libya', 14 June 2011, Available at: http://mg.co.za/article/2011-06-14-zuma-lashes-nato-for-abusing-un-resolutions-on-libya

Mann, Michael Mann, *The Dark Side of Democracy: Explaining Ethnic Cleansing* (Cambridge: Cambridge University Press, 2005).

Månsson, Katarina, 'Use of Force and Civilian Protection: Peace Operations in the Congo', *International Peacekeeping*, 12, no. 4 (2005), pp. 503–519.

Månsson, Katarina, 'Integration of Human Rights in Peace Operations: Is There an Ideal Model?', *International Peacekeeping*, 13, no. 4 (2006), pp. 547–563.

Marshall, Monty G. and Benjamin R. Cole, *Global Report 2014: Conflict, Governance and State Fragility* (Vienna, VA: Center for Systemic Peace, 2014).

Melander, Eric, Therese Pettersson and Lotta Themner, 'Organised Violence, 1989–2015', *Journal of Peace Research*, 53, no. 5 (2016), pp. 727–742.

Melvern, Linda, *A People Betrayed: The Role of the West in Rwanda's Genocide* (London: Zed Books, 2000).

Menon, Rajan, *The Conceit of Humanitarian Intervention* (Oxford: Oxford University Press, 2016).

Midlarsky, Manus, *The Killing Trap: Genocide in the Twentieth Century* (Cambridge: Cambridge University Press, 2005).

Mill, John Stuart, 'A Few Words on Non-Intervention' [1859], in John Stuart Mill, *Essays on Politics and Culture* (edited by Gertrude Himmelfarb) (Gloucester: Peter Smith, 1973).

Mills, Kurt, *International Responses to Mass Atrocities in Africa: Responsibility to Protect, Punish and Palliate* (Philadelphia, PA: University of Pennsylvania, 2015).

Mishra, Pankaj, *Age of Anger: A History of the Present* (New York: Farrar, Straus and Giroux, 2017).

Mitton, Kieran, *Rebels in a Rotten State: Understanding Atrocity in the Sierra Leone Civil War* (Oxford: Oxford University Press, 2015).

Moellendorf, Darrel, *Cosmopolitan Justice* (Boulder, CO: Westview, 2002).

Moorehead, Caroline, *Dunant's Dream: War, Switzerland and the History of the Red Cross* (New York: Carroll and Graf, 1998).

Morjane, K., 'The Protection of Refugee and Displaced Persons', in ed., B. G. Ramcharan, *Human Rights Protection in the Field*, (The Hague: Brill, 2006).

Morris, Justin, 'Libya and Syria: R2P and the Spectre of the Swinging Pendulum', *International Affairs*, 89, no. 5 (2013), pp. 1265–83.

Morris, Justin, 'The Responsibility to Protect and the Great Powers: The Tensions of Dual Responsibility', *Global Responsibility to Protect*, 7, no. 3–4 (2015), pp. 398–421.

Moses, A. Dirk, 'The United Nations, Humanitarianism and Human Rights: War Crimes/Genocide Trials for Pakistani Soldiers in Bangladesh', in *Human Rights in the Twentieth Century*, ed. Stefan-Ludwig Hoffman (Cambridge: Cambridge University Press, 2011).

Mueller, John E., *The Remnants of War* (Ithaca, NY: Cornell University Press, 2007).

Murdie, Amanda M. and David R. Davis, 'Shaming and Blaming: Using Events Data to Assess the Impact of Human Rights INGOS', *International Studies Quarterly*, 56, no. 1, (2011), pp. 1–16.

Myint-U, Thant, *The River of Lost Footsteps: Histories of Burma* (New York: Farar, Straus and Giroux, 2006).

Naimark, Norman, *Stalin's Genocides* (Princeton, NJ: Princeton University Press, 2011).

Nsia-Pepra, Kofi, *UN Robust Peacekeeping: Civilian Protection in Violent Civil Wars* (London: Palgrave, 2014).

Nathan, Laurie, 'Correspondence: Civil War Settlements and the Prospects for Peace', *International Security*, 36, no. 1 (2011), pp. 202–210.

Nolan, Cathal J., *The Allure of Battle: A History of How Wars Have Been Won and Lost* (Oxford: Oxford University Press, 2017).

O'Brien, Emily, with Richard Gowan, *The International Role in Libya's Transition: August 2011–March 2012*, Report of the Centre on International Cooperation, New York University, July 2012.

O'Hanlon, Michael and Peter W. Singer, 'The Humanitarian Transformation: Expanding Global Intervention Capacity', *Survival*, 46, no. 1 (2004).

Olsson, Louise and Theodora-Iseme Gizelis, *Gender, Peace and Security: Implementing UN Security Council Resolution 1325* (London: Routledge, 2015).

Orford, Anne, *International Authority and the Responsibility to Protect* (Cambridge: Cambridge University Press, 2011).

Pape, Robert A., 'When Duty Calls: A Pragmatic Standard of Humanitarian Intervention', *International Security*, 37, no. 1 (2012), pp. 41–80.

Paris, Roland, 'The "Responsibility to Protect" and the Structural Problems of Preventive Intervention', *International Peacekeeping*, 21, no. 5 (2014), pp. 569–603.

Pattison, James, *Humanitarian Intervention and the Responsibility to Protect: Who Should Intervene?* (Oxford: Oxford University Press, 2010).

Pattison, James, *The Alternatives to War: From Sanctions to Nonviolence* (Oxford: Oxford University Press, 2018).

Pinker, Steven, *The Better Angels of Our Nature: The Decline of Violence in History and its Causes* (New York: Allen Lane, 2011).

Power, Samantha, *A Problem from Hell: America and the Age of Genocide* (New York: Basic Books, 2002).

Prunier, Gerard, *The Rwanda Crisis: History of a Genocide* (London: C. Hurst and Co., 1998).

Prunier, Gerard, *Darfur: The Ambiguous Genocide* (London: Hirst, 2005).

Prunier, Gerard, *Africa's World War: Congo, the Rwandan Genocide and the Making of a Continental Catastrophe* (Oxford: Oxford University Press, 2008).

Puri, Hardeep Singh, *Perilous Interventions: The Security Council and the Politics of Chaos* (New York: Harper Collins, 2016).

Ramsey, Paul, *The Just War: Force and Political Responsibility* (Lanham, MD: Rowman and Littlefield, 2002).

Rawls, John, *A Theory of Justice* (Cambridge, MA: Harvard University Press, 1971).

Regan, Patrick, 'Third-Party Interventions and the Duration of Intrastate Conflict', *Journal of Conflict Resolution,* 46, no. 1 (2002), pp. 55–73.

Reike, Ruben, 'The Responsibility to Prevent: An International Crimes Approach to the Prevention of Mass Atrocities', *Ethics & International Affairs,* 28, no. 4 (2014), pp. 451–476.

Reike, Ruben, 'Libya and the Prevention of Atrocity Crimes', in Serena K. Sharma and Jennifer Welsh (eds), *The Responsibility to Prevent* (Oxford: Oxford University Press, 2015).

Reno, William, *Warfare in Independent Africa* (Cambridge: Cambridge University Press, 2011).

Reuters News, UN General Assembly Approves $5.5 Billion Budget for 2014/2015', by Michele Nichols, 27 December 2013, *Reuters*, Available at: www.reuters.com/article/2013/12/27/us-un-budget-idUSBRE9BQ0JX20131227

Richmond, Oliver, *Failed Statebuilding: Intervention, the State and the Dynamics of Peace Formation* (New Haven, CT: Yale University Press, 2014).

Riddell, Kelly and Jeffrey Scott Shapiro, 'Hillary Clinton's 'WMD' Moment: US Intelligence Saw False Narrative in Libya', *The Washington Times,* 29 January, 2015, Available at: http://www.washingtontimes.com/news/2015/jan/29/hillary-clinton-libya-war-genocide-narrative-rejec/

Risse, Thomas and Stephen Ropp, 'Introduction and Overview', in Thomas Risse, Stephen Ropp and Kathryn Sikkink (eds), *The Persistent Power of Human Rights: From Persistence to Compliance* (Cambridge: Cambridge University Press, 2013).

Roberts, Christopher, *The Battle for Syria: International Rivalry in the New Middle East* (New Haven, CT: Yale University Press, 2016).

Rogin, Josh, 'How Obama Turned on a Dime Toward War', 18 March 2011, Available at: http://thecable.foreignpolicy.com/posts/2011/03/18/how_obama_turned_on_a_dime_toward_war

Rohde, David, *Endgame: The Betrayal and Fall of Srebrenica, Europe's Worst Massacre since World War II* (New York: Penguin, 2012).

Rosenberg, Sheri, Tiberiu Galis and Alex Zucker (eds), *Reconstructing Atrocity Prevention* (Cambridge University Press, 2015).

Rousseff, Dilma, Statement by H.E. Dilma Rousseff, President of the Federative Republic of Brazil, at the Opening of the General Debate at the 67th Session of the United Nations General Assembly, New York (25 September 2012)., Available at: http://gadebate.un.org/sites/default/files/gastatements/67/BR_en.pdf.

Rummel, R. J., *Death by Government* (Piscataway, NJ: Transaction, Piscataway, 1994).

Rummel, R. J., *Statistics of Democide* (Piscataway, NJ: Transaction, 1997).

Saunders, Doug, 'Why Louise Arbour is Thinking Twice', *The Globe and Mail,* 28 March 2015, Available at: http://www.theglobeandmail.com/globe-debate/why-louise-arbour-is-thinking-twice/article 23667013/

Sands, Philippe, *East West Street: On the Origins of Genocide and Crimes Against Humanity* (London: Weidenfeld and Nicolson, 2016).

Savage, Charlie and Eric Schmitt, 'Trump Eases Combat Rules in Somalia intended to Protect Civilians', *New York Times*, 30 March 2017, Available at: https://www.nytimes.com/2017/03/30/world/africa/trump-is-said-to-ease-combat-rules-in-somalia-designed-to-protect-civilians.html

Security Council Report, *Protection of Civilians in Armed Conflict: Cross Cutting Report*, Security Council Report, New York, 2015.

Seybolt, Taylor, *Protection of Civilians in Armed Conflict: Cross Cutting Report*, Security Council Report, New York, 2007.

Shane, Scott and Jo Becker, 'A New Libya, with 'Very Little Time Left'', *New York Times*, 27 February 2016, Available at: http://www.nyti.ms/212ZDkW

Sharma, Serena K., *The Responsibility to Protect and the International Criminal Court: Protection and Prosecution in Kenya* (London: Routledge, 2015).

Schabas, William, *An Introduction to the International Criminal Court* (Cambridge: Cambridge University Press, 2008).

Schabas, William, *Genocide in International Law: The Crime of Crimes* (Cambridge: Cambridge University Press, 2009).

Schabas, William, *Unimaginable Atrocities: Justice, Politics and Rights at War Crimes Tribunals* (Oxford: Oxford University Press, 2012).

Schachter, Oscar 'The Legality of Pro-Democratic Invasion', *American Journal of International Law*, 78, 1984, pp. 645–650.

Schneider, Gerald and Margit Bussmann, 'Accounting for the Dynamics of One-Sided Violence: Introducing KOSVED', *Journal of Peace Research*, 50, no. 5 (2013), pp. 635–644.

Serena Sharma and Jennifer Welsh (eds), *The Responsibility to Prevent: Overcoming the Challenges of Atrocity Prevention* (Oxford: Oxford University Press, 2015).

Shaw, Malcolm N., *International Law* 5th edition (Cambridge: Cambridge University Press, 2003).

Shaw, Martin, *War and Genocide: Organized Killing in Modern Society* (Oxford: Polity, 2003).

Shue, Henry, 'Mediating Duties', *Ethics*, 98, no. 4 (1988), pp. 687–704.

Shue, Henry, *Basic Rights: Subsistence, Affluence and US Foreign Policy*, 2nd edition (Princeton, NJ: Princeton University Press, 1996).

Sikkink, Kathryn, *The Justice Cascade: How Human Rights Prosecutions are Changing the World* (New York: Norton, 2011).

Simms, Brendan, ed., *Humanitarian Intervention: A History* (Oxford: Oxford University Press, 2013).

Simon, Bernd and Bert Kalndermans (2001), 'Politicized Collective Identity: A Social Psychological Analysis', *American Psychologist*, April 2001.

Slim, Hugo, 'Using What We Know: Politicizing Knowledge and Scholarship to Stop Group Violence', *Social Science Research Council*, 22 December 2006.

Slim, Hugo, *Killing Civilians: Method, Madness and Morality in War* (London: Hurst and Co., 2007).

Snyder, Jack, *From Voting to Violence: Democratization and Nationalist Conflict* (New York: W.W. Norton and Company, 2000).

Snyder, Jack and L. Vinjanmuri, 'Trials and Errors: Principle and Pragmatism in Strategies of International Justice', *International Security*, 28, no. 3 (2003–4), pp. 5–44.

Snyder, Timothy, *Bloodlands: Europe Between Hitler and Stalin* (New York: Basic Books, 2010).

Snyder, Timothy, 'Hitler vs. Stalin: Who Killed More?', *New York Review of Books,* 10 March 2011.

Spangaro, Jo, Chinelo Adogu, Geetha Ranmuthugala, Gawaine Powell Davies, Lea Steinacker, and Anthony Zwi, 'What Evidence Exists for Initiatives to Reduce Risk and Incidence of Sexual Violence in Armed Conflict and Other Humanitarian Crises? A Systematic Review', *PLos ONE,* 8, no. 5, (2013).

Stephen, Chris, 'Five Years After Gaddafi, Libya Torn by Civil War and Battles with ISIS', *The Guardian,* Tuesday 16 February 2016, Available at: https://www.theguardian.com/world/2016/feb/16/libya-gaddafi-arab-spring-civil-war-islamic-state

Stewart, Frances, ed., *Horizontal Inequalities and Conflict: Understanding Group Violence in Multiethnic Societies* (London: Palgrave, 2008).

Stewart, Frances and Armin Langer, 'Horizontal Inequalities: Explaining Persistence and Change', in *Horizontal Inequalities and Conflict: Understanding Group Violence in Multiethnic Societies,* ed. Frances Stewart (London: Palgrave, 2008).

Stewart, Frances, 'The Causes of Civil War and Genocide: A Comparison', in Adam Lupel and Ernesto Verdaja (eds), *Responding to Genocide: The Politics of International Action* (Boulder: Lynne Rienner, 2013).

Straus, Scott, *The Order of Genocide: Race, Power and War in Rwanda* (Ithaca: Cornell University Press, 2008).

Straus, Scott, *Making and Unmaking Nations: War, Leadership and Genocide in Modern Africa* (Ithaca, NY: Cornell University Press, 2015).

Summer, John G., *Hope Restored? Humanitarian Aid in Somalia* (Refugee Policy Group, 1994), Available at: http://pdf.usaid.gov/pdf_docs/PNABZ357.pdf

Sutter, Daniel, 'The Deterrent Effects of the International Criminal Court', *New Political Economy,* 23, no. 1 (2006), pp. 9–24.

Téson, Fernando, 'The Liberal Case for Humanitarian Intervention', in J. L. Holzgrefe and Robert O. Keohane (eds), *Humanitarian Intervention: Ethical, Legal and Political Dilemmas* (Cambridge: Cambridge University Press, 2003).

Teitel, Ruti G., *Humanity's Law* (New York: Oxford University Press, 2011).

Thakur, Ramesh, *The United Nations, Peace and Security: From Collective Security to the Responsibility to Protect* (Cambridge: Cambridge University Press, 2006).

Thakur, Ramesh, *The Responsibility to Protect: Norms, Laws and the Use of Force in International Politics* (London: Routledge, 2011).

Thakur, Ramesh, 'R2P after Libya and Syria: Engaging Emerging Powers', *The Washington Quarterly,* 36 (2) 2013, pp. 61–76.

Thayer, Bradley, 'Humans, Not Angels: Reasons to Doubt the Decline of War Thesis', *International Studies Review,* 15, no. 3 (2013), pp. 411–416.

Themner, L. and Peter Wallensteen, 'Armed Conflict: 1946–2013', *Journal of Peace Research,* 51, no. 4 (2014), pp. 315–527.

Toft, Monica Duffy, 'Ending Civil Wars: A Case for Rebel Victory?', *International Security,* 34, no. 4 (2010), pp. 7–36.

Tomasky, Michael, 'Gaddafi's Speech', *The Guardian,* 17 March 2011, Available at: https://www.theguardian.com/commentisfree/michaeltomasky/2011/mar/17/usforeignpolicy-unitednations-libya-it-will-start-fast

de Torrente, Nicolas and Fabrice Weissman, 'A War Without Limits: Somalia's Humanitarian Catastrophe', *Harvard International Review,* 30, no. 4 (2009).

UCDP/PRIO Armed Conflict Dataset version 4–2016.

Ulfelder, Jay, 'Genocide is Going Out of Fashion', *Foreign Policy,* 14 May 2015.

United Kingdom Parliament, *Libya: Examination of Intervention and Collapse and the UK's Future Foreign Policy Options,* 9 September 2016, Available at: https://www.publications.parliament.uk/pa/cm201617/cmselect/cmfaff/119/11905.htm

United Nations, *The Arms Trade Treaty* (2013).

United Nations, *Responsibility to Protect: Timely and Decisive Response – Report of the Secretary-General,* UN Doc. A/66/844-S/2012/578, July 25.

United Nations, *Fulfilling our Collective Responsibility: International Assistance and the Responsibility to Protect* (New York: United Nations, 2014), Doc no. A/68/947-S/2014/449.

United Nations, *Mobilizing Collective Action: The Next Decade of the Responsibility to Protect: Report of the United Nations Secretary-General,* A/70/999-S/2016/620, 22 July 2016.

United Nations, doc. S/1998/318, 13 April 1998.

United Nations, Doc. S/PV.6491, 26 February 2011.

United Nations, Doc. S/PV.6498, 17 March 2011.

United Nations, Doc. S/PV.6531, 10 May 2011.

United Nations, Doc. S/PV.7216, 14 July 2014

United Nations General Assembly, '2005 Summit Outcome Document', A/60/L.1, 20. September 2005.

United Nations General Assembly, Resolution 66/253 (21 February 2012)

United Nations News Centre, 'UN Rights Council Recommends Suspending Libya, Orders Inquiry into Abuses', 25 February 2011, Available at: http://www.un.org/apps/news/story.asp?NewsID=37626#.V5H9jzcX5Y8

United Nations OCHA, *Global Humanitarian Overview 2016* (Geneva: OCHA, 2016).

United Nations Office of Internal Oversight Services, *Evaluation of the Implementation and Results of Protection of Civilians Mandates in United Nations Peacekeeping Operations,* A/68/787, 7 March 2014.

United Nations Press Release, 'UN Secretary-General Special Adviser on the Prevention of Genocide, Francis Deng, and Special Adviser on the Responsibility to Protect, Edward Luck, on the Situation in Libya', 22 February 2011, Available at: http://www.un.org/en/preventgenocide/adviser/pdf/OSAPG,%20Special%20Advisers%20Statement%20on%20Libya,%2022%20February%202011.pdf

United Nations Press Release, 'Fifth Committee Recommends $5.4 Billion Budget for 2016–2017 Biennium as it Concludes Main Part of Seventieth Session', *United Nations Meetings Coverage and Press Releases,* 23 December 2015, Available at: http://www.un.org/press/en/2015/gaab4185.doc.htm

United Nations, 'Yemen Emergency Food Security and Nutrition Assessment – 2016 Preliminary Results', 8 February 2017, Available at: http://fscluster.org/yemen/document/yemen-emergency-food-security-and-0

United Nations Security Council Resolution 751 (1992a).

United Nations Security Council Resolution 794 (1992b).

United Nations Security Council Resolution 929 (1994a).

United Nations Security Council Resolution 940 (1994b).

United Nations Security Council, Minutes, S/PV.3989 (26 March 1999).

United Nations Security Council, Resolution 1973 (17 March 2011).

United Nations Security Council Resolution 2098 (2013).

United Nations Security Council Resolution 2042 (2012), Annex: Six-Point Proposal of the Joint Special Envoy of the United Nations and the League of Arab States.

United Nations Security Council Resolution 2043 (21 April 2012).

United Nations Security Council Resolution 2149 (10 April 2014).

United Nations, *Somalia – UNOSOM II, Facts and Figures*, Available at: http://www.un.org/en/peacekeeping/missions/past/unosom2facts.html

United Nations High Commissioner for Refugees, *Global Trends: Forced Displacement in 2014* (Geneva: UNHCR, 2016).

United Nations High Commissioner for Refugees, *Global Trends: Forced Displacement in 2015* (Geneva: UNHCR, 2016).

Valentino, Benjamin A., *Final Solutions: Mass Killing and Genocide in the Twentieth Century* (Ithaca, NY and London: Cornell University Press, 2004).

Valentino, Benjamin A., 'Why We Kill: The Political Science of Political Violence against Civilians', *Annual Review of Political Science,* 17 (2014), pp. 89–103.

Valentino, Benjamin A. and Paul Huth, 'Mass Killing of Civilians in Time of War', in J. Joseph Hewitt, Jonathan Wilkenfield and Ted Robert Gurr (eds), *Peace and Conflict 2008* (Boulder, CO: Paradigm 2008).

Verwey, Wil, 'Humanitarian Intervention in the 1990s and Beyond: An International Law Perspective', in *World Orders in the Making: Humanitarian Intervention and Beyond,* ed. J. N. Pierterse (London: Macmillan, 1998).

von Hippel, Karin, *Democracy by Force: US Military Intervention in the Post-Cold War World* (Cambridge: Cambridge University Press, 2000).

von Treitschke, Heinrich, *Politik* (Leipzig: Insel, 1899), vol. 2.

Wallensteen, Peter and Isak Svensson, 'Talking Peace: International Mediation in Armed Conflicts', *Journal of Peace Research,* 51, no. 2 (2014), pp. 315–327.

Waller, James, *Confronting Evil: Engaging our Responsibility to Prevent Genocide* (Oxford: Oxford University Press, 2016).

Walzer, Michael, *Just and Unjust Wars: A Philosophical Argument with Historical Illustrations* (New York: Basic Books, 1977).

Walzer, Michael, *Spheres of Justice: A Defence of Pluralism and Equality* (Oxford: Basil Blackwood, 1983).

Walzer, Michael, *Thick and Thin: Moral Argument at Home and Abroad* (New Haven, CT: Yale University Press, 1994).

Weinstein, Jeremy M., *Inside Rebellion: The Politics of Insurgent Violence* (Cambridge: Cambridge University Press, 2007).

Weiss, Thomas G., 'The Sunset of Humanitarian Intervention? The Responsibility to Protect in a Unipolar Era', *Security Dialogue,* 25, no. 2 (2004), pp. 135–153.

Weiss, Thomas G., *Humanitarian Intervention,* 2nd edition (Cambridge: Polity, 2012).

Weiss, Thomas G. and Don Hubert, *The Responsibility to Protect: Supplementary Volume to the Report of the International Commission on Intervention and State Sovereignty,* International Development Research Centre, Ottawa, 2001.

Welsh, Jennifer M., 'Conclusion: Humanitarian Intervention after 11 September', in Jennifer M. Welsh (ed.), *Humanitarian Intervention and International Relations* (Oxford: Oxford University Press, 2004).

Welsh, Jennifer M., *Humanitarian Intervention and International Relations* (Oxford: Oxford University Press, 2006).

Welsh, Jennifer M., *The Return of History: Conflict, Migration and Geopolitics in the Twenty-First Century* (Toronto: House of Anansi Press, 2017).

Wheeler, Nicholas J., *Saving Strangers: Humanitarian Intervention in International Society* (Oxford: Oxford University Press, 2000).

Wheeler, Nicholas J. and Justin Morris, 'Humanitarian Intervention and State Practice at the End of the Cold War', in Rick Fawn and Jeremy Lankins (eds), *International Society After the Cold War: Anarchy and Order Reconsidered* (London: Macmillan, 1996).

Wheeler, Nicholas J. and Justin Morris, 'Justifying the Iraq War as a Humanitarian Intervention: The Cure is Worse than the Disease', in Ramesh Thakur and Waheguru Pal Singh Sidhu (eds), *The Iraq Crisis and World Order* (Tokyo: UN University Press, 2006).

Williams, Paul D., 'From Non-Intervention to Non-Indifference: The Origins and Development of the African Union's Security Culture', *African Affairs*, 106, no. 423 (2007), pp. 253–279.

Wills, Siobhan, *Protecting Civilians: The Obligations of Peacekeepers* (Oxford: Oxford University Press, 2009).

Wills, Siobhan, *Protection of Civilians* (Oxford: Oxford University Press, 2011).

Wright, Ronald, *A Short History of Progress* (Toronto: House of Anansi Press, 2004).

Young, Oran, 'International Regimes: Toward a New Theory of Institutions', *World Politics*, 39, no. 1 (1989), pp. 104–122.

Zartman, I. William, 'The Timing of Peace Initiatives: Hurting Stalemates and Ripe Moments', *Global Review of Ethnopolitics,* 1, no. 1 (2001), pp. 8–18.

Zartman, I. William, *Cowardly Lions: Missed Opportunities to Prevent Deadly Conflict and State Collapse* (Boulder, CO: Lynne Rienner, 2005).

Zartman, I. William, M. Anstey and P. Merts. (eds), *The Slippery Slope to Genocide* (Oxford: Oxford University Press, 2012).

Index

In this index *t* indicates table

Printed by Printforce, the Netherlands